The
Wonder
Trail

The

Wonder
Trail

True Stories from Los Angeles

to the End of the World

Steve Hely

DUTTON
→ est. 1852 ←

An imprint of Penguin Random House LLC
375 Hudson Street
New York, New York 10014

LIBRARY OF CONGRESS CATALOGING-IN-PUBLICATION DATA
Names: Hely, Steve.
Title: The wonder trail : true stories from Los Angeles to the end of the world / Steve Hely.
Description: New York, New York : Dutton, 2016.
Identifiers: LCCN 2015038442| ISBN 9780525955016 (hardcover) | ISBN 9780698404236 (ebook)
Subjects: LCSH: Hely, Steve—Travel—Central America. | Hely, Steve—Travel—South America. | Central America—Description and travel. | South America—Description and travel. | Central America—Social life and customs. | South America—Social life and customs. | Curiosities and wonders—Central America. | Curiosities and wonders—South America. | BISAC: TRAVEL / South America / General. | TRAVEL / Essays & Travelogues. | HUMOR / Form / Essays.
Classification: LCC F1433.2 .H45 2016 | DDC 917.2804—dc23
LC record available at http://lccn.loc.gov/2015038442

Printed in the United States of America
10 9 8 7 6 5 4 3 2 1

Set in Warnock Pro
Designed by Alissa Rose Theodor

All photos and maps courtesy of the author unless otherwise noted.
Drawing on page 90 by Frederick Catherwood.

To tell the tale of the journey is to go on it a second time.

—PONCE DE LEÓN

Oh, there's the whole universe.

When I closed my eyes, I could see it. Just beyond the parades of dancing animals and dinosaurs.

The whole everything of the cosmos. Expanding out in every direction. Beyond the stars, through the galaxies, to the bright edge of everything, and infinity. In, too, inside my brain and my body, down to my very molecules, until they became galaxies of particles, infinities of their own.

I did know where I was, don't get me wrong. Like if you'd asked me, I could've told you I was lying on my back on the wood floor of the shaman's house, under a mosquito net, about an hour's walk from that village, San something, on the Rio Amazonas. Two hours' boat ride or so, plus an hour walk, from Iquitos, Peru. So if there was an emergency, I could . . . I dunno, walk two or three miles, until I got service, and text . . .

Eh, forget emergencies. I felt better and safer than I had in a long time. Geography, where I was, that all seemed like a meaningless detail right now, when, if I could just keep my eyes closed, the whole meaning of everything would be revealed. Any question I ever had could be answered. Cosmic harmony would wash over me and swallow me like an ocean.

If I could just remember: What was I looking for, again?

What Kind of Book Is This?

This is the story of a trip, from Los Angeles to Patagonia. True tales and stories and adventures collected by a traveler. As long as there've been books, this has been a kind of book.

Who Should Read This Book?

- Anyone taking a trip
- People who would like to take a trip but can't, because they're stuck, like at work or in a waiting room someplace or at home with their kids, but wish they could take a trip
- Anyone who can happily remember taking a trip
- Or anyone who hates taking trips. They can read it, laugh at the discomfort of the traveler, and experience the best parts of a trip without ever even getting up.

So: People taking trips, people who aren't taking trips, people who like trips, and people who don't like trips should all enjoy this book.

Plus:

On this trip, I went through Mexico, Central America, and the western half of South America. So this book should also appeal to:

- People who don't know much about the places south of the United States but are curious
- People who know a lot about that part of the world should also read this book, so they can scoff at my many naive impressions and misunderstandings.

So: People who do and do not know a lot about Latin America should also read this book.

Plus, just general fans of books.

Or people who are new to books—why not start with this one?

Also: Young Adults

Young adults read lots of books, I'm told. Teens and preteens. This could be a good one for them. I write at a level suitable for a clever ten-year-old.

Contents

The Beginning / Los Angeles

Mexico

Central America—Guatemala, El Salvador, Nicaragua, Costa Rica, and Panama

Around the Darién Gap and Colombia

The Amazon and Peru

The Galápagos and Bolivia

Chile and Patagonia

The Beginning / Los Angeles

A Travel Book

There were stories like this way before there were books.

I'll bet you the cave paintings they find in France, all those bison and horses running around, those were illustrations for tales of trips. Maybe they also served as base camp for kinds of mental or spiritual trips, shamanic trips, practice trips.

What we call humans climbed out of the trees, two million years ago let's say, in eastern Africa. We started walking and we haven't stopped. We filled up the Earth, every crevice and corner. Now we're poking about looking for new Earths.

Campfire stories aren't always about trips, it's true—sometimes they're about Hook-Hand Man, for instance—but then again you're already camping. You're reenacting the major activity of human history: walking the Earth.

For as long as there have been books, there have been books about trips. In the Sumerian *Epic of Gilgamesh*, King Gilgamesh and his grass-eating, wild-haired buddy Enkidu are off to the Cedar Forest by tablet 4.

In fairness, Gilgamesh and Enkidu aren't just going on vacation—they're going to kill the monstrous giant Humbaba because it will make them even more famous. Gilgamesh is already famous—back in tablet 1, it's established that he's had sex with every single hot woman in Uruk, to the point that it's a problem. But he feels called to go on an adventure.

Maybe the first person to take a trip just to write about it was Herodotus, who lived in Greece, or maybe western Turkey, in the fifth century BC. He went across the Mediterranean to have a look at Egypt.

Herodotus showed the way to write this kind of book: Put in anything interesting you come across. He believed anything anybody told him, like for example that in Central Asia, there are enormous ants that dig up gold. This might sound ridiculous, but it may even be half-true. The pro-

Herodotus historians will inform you that the Brogpa people of Ladakh, in far northern India, sometimes collected gold dust from burrows dug by Himalayan marmots. It doesn't matter. Herodotus's point was that the world was interesting, and if you had a look at it, and told people what you saw and heard, they'd be interested, too.

He was right. The story goes that Herodotus got back to Greece with his pages and went immediately to the Olympic Games, where he read his work out loud in an arena and was celebrated by the crowd with thunderous applause.

That's what later Greek writer Lucian claimed, anyway. Lucian might've been joking, come to think of it, or making fun of Herodotus in some weird, jealous way. You can feel the professional envy dripping off Lucian: "There was no man who had not heard his name . . . he had only to appear, and fingers were pointing at him."

Lucian was so pissed, in fact, that he wrote *True History*. As best as I can tell, *True History* was meant to be a wicked, brutal parody of Herodotus's travel stories. Lucian goes on and on about how when *he* was traveling, he saw a river of wine and a cheese island, and he visited the morning star where dog-faced men fight each other on flying acorns.

I won't make anything up, though. Everything I put in this book is true. I saw it or heard it or experienced it myself, or else it's something I learned that I looked into and I believe to be true.

There's no need to make up experiences. Why do that extra work of imagining? If you just go out into the world far enough, you'll find plenty that's crazy and worth putting down.

Ancient China was full of travel tales. In the 1600s, Xu Xiake went all over China, along the way earning extra money from Buddhist abbots who would pay him to gather and write the history of local monasteries. There's enough odd and exaggerated stuff in Chinese travel literature to fuel a whole industry of people who believe ancient Chinese sailors were hanging out in San Francisco Bay by the 1400s.

Then there was Rustichello da Pisa, who'd had some success writing a romance about King Arthur before he got thrown into a dungeon in

Genoa around the year 1284. His cellmate was a guy named Marco Polo, who, it turned out, had traveled farther than anyone else alive, all the way to the court of Kublai Khan in what's now Beijing.

Or had he? Some scholars suspect he made a lot of it up. But in any case, Rustichello saw a chance to make a quick buck ghostwriting, and the result is that Europe heard about China.

Soon the great age of exploring began. In 1492, Columbus discovered something. It was unclear what, but the desperate and adventurous went to find out. Alcoholic bastard sons of minor nobles in Spain went to South America, lucked into lopsided victories over the locals, and made themselves lords of spectacularly wealthy kingdoms. Others got lost in the jungle and went insane. Magellan set off around the world on a leaky wooden boat that he had barely any idea how to navigate. He got himself speared to death in the Philippines by natives who guessed, correctly, that he was up to no good, but the survivors of his expedition became the first people to circumnavigate the Earth.

From there traveling and travel writing were unstoppable. People couldn't get enough. The English went particularly nuts with exploring, maybe because they were from a cold, dreary island where nothing fun ever happened, and meanwhile the first English captains to reach Tahiti were writing stupefied entries in their logbooks about what Tahitian women had just taught them about blow jobs.

The American scholar Paul Fussell wrote a whole book, *Abroad*, about this history of English travel writing, about sensitive aristocrats and shell-shocked survivors of World War I who set out for the tropics, for the desert, for the source of the river Oxus, and for the peaks of the Himalayas. There were so many English writers taking trips that they'd run into each other. Eric Newby was trekking around Afghanistan writing *A Short Walk in the Hindu Kush* when he ran into the legendary explorer Wilfred Thesiger, who was living with a local tribe and who told Newby the route he was taking was for pussies.

Travel books were a massive form of entertainment in the nineteenth century. Robert Louis Stevenson commissioned one of the world's first sleeping bags so he could write his bestseller *Travels with a Donkey in the Cevennes.* Herman Melville got famous writing about his real-life adventures with cannibals in the Marquesas, and then went broke when he switched to fiction. The freelance reporter Henry Stanley went to Africa to find lost do-gooder doctor David Livingstone. All along the way back, he got chiefs to sign contracts they didn't understand, which he then sold to the king of Belgium, who used them to claim the entire Congo.

For most of human history it was a lot easier for men to chuck whatever they were doing and wander off somewhere. But the stories of women who did it are incredible. There's an old theater near my house in Los Angeles where a packed audience heard a speech from Amelia Earhart, who soon thereafter took off on a flight around the world she never came back from.

Lately, women have been dominating the field, perhaps because they've realized the emotional journey is more important than the physical one. Elizabeth Gilbert and Cheryl Strayed wrote massive bestsellers that are on the surface about geographical trips but are really about journeys of growth and restoration.

(There's much more about female travel writers tucked in at the end of this book.)

The world has changed so dramatically in the past ten to twenty years it's difficult to contemplate. One result has been that firsthand reports, dispatches, and images from anywhere in the world are about a thousand times easier to get than they were when I was a boy poring over the murals of Bonampak and the Amazon in *National Geographic.*

But I think I still have something to offer.

It seems like there might be some ground for me to stake out in the realm of travel reporting. Somewhere between a hard-nosed reporter who's camping out with the dwellers of the garbage dumps of Nicaragua, and Rick Steves, who tells PBS viewers where to find Stockholm's best cinnamon buns.

How I Came to Write This Book

Leaving my house, heading south, and going all the way down the globe to the very bottom tip of the Western Hemisphere. That was an idea I'd had for a while. To be able to draw a line of travel down the side of Central and South America seemed like it would be satisfying.

And then one day a sign appeared. A map on the wall of my local coffee shop. It was a big colored relief map like you'd hang on the wall of a sixth-grade classroom, showing Central and South America. Everywhere from Mexico down to the end, to Tierra del Fuego. Everything south of where I was.

Just a bit of hipster style, really, nostalgic-retro interior decoration. The map was in bright 1970s colors, covering the concrete wall.

But to me it was like a dare.

Maybe I should go down there.

First I said that to myself.

Then I started saying it to other people: "I'm gonna leave my home and go south."

"South where?"

"I dunno, everywhere south, until I get to the bottom. Across Mexico, Central America, and South America down to the Straits of Magellan."

If this was a bad idea, no one told me. I live in Los Angeles. In Los Angeles, nobody ever tells you if your idea is bad.

Los Angeles, I'm Yours

Los Angeles is fantastic. In LA, dreams erupt out of the ground like water gushing from fountains, and it's sunny every day. The beach is there, the mountains are there, but it doesn't matter if you never go to either of them. Many people don't. They prefer to mix it up and eat and drink and party at the exploding carnival camped out in the valley by the Pacific, the most wonderful carnival in the history of the world.

Before I moved to Los Angeles, a friend told me, "In Los Angeles, a complete idiot becomes a millionaire every single day. Don't come here if you'll hate that. Come here if you'll love that."

Well, it scared me a little, but I decided I'd love it, too. I came. He was right. It's stupefying and wonderful.

Carved into a monument in Pershing Square in downtown Los Angeles, I mean as close as possible to the exact old civic heart of the city, presumably the most sensible and stodgiest place in the city, a short walk—walk!—from the courthouse and City Hall, is a true story, from journalist Carey McWilliams's 1946 book *Southern California Country*. McWilliams says—again, his words describing this are carved in stone in the heart of Los Angeles—he got blackout drunk one night, woke up at the Biltmore Hotel where some friends had carried him, stepped outside to the park, and saw a blond woman hike her skirt up, get into the fountain, and start singing while "grimacing and leering old goats" cheered her on. "Here indeed was the place for me," says McWilliams, "a ringside seat at the circus."

That's what you get in LA, you get a ringside seat at the circus, and I love the circus.

Don't get me wrong, there are times when Los Angeles drives me crazy. That's my fault. That's because I came here from Massachusetts and sometimes my stubborn mind wearies itself out working away, working its feeble little gears of logic to try to figure out questions like *What is happening?* That is a terrible instinct, a curse, really. It's never gotten me anywhere but frustrated. Los Angeles doesn't make sense, it's not supposed to. If it ever did, it gave up long ago. Sometimes somebody tries to make sense, to implement some plan. The result is always ridiculous, any work on it ends up abandoned, one more absurd and baffling ruin to point out and idly wonder about and tease until it's another chunk of beloved eccentric ephemera on the landscape, something you smile at from the 101 as you whizz past.

No, Los Angeles operates on dream logic. People come out here because of dreams and then they work in the field of dreams at huge dream companies that try to make and bottle and sell dreams. Which is of course impossible. You can have no idea what dream people want, what dream they're having, but somehow everything works out and everybody who does it in the right spirit, accepting that it's all a dream, seems to me to get some version of what they were after.

There are the movie and TV and music businesses, sure, but my opinion is that's not even where the biggest dreamers are. Close to the core, those businesses get kind of conservative, actually, from what I've seen of the inside of them. But real estate? Technology? The energy business, design, fashion, art, communications? Those people have no limit. You can easily meet well-groomed people in very nice clothes who will tell you they intend to die in space or their children's bodies will be kept in silicon isospheres while their consciousness experiences the singularity through neurotech. Then they might tell you they've been distilling their own mescal and offer you some.

Everywhere, there are tacos and delicious cheeseburgers and cold-pressed juices and Salvadoran pupusas and Korean barbecues, and every week somebody tells you to drive out to some mysterious suburb like San Gabriel or Alhambra to get a soup just like they make it in the southern beach villages of Thailand, or a special tea dumpling you could only get in Sichuan. And the fruits and vegetables! In Los Angeles, it's legal to pick any fruit that hangs over the sidewalk. No one minds because there's so much of it! I used to walk up the street from my house and pluck grape-fruits. There are palm trees and cactuses, and in the hills there are deer and coyotes.

For some people this dream is too much, too intense. Scary, even. They try to warn everyone that dreams sometimes turn into nightmares. There are police helicopters overhead and there's not enough water, the hills could slide into the ocean at any minute, and who knows what's coming from south over the border?

To these doom prophets most people shrug and say "Maybe!" Sure, maybe in your twenties you read the pessimistic LA urbanist Mike Davis or talk to people at parties about the Manson family and *Blade Runner*, but you can't take it too seriously. Keep some of it on your shelf as a souvenir and then move on to Reyner Banham, who drove around in the 1970s filming himself marveling to his English countrymen at how fantastic everything was. Or pick up Joan Didion, who stared hard in the face at everything terrible about Los Angeles but then went off to vacation in Hawaii with the shitloads of money she made writing movies that never even happened.

The English painter David Hockney came to Los Angeles in 1963 and he said, "Within a week of arriving there in this strange big city, not knowing a soul, I'd passed the driving test, bought a car, driven to Las Vegas and won some money, got myself a studio, started painting, all within a week. And I thought, it's just how I imagined it would be." I quoted that one time to a woman I knew in New York, and she said to me, "Yes, everyone from Los Angeles is always bringing up that quote."

A few years later she moved to Los Angeles to work for a guy who's trying to pioneer electric cars, travel through space, and build a hyper-tube to San Francisco.

Don't Wake Up LA!

D on't get me wrong: I kind of agree with the doomsayers. If anything, I think it's *worse* than they do. From what my eyes have seen, the apocalypse is well under way and spilled long ago into Los Angeles County. The local news is nothing but fires and murders and gangs of barbarians and people driven mad with rage, and law enforcement overwhelmed or driven themselves to madness. Drive out to Palmdale or Lancaster and see cities that were sold as bountiful beacons of promise now dusty half ruins overrun by wild dogs. Drive out to Mojave and you're in full-on Mad Max country. Beyond that, the desert is mostly owned by the federal government, which long ago gave up stopping weirdos from ripping around on it on their ATVs, except on those stretches the military uses to do practice bomb runs and/or build mock Iraqi towns to invade.

For a while I got interested in fly-fishing. It was fun, but the real lesson I took from it is how far from Los Angeles you have to go to be near even a minor stretch of running water, even a stream. We used to drive 266 miles to get to the nearest fishable river. Los Angeles, just the city, has 3.8 million people or so, and it has nowhere near enough water to drink, let alone to water everyone's yards and grapefruit trees and fill everybody's swimming pools. Los Angeles is a dry place, it's a desert culture. That's why the first thing that happens whenever you go to an important meeting is someone offers you a bottle of water. As with desert tribes, offering water is a sign of power. The last true tyrants of Los Angeles understood this, and that's why all along the banks of that fishable river 266 miles away, you see signs that read PROPERTY OF LOS ANGELES DEPARTMENT OF WATER AND POWER, because they bought/stole it a hundred years ago and drained whole lakes and valleys and pumped water over miles of hills and through mountains and sent it gushing down the great concrete aqueducts into Los Angeles.

So: Yeah, I get it. My one point might be it's too simple to say there's *a catastrophe coming.* I'd say *the catastrophe's already happening.* We're in it, this is it, the whole thing's a catastrophe. And you know what? People are still desperate to come here. Most of them who make it want to stay. It's possible Los Angeles has its doom coming. But I doubt it's anything we can predict or do anything to prevent. If the whole thing ends, it'll be with a big sudden jolt—like waking up from a dream.

Where I Was From

Before LA, I lived in New York City. I moved there in 2003, probably in the last generation when kids just out of college could afford to live in Manhattan. On an island! In Manhattan, every single street is interesting. There are whole neighborhoods just for partying, blocks and blocks with a bar on every one. You could drink in the courtyard of one bar on Saturday afternoon and stumble up the steps and into the sunlight from another bar on Sunday morning and round the corner and there are your friends having brunch right there, and on the way home, there's a store to sell you Advil and toilet paper and Gatorade and there's Julianne Moore walking her dog.

New York is wonderful, all praise to New York. But when I've gone back there it's felt fun but a little off somehow, like it's becoming a theme park of itself. Some people are enjoying the theme park but some people are grumbling because it isn't the theme park they wanted or were sold or the ticket was too expensive. Or they're just tired because they're not part of the theme park of New York at all. New York's just the place they live in, but the theme park's taken over all the good stuff, so it's just a long train ride to work every day.

That's what it seems to me, anyway. But if somebody asks me, "Which one do you like better, New York or LA?" I say, "They're both great!" while also fretting because this conversation is off to a boring start.

But where I'm really from is Massachusetts. Sometimes in a brief exchange I might shorthand and say I'm from Boston. That has the danger of giving the wrong idea, like I grew up with a bunch of Irish drunks and armed robbers who never pronounced the letter *r*, when really I grew up in a pretty nice suburb. There were plenty of Irish drunks, though.

Boston is clannish, tribal, and boastful. It makes sense if you imagine it as being more an Irish town than an American city. If you follow the stories of Boston sports teams, you realize they're written and told in the same dramatic, histrionic way the Irish tell their history, maudlin, weeping years of famine and then wild, outrageous victories behind stupendous white heroes. Even the greatest black athlete in Boston history was named Bill Russell. But what comes with that, too, is Irish Catholicism, a thick, long-brewing stew of guilt and self-pity and -aggrandizement and -aggrievement. Mix *that* in with the pockets of Italians and the French Canadians and the Jews and the immigrants and the black people and it *does* make everybody funny.

There's also the whole Puritan strain, which runs from the witch-hanging founders of Boston, the Pilgrim fathers who arrived and straight-up declared they were here to set up God's shining city on a hill and then went to work translating the Bible into Algonquin. Their children and grandchildren turned this drive toward generating uptight and industrious families and building empires of mills and whale ships, leaving their names behind on the dorms at Harvard as their trust-funded descendants slipped into the decadences of the time, like schizophrenic poetry and art collecting.

Combine these two traditions and what you get is an insane self-regard. I mean it's really so delusional as to be endearing, the regard in which Boston people hold Boston. When I was young, it was once reported in *The Boston Globe* that Supreme Court Justice David Souter of New Hampshire, while walking in Boston's Public Garden, remarked, "Who needs Paris when you have Boston?" and many Boston readers heartily agreed. People in Boston call it the hub of the universe and the Athens of America and they pretend they're joking, but they're not. If anything, they think that's a bit too much of a compliment to Athens, which they hear has fallen into a scuzzy shambles lately, not that they've bothered to go. This insane Bostonian self-regard is also why people who went to Harvard get weird one way or another when it's time to tell you they went there. It's because they're so certain of the godlike power Harvard's name will mean to *you* that they get self-conscious. They think they're being, like, humble or courteous, but thinking that just shows how insanely highly they regard Harvard. It's a truly, psychopathically Puritan way of self-aggrandizing while also *simultaneously* self-congratulating for, of all things, *modesty*! Truly unbelievable. (I went to Harvard.)

New England is brutally cold and harsh, the soil is rocky and stingy. In the summer the air can get heavy and thick and humid for weeks at a time, only releasing now and again in a violent thunderstorm. There's every sign that God is showing no favors to this place, which of course is just how the Catholics and the Puritans like it. They convince themselves this is all edifying, that God, like a tough coach, is giving them just as much as they can handle because He wants to make them stronger. He loves them so much He gives them lots to complain about. When there's a perfect day, in October or May, it's true there's nothing like New England, it's so beautiful. But that's a bit like eating a pound of cold broccoli every night and then rewarding yourself with a single bite of a chocolate macaroon from the world's best bakery. It doesn't make a *ton* of sense.

This is all to explain why when I got to California it kind of blew my head off.

Here was a place where every day was gorgeous. When it rained, every rare once in a while, even that was thrilling fun. Everybody freaked out and water gushed down the canyons. The next day it was green everywhere and the air was so clear you could see Catalina Island from the hills.

But it wasn't just the climate. The whole way of seeing the world was upside down. In New England, nobody has a positive attitude. Why would you? It'll be winter again soon, and that's gonna be a friggin' nightmare (pronounced "nightmayh") so suck it up and get on with it. You're lucky to be walkin' around.

But in California? Dude! If you're not crushing it? Your problem must be you're not projecting enough positive vibes! Or else your vision isn't epic enough. Every day, somebody will tell you about a juice cleanse or cultish exercise and how amazing it's making them feel. Every single conversation has at least some element of delusion. You might spend a very happy morning talking to five or six people about a project everyone knows is never going to happen. But everybody has a good time, so who cares? You get a bottle of water when you arrive and parking validation when you leave.

People in Boston are more buttoned up than people in Los Angeles, that's for sure. I mean literally: They button up more of their buttons. That probably started just because it's colder in Boston, but something like that can grow into a whole philosophy, whole ideas of restraint and propriety and decency. There are lots of ideas like that in Boston.

There are none of those ideas in Los Angeles. To suggest them is to be kind of rude, actually. Suggesting, for instance, that filming yourself having sex is a less "respectable" job than, say, being a public school principal is a mark of deep confusion, if not very wrong, malevolent, "judgy" thinking. That can go too far, of course, it can get a little crazy, and for someone from New England, it can be disorienting. But the value at the root of it is tolerance, acceptance, openness to possibility, the belief that there's a whole wide range of realities, maybe not just yours. In a way it's a kind of moral humility. At its best, that openness is what makes Los Angeles so great.

Sometimes, people from elsewhere in the world tell me that they've heard the people in LA are "fake." That's totally true. People are working to put across some invented image all the time. Literally, a lot of them are acting. You don't just stop doing that after work. People are auditioning for you all the time. For what part, you often have no idea. *They* may not know. You do get the feeling, all the time, that you're a bit player in somebody else's whacked-out reality show.

But mostly, I think the fakeness is a kind of politeness. Courtesy. There are lots of people in LA who are working very hard on wild, creative endeavors. Lots of wild, creative endeavors turn out to be disasters. Many more, probably most, turn out to be just . . . nothing, mixed-bag experiments presented to a public that shrugs, says "Okay," and moves on. One in ten thousand will be a stupendous, world-changing success. But do not trust anyone who tells you they know which one it will be. No one knows. If you're right more often than you're wrong you're a genius. If you're right *once* you might be a genius. You can be wrong ten times and then really right once and retire in comfort to Ojai.

So people default, sensibly enough, to a generic, noncommittal sunni-ness. What else is there to do? Somebody tells you an idea that sounds insane, that you suspect will lead them, at best, to skulking, humiliated retreat and, at worst, to major public embarrassment and all you can do is say, "Sounds great!"

You could say this is a kind of moral cowardice. Maybe it is. But I think it's a kind of modesty, an acceptance that this is all beyond logic, and that all you can do is root for good things and make honest efforts and be around fun people. And maybe it's a kind of respect for anybody who's bold enough to spend their life running after some illusory vision.

Even if their vision sounds *super* stupid.

So Why Was I Restless?

I don't know, but I was.

I had a great life in Los Angeles, writing for TV shows like *The Office* and *American Dad*. When you write for a TV show, you get something called hiatus. *Hiatus* is a word television people—not just writers but other kinds of con artists like actors and (most amazing con artists of all) producers—got together and made up because "two to three months of vacation" would induce outrage in the general public. The trick worked, which shows you the power in naming things, and so people who work on TV shows get huge amounts of time off.

When I was twenty-seven, I used my hiatus to travel all the way around the world by ship and train. A TV writer friend of mine—you may have heard of him, his name, Vali Chandrasekaran, lives in infamy—and I cooked up the idea of having a race around the world. We'd leave Los Angeles. I'd go west, Vali would go east, and the first person to make it all the way around the globe would win a bottle of expensive Scotch. The only rule was no airplanes.

What happened next is recorded in our book, *The Ridiculous Race*. It was a great adventure for me: I saw whales breaching off the volcanic Aleutian Islands from the deck of a cargo ship, road-tripped across China with my beautiful translator and two prostitute-loving drivers, stayed with a nomad family in Mongolia, took the Trans-Siberian Railway through days' worth of forests to Moscow, partied with Swedish celebrities, visited very distant relatives in the mountains of Italy, ate in Paris, sailed from Southampton to New York on the *Queen Mary*, and rode with a truck driver across the United States and back to LA the long way.

That should've cured me, but it didn't. I was still itchy. Every chance I got I went someplace interesting. Cuba, Vietnam, India, Dubai, Texas. None of it fixed whatever wanderlust or curiosity monster was eating me.

All that happened was I got more ideas of places to go. My work was really interesting and fun, but still I'd catch myself staring out the window, wondering what it was like in the Mauritius islands or Mali or Micronesia.

Maybe I have some kind of genetic wandering disease. There might be a strain of that in Americans.

Now I couldn't stop thinking about going south to the bottom of the map.

Maybe lots of people get ideas like this, daydream about them. Some obvious excuse comes up, or the dream passes, and they never do it. Probably their lives are no less happy for it.

For me, there was no excuse. By luck, good or bad, or choice, wise or stupid, or some swirly combination of it all, I was at that moment thirty-four and completely free of commitment. What came instead, in fact, was an odd, accidental gap in work, maybe three months before my next TV writing job started.

This was a lucky break like nobody ever gets. I had to go someplace.

Mexico
Mayan Stuff
Waterfalls?
Canal
Volcanoes?
Coffee?
Easter?
Galápagos
Amazon River
Machu Picchu
Lake Titicaca
Maps not 100% accurate Do not use for navigation
Atacama Desert
Andes
Patagonia

The Wonder Trail

My idea was to get to the bottom of the continent. Puerto Williams, in Tierra del Fuego, at the southern tip of Chile, claims to be the southernmost city in the world, and most reasonable people agree. That was my target, but there was a whole lot of world to see on the way.

Now, if I were a real hero, I would never once leave the ground. I would travel by bus and horse and foot and train and boat. But: In this part of the world, there are very few trains, at least trains that carry humans instead of loads of coal and nitrate.

Bus, horse, foot, boat, I'd try all the rest, but in three months. I'd never make it. Plus, there were the wonders. I wanted to see:

- [ ] the Mayan villages of southern Mexico
- [ ] the ruins of the ancient Mayan cities
- [ ] at least one good waterfall
- [ ] the volcanoes of Central America
- [ ] the best coffee in the world
- [ ] the Panama Canal
- [ ] some traditional and strange Easter festival
- [ ] the Amazon jungle
- [ ] Machu Picchu
- [ ] the Galápagos
- [ ] the Andes
- [ ] Lake Titicaca
- [ ] the Atacama Desert of Chile

And at last to the wind-worn plains and jagged mountains and dramatic coast of Patagonia. It seemed like there was a trail of wonders that led down to the bottom of the globe.

Now, look, three months isn't long. I couldn't see it all. There's a fork in the road there, south of Panama. I chose west.

That meant I'd miss Brazil, Argentina, Uruguay, Venezuela, Suriname, Guyana, and French Guiana.

I know. I'm sorry. Suriname is worth seeing for its toads alone. I skipped Belize, too. Belize, once known as British Honduras, is a whole interesting weirdness of its own. Another time, Belize.

So: west. I made one plan for where to be at Easter, and then I went to work on how to cross the Darién Gap, the most lawless and dangerous stretch of this trail.

Beyond that: Well, you can't plan too much for this kind of thing. Sooner or later you just go.

Possible Alternate Title for This Book:

A Gift to Those Who Contemplate the Wonder of Cities and the Marvels of Traveling

Didn't think up that title myself, actually. That's the title of Ibn Battuta's book. He dictated it in the year 1355. Ibn Battuta was probably the most widely traveled man in the world before Magellan. When he was twenty-one, he left his home in Morocco on a pilgrimage to Mecca. He didn't make it back home again for twenty-four years.

In that time, he visited China and Vietnam and Malaysia, he crossed the Sahara a few times and maybe went to Russia. Along the way he got married three times. Battuta was a proper Muslim. In his book he complains about topless women everywhere. On the paradise island of the Maldives, he basically got kidnapped by King Omar, who liked him so much he not only made him be chief judge, he also insisted Battuta marry his prettiest sister. Battuta, meanwhile, sat around stewing that no one listened to his complaints about the topless women.

Look, I'm not saying I expected that would happen to me on this trip. I'm saying I was open to it.

It's a tiny bit presumptuous to call your book a gift. I'm far from comparing myself to Ibn Battuta, who was obviously one of the coolest men who ever lived (if a bit uptight about tits). But it wasn't lost on me that I'm *lucky*. I don't mean to brag or tempt fate. What I mean is, I was in the position to take this trip because I was born lucky. I was born where I was and when I was, I got a chance to get the best education in the world, to follow my passions and go down the roads I thought looked most delightful and interesting. I was a young (well, young-ish, even one more year and it might get creepy, I had to go *now*) healthy white man in America who made more money than he needed just by doing what he loved and would've done anyway.

That's not because there's all that much that's special and amazing about me. It's because I'm lucky. The world is wild and arbitrary, so much of it is based on luck. If there's a moral to a book about the southern half of the Western Hemisphere, it might be "life isn't fair." I don't know what you should do about the inequality of luck that exists in the world. That's probably the greatest moral issue of our time.

The one thing I do know is that if you're lucky, you should try to share it. That's the point of this book. To make out of my journey some informative entertainment, and I hope you enjoy it.

So:

I got a backpack, threw in a few shirts, socks, underpants, a first-aid kit, malaria pills, cigarettes (I've found you can always start a conversation if you have cigarettes), and a couple of good books, and I went south.

When you go south from the United States, the first place you come to is Mexico.

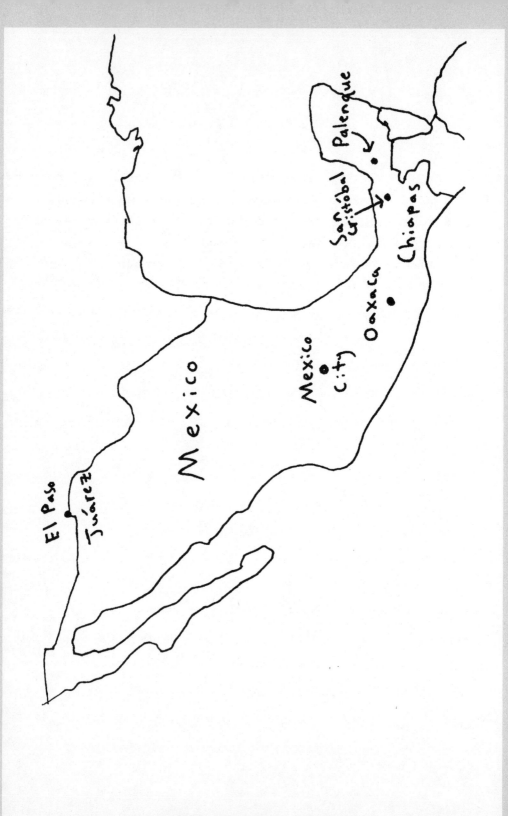

Mexico

Spanish Level: *De Gravedad*

Before my trip, I'd signed up for an eight-week Spanish course at the Beverly Hills Lingual Institute, but truth be told, between the awful fluorescent lights and the persistent sweatiness of my teacher, it reminded me of everything bad about school and I skipped half the classes.

With discipline, I made up for this by practicing with an iPhone app called Duolingo. Duolingo is like a little video game that teaches you a language. You are encouraged to learn by a cartoon bird. The bird is happy if you do well. If you skip too many days in a row, the bird grows sad. The bird will cry, and grow sadder and sadder. Soon the bird was so sad I couldn't bear to look at it and I stopped practicing.

No worries. Immersion is the best way to learn anyway. On the streets of San Cristóbal and Medellín, Spanish will flow into my ears and soon out my mouth. That's what I decided, possessing as I did a rich, imaginative mind gifted and honed to make excuses for laziness.

With confidence I went to LAX, said, "*Uno person por Mexico DF*," and boarded my flight.

There was a boy in the window seat in the row across from me. He was with his father, who sat, tired but calm, as the boy leaned forward as hard as he could against his seat belt to look out the window. The boy had Down syndrome, but you could tell he was a wonderful boy and his father loved him very much. His father was one of the most patient and gentle fathers I've ever seen, having so much calm it couldn't help but calm the boy himself when he would get excited.

As I watched this, I was moved in the deepest places of my heart. I tried to listen to the soft words the father exchanged with the boy, the patient answers to his simple questions.

Then I fell into a panic.

I can't understand most of this. Oh God. My Spanish comprehension, let alone my speaking, is way below the level of an eight-year-old with Down syndrome.

Maybe it was lucky I was skipping half of Mexico.

The Bad North of Mexico

S ome of the best writing in the world, the best fiction and the bravest journalism, is about the border country of northern Mexico. Cormac McCarthy, Roberto Bolaño, Charles Bowden, Don Winslow, Ambrose Bierce, these are some of the ones I learned about it from: hard guys looking hard at a hard place.

It's very strange country for sure. Tough country, dry and hot and dusty. On top of that, there's a border there, a line violently imposed and held that didn't used to be there.

From the Atlantic Ocean to El Paso, Texas, the border follows the Rio Grande, but that doesn't make it natural. Comanches, Apaches, Jumanos, and people before them walked and camped and crossed all over this land for 11,000 years before there was a border. After the Republic of Texas had joined the United States, and the US Army had raised the American flag over Mexico City, the border was created. By no accident, most of the good stuff was in the US and the shitty part was in Mexico.

Don't get me wrong. There's a lot of Mexico that's wonderful and interesting. My goal was to get to that part of Mexico as quickly as possible. I'd already seen as much of the bad stuff as I cared to.

In a previous burst of restlessness, years back, I took a bus from Los Angeles to Mexico City. My idea was that maybe I'd see "the real Mexico." I think I did, and I didn't like it. I changed buses in Ciudad Juárez. This was in 2008, when the mayor and the chief of police of Juárez had fled the city. What I saw mostly was the bus station, which armed soldiers with automatic weapons discouraged me from leaving. This was when Juárez was still the world's murder capital, with drug war killings piled onto what some suspected was a diabolical serial killer, or killers, who was murdering some unknown number of young women from the city's maquiladoras—"assembly factories," or "sweatshops." What I saw once I got on the bus were streets that looked half-abandoned as the sun rose on the dismal paint of lifeless-looking stores, but it was very early in the morning, so who knows? Since then, I'm told that Juárez, murders much reduced, is having a mini renaissance. I hope so. When the mini renaissance has taken full hold, maybe I'll go back.

What I saw for two days *on* the bus were Mexican men in white straw cowboy hats sleeping through Spanish-dubbed American movies like *Alex Rider: Operation Stormbreaker*.

What I saw *outside* the bus was dry, rough desert. Off to the side of the road, across the dust and brown earth, we passed a prison. *Wow*, I thought to myself, *inside of that prison is one of the top places on Earth I never want to be*. Some months later I read an article about a riot in the prison where twenty people died.

Our bus stopped in a town called Villa Ahumada. The bus driver, without a word, stopped the bus and vanished into the town. It was three hours until he came back, and we took off without explanation. Not more than two weeks later in a Mexican newspaper I read about how a drug gang had ridden into Villa Ahumada and shot it up. The entire police department fled.

After two days the bus arrived in Mexico City, where I went to see a bullfight. The bullfight was no joke. The Plaza México holds 45,000 people. I'd say it was 40 percent full when the events got started, just as the sun was starting to go down. It's wrong to call a bullfight a fight. It's not a fight, it's a sacrifice. A dangerous sacrifice maybe, but it's always gonna end with a human killing a bull for the benefit of a crowd.

This bullfight wasn't even a good one by bullfight standards. The third and final bull ended his days up against a clumsy matador who was failing to do his job, which is, literally, to kill. The crowd was not helping. They were booing. People threw programs and seat cushions into the ring. Ugly, the whole scene. No one could've enjoyed it. The bull was killed, finally, after enough time for the crowd to make clear what they were feeling. *Disgust.*

That wasn't one of my best trips.

If you go looking for horrible things to see in Mexico, you can find them. I'm not a journalist. I decline to take that on as my job. I'm an entertainment writer, weekend library historian, and amateur explorer.

My job's to discover wonderful things, I decided. So I began my Great Southern Expedition by flying right to Mexico City, where the craziest action and wildest ideas have been since at least the days of the Aztecs.

If You Have One Hour in Mexico City:

D o this: Start at the Plaza de la Constitución.
    (I will assume you can teleport yourself there. If your hour starts at, say, the airport, then forget it, you're done.)

Here is the Plaza de la Constitución, a huge paved square with an almost-as-huge Mexican flag flying over it. In 1847, the American flag flew over this square, when the US Army invaded and drove their way into Mexico City. Robert E. Lee and Ulysses Grant were both there. But after slicing off what they wanted of the northern part of Mexico, the US Army went back home and a few years later, American veterans of Mexico spent their excess energy killing each other in the Civil War.

Now have a look at that enormous church on the north side. That is Mexico City's Metropolitan Cathedral, largest in the Western Hemisphere. Inside it's crazy. There's a whole lot to see: You can stop at the shrine of the Niño Cautivo if you need to pray for someone who's kidnapped. But with just an hour, stay outside. Have a look at the whole size of the thing.

Now notice how the cathedral is leaning. This is because it's sinking, because the ground you're standing on was once in the middle of an enormous lake.

Hard to believe, but this is true. Where we are was on an island in that lake. On the island, there was a city, and in the year 1519, it may have been the biggest city in the world.

This was built by the Aztecs, though that's no longer the preferred nomenclature. Let's say, instead, it was built by a people who were called the Mexica.

Their temple—the temple of the Mexicans, the Aztecs—stood right in the middle of the island. It was enormous. A Spanish soldier named Bernal Díaz del Castillo stood on top of the temple in its last days. Just to walk up the stairs was exhausting. Díaz says that at the top there was a massive statue of a dragon "and other hideous figures." He says there was a stone altar, and the day he went up, it was wet with blood from humans who'd been sacrificed that very day. But to him, that wasn't even the scary part. Writing fifty years later, he still remembered how stunned he was when he looked *out*.

You'd see for miles. You'd see the city. You'd see the marketplace and "the swarm of people, buying and selling." Díaz says you could hear the noise of the marketplace from three miles away. Men with him said it reminded them of Constantinople or Rome. You'd see streets of houses with flat roofs, and smaller temples everywhere, on out to the three causeways that led out of the island, across the lake, but the lake would be full of boats, and on the shores of the lake would be many *more* towns and towers and temples, on and on.

That was Tenochtitlán, or Mexico, the city of the Mexicans. Two years later it was destroyed, it was burned to the ground and the stone buildings were torn down, knocked down, and almost everyone who lived there was dead. That was maybe 100,000 people, and their bodies were spread out so thick across the city that you could walk through the streets, from one end of the island to the other, stepping only on their dead bodies.

That was here. That was right under where you're standing. That was Tenochtitlán, and it became Mexico City.

No sooner was it destroyed than it started to grow again. Like a seed from the ash of a wildfire.* It grew so fast, if you watched it from the tower of the cathedral—well, first of all, you'd see construction the whole time because they started the cathedral in 1573, and they weren't done until 1813—you'd see earthquakes and fires and riots and cannon fire, but then, very fast, you'd see the city explode in size, going all up the mountainsides in wild, unplanned neighborhoods that are *still* going up fast. Yes, you'd see all that from the cathedral, you'd see the rise of these incredible neighborhoods around you.

---

*Just assuming seeds from wildfire ash grow fast, don't really know, not gonna look it up.

It all rose up from the ruins of Tenochtitlán because the Spanish were *genius conquerors*. They knew the way to conquer. They knew all you had to do to conquer a nation was:

> 1) knock down their gods,

> 2) put up your gods,

and then

> 3) that's it.

That's it, that's all you need to do. Knock down their gods, put up your gods. Game over after that. Don't sweat the details, either. If they want your gods to look kinda like their gods? Fine. Get their guys to paint it, the Mexicans were amazing painters. Get their guys to do almost everything. Relax and count the money.

That's how the Spanish "conquered Mexico." The more you study it, the less it seems like they really conquered it—the Spanish king had lost it by, oh, 1821 or so. Plus, it happened so fast of course that everybody got mixed up, racially. There were kids who were half Spanish and half—oh, let's pretend she was a Mexican princess and not look back much further, and then their kids and their kids and so on until there was, of course, a whole new place.

That's Mexico, and you're in its capital. If you turn around, you will see the presidential palace. Astounding, no? But you only have an hour, so come with me down the busy street to El Moro Churrería, where you can have one of four kinds of hot chocolate: *mexicana* (lightest of all), *francia* (darker, but with a hint of vanilla), *española* (thick and extra sweet), or *suiza* (with extra cream).

I say if you're only here once, then goddammit be a champion and order all four, find a friend if you have to, won't be hard, and dip in those churros they give you and admire the white tile floor, you have to admit a classy touch. This place has been here since the 1930s, what a wondrous refuge from the busy city, and yet through the window, you can watch all the city pass by on the wide Eje Central Lázaro Cárdenas. The last Aztec emperor, Montezuma, used to drink hot chocolate before visiting his many wives.

Uhp! Boom hour's up. That's it, you're teleporting out.

But as you shimmer away, think about how baller that is of the Spanish. Where they put the cathedral. They put it right on top of the smoking (okay, maybe not smoking but the) ruins of the Mexican temple, right in its rubble. Right on top of your temple we will put our temple, BIIIITCH!

Except look at that cathedral—just real quick, remember it, and wonder if it doesn't look more than anything like an Aztec temple, like a Mexican temple, like just a twisted version of what was there before?

This was my third time in Mexico City, and my third time at El Moro Churrería. Over the years, I'd tried to learn, as best I could, how Mexico City got to be the way it is.

In the year 1519, this was the biggest city in the Western Hemisphere.

The First White People in Mexico

W ait, let's say:

The First Europeans in Mexico

B ecause talking about "white people" and what *that* even means gets thorny awful fast.

Race in Mexico is very tricky, just like it is in the USA. You start making decisions about what race somebody is and before you know it, you're unsticking yourself from ugly arguments that have been going on for four hundred years at least.

It's silly. One of the first two Europeans in Mexico had mixed-race kids, and after that, forget about sorting out who's white.

The first Europeans in Mexico washed up after a shipwreck. When Columbus hit the New World he hit the Caribbean, and that's where the Spanish Empire started setting up shop. Soon they'd found Panama. They knew there was more, the navigators sensed it. In 1511 a Franciscan monk named Jerónimo de Aguilar was sailing from Panama to Santo Domingo, where he was involved in a lawsuit with some guy. There were others on the ship, all kinds of adventurers, men and women. When their ship was wrecked, fifteen of the men and two women managed to get to the shore of Mexico. But it was bad times for them there.

They were captured by local natives, a people who called themselves the Calachiones. They spoke a Mayan language. Some of the shipwreck-ees got made into human sacrifices, offered to various gods. The two women were made to grind corn (and who knows what else) and died of overwork.

The only two survivors were Jerónimo the monk and a sailor named Gonzalo Guerrero. Jerónimo was made into a slave. He had to haul water and chop wood and work in the cornfields and haul heavy loads. The whole time, he stuck to his monkish vows, which baffled the local chief. Once, to test him, the chief made him spend the night in a hammock with a hot fourteen-year-old girl who'd been told to try to have sex with him.* Jerónimo fought temptation all night. When he got back, the chief was really impressed (according to Jerónimo).

Gonzalo the sailor, on the other hand, joined the natives, got a face tattoo, two ear piercings, and a native wife, had three kids, and became a famous warrior renowned for his bravery.

Seven years after the shipwreck, Jerónimo was sitting around his village, when some Indians showed up carrying letters they'd been given by strange men who'd landed on a nearby island. Letters in Spanish.

Jerónimo was ecstatic. He sent a message to Gonzalo saying something like "Oh my God! We're saved!" Gonzalo wrote back (I paraphrase), "Um, actually, I'm good here with my wife and kids." Jerónimo wrote back, "What about your eternal soul?!" to which he never heard from Gonzalo, who disappeared into the Mexican jungle. Years later Gonzalo's naked and tattooed body was found after a battle in what's now Honduras. He'd died helping his new Mayan countrymen fight off the Spanish.

Having tried his best with his countryman and gotten nowhere, the excited monk went down to the beach, where Hernán Cortés was just finishing up having some of the men in his expedition flogged.

---

*Not making this up. See *The General History of the Vast Continent and Islands of America, Commonly Call'd the West-Indies, from the First Discovery Thereof: with the Best Accounts the People Could Give of Their Antiquities,* written by Antonio de Herrera y Tordesillas. I'm reading the English translation by John Stevens.

Cortés the Killer

You may have heard of Cortés. Hernán Cortés, he is usually called now, though he sometimes signed his name as Ferdinando. I'm not sure what people called him. Almost nobody called him by his first name, I'm sure of that.

He was the man who led 508 Spanish soldiers and fifteen horses from the shore and through the jungle and across mountain passes in the snow and down into the very heart of Mexico, where they destroyed and burned to the ground the capital city of an empire of hundreds of thousands, and filled the rivers that fed the lake with dead bodies.

I say soldiers, but most of them, before they signed on with Cortés, were just guys. By the time they were done, they'd all seen human heads cut off, among a thousand other horrors, if they were still alive, which half of them weren't.

Cortés was born in a town called Medellín. His dad was a kind of low-level nobleman, a hidalgo. When he was a young man, Cortés left Spain and went to the Spanish colony on Cuba. There he promised a girl he'd marry her. Then he maybe hooked up with her sister for a while, tried to weasel out of the engagement, and was finally more or less forced to marry her. Then, years later, he maybe murdered her.

That was his personal life. In his professional life, Cortés was also pretty treacherous. In his early twenties, Cortés helped Diego Velázquez take over Cuba, and then he several times conspired against Velázquez. He kept getting locked in irons and then escaping. Finally he and Velázquez patched things up. Cortés got some land in Cuba and some gold mines, and made himself rich, but along the way he was so vicious to the enslaved natives that even other conquistador types were kinda weirded out.

There is no question Cortés was also insanely brave. Even if you detest

Cortés, you have to give him that. It's easy to see why he was thought to be demonic, because he moved across the countryside like an angel of death. There was no force that could stop him, and what trailed him in the villages and towns of those who opposed him was death and desolation and fear.

He was personally terrifying. He can seem psychotic. And yet in the letters he sent to his "Very High, very Powerful, and most Excellent Prince very Catholic and Invincible Emperor King and Lord," he tells of his conquest in a very calm and rational way. He seems to have been a genuine religious fanatic, stern, determined, and violent in his mission to exterminate the idolatry he believed he found everywhere he went.

He was not fucking messing around. That was the message that began to reach Montezuma, emperor of the Mexicans, when Cortés landed on the coast in the year 1519.

Montezuma of the Mexicans

Let me apologize in advance for possibly using the wrong terms. The single book I read that I thought about most, almost every day in Central and South America, is *1491: New Revelations of the Americas Before Columbus* by the great Charles C. Mann. He suggests that *Aztec* is an inaccurate term. The empire Cortés found he calls the Triple Alliance, and the dominant partner in the Triple Alliance was the Mexica, and their emperor was Montezuma.

Much of what we can say about the Mexica comes from a book called the *Florentine Codex*. It's called that because it turned up in a library in Florence, Italy, in 1793. The words of the *Florentine Codex* are written in Nahuatl, the language of the Mexica. They were written there by a Spanish monk who was trying to understand the native people he'd found. There are twelve volumes of the *Codex*, and even if you can't read Nahuatl, you can follow the book—it's all available online—like a graphic novel or a comic book because the *Florentine Codex* is full of illustrations, hundreds of them, vivid and incredible.

For eleven volumes you look at pictures of the whole spectrum of Mexica life. The gods, the ways of living, hunting, fishing, lush drawings of plants. Old legends and stories. Beautiful princesses, styles of clothes, beautiful landscapes of special places. Then you come to volume 12.

The illustrations change. Horses. The Spanish coming. The Spanish firing guns. Indians with their arms, legs, and heads chopped off.

Montezuma was about forty when Cortés landed. Himself the son of a dominating ruler—he was actually Montezuma II—he was a canny operator at the head of a vast and violent kingdom or theocracy or dictatorship or something. The Mexica were no joke. They'd come into the great Valley of Mexico with its enormous lake sometime around the year 1323, when their wizard had a vision of an eagle eating a snake on a cactus.

Where they saw that, they would found a city and build an empire. They saw it, they built Tenochtitlán, and then they conquered everything around. By the time of Cortés, everyone for two hundred miles paid tribute to Montezuma.

The Mexica had themselves conquered an empire. The tribes and peoples that Cortés encountered didn't always think he was the worst option. Enemies of the Mexica came to pay tribute to the Spanish, and told them that Montezuma's guys came to their villages and took everything they wanted, including wives and daughters.

From the frontiers of his country, word came to Montezuma that some new guys were coming. You can see this rendered in drawings in creative and inventive ways in the *Florentine Codex*. Montezuma consults omens.

Meanwhile, in the *Florentine Codex*, there appear drawings of Mexicans with a new disease, smallpox, that seemed to follow the Spanish.

The Fall of Tenochtitlán

B ernal Díaz was there when Cortés and Montezuma met. When he was eighty-four, Díaz sat down and wrote or dictated what he remembered of the greatest adventure of his life, one of the wildest and most violent adventures anyone ever experienced.

The book Díaz wrote, *The Conquest of New Spain*, is one of the most incredible true stories I've ever read. It's like a lost volume from an epic series of fantasy novels: deranged battles, massacres, human sacrifices, abandoned temples, plagues, landscapes wondrous and horrible. Writing fifty years later, Díaz can scarcely believe he survived it all. I read the translation by J. M. Cohen, and even he admits he left out more good parts—he's a gentleman, that J. M. Cohen.

As much as I don't like Cortés, I gotta say I admire Díaz. Who was he on the expedition? A nobody, basically. Respected but not consulted on anything. Why did he write his book? He dictated it, actually, because with old age he'd gone blind and deaf. He says unfortunately he had no wealth to leave to his children and descendants "except this true story," which he promises to tell "plainly, as an honest eyewitness, without twisting the facts in any way."

By the time Díaz and the other men with Cortés climbed the mountains to the east of the Valley of Mexico, where the peaks were covered with snow, the men with Cortés had survived battle after battle, including disputes with each other. Natives they passed had warned them they would all be killed and cooked with chillies. As they climbed the mountain, they found the paved road of the Mexica Empire blocked by trees. But natives of the country who'd gambled on the new guys or been forced into their service told them to keep going. Then they came at last to a ridge where they could all see down into the Valley of Mexico.

"We were astounded," says Díaz. "Some of our soldiers asked whether it was not all a dream. It was all so wonderful that I do not know how to describe this first glimpse of things never heard of, seen or dreamed before."

How many people were in the city Díaz saw? Maybe 200,000, say some scholars. Maybe 100,000, maybe 50,000, with another 100,000 in the towns around.

The lake was ringed with towns. But right in the middle of the lake was the island city where the stone buildings towered up. The water of the lake, which was maybe fifty miles across, was thick with boats.

On one of the causeways that led to the city, Montezuma invited Cortés and the Spanish to follow him into the city.

What was his plan? Maybe to trap the Spanish and kill them? Maybe to convince them to leave? Maybe he wasn't sure.

Díaz never forgot what he saw in Tenochtitlán. In the streets of the city, there were sellers of silver and gold and feathers and slaves and birds and rabbits and fruit and pitch pine and cloth and rope and sandals and the skins of jackals and jugs and honey and boards and cradles and furniture and axes. There were vendors who sold human shit, which was used for tanning. There were women who cooked all kinds of food. Díaz goes on and on listing things, before giving up and saying he can never describe it all. He says you could hear the noise from the central market from three miles away. There were gardens and an aqueduct that brought in fresh water. Díaz says Montezuma had zoos full of animals, and dwarves and clowns to amuse him, and stilt walkers and acrobats. He says there were so many of these people that they filled a whole neighborhood—Tenochtitlán's Hollywood.

Less than two years later the whole place would be destroyed.

If you want to know how that happened, you can read Díaz, who somehow survived. He describes days and nights of battle, heads chopped off and thrown at the enemy, fires, buildings destroyed, the Spanish constructing rolling wooden attack towers, trying and failing to build a catapult, fighting from house to house, watching as their comrades had their hearts cut out and their arms and legs chopped off and their faces cut off.

Meanwhile thousands of natives were arriving and joining the fight. Maybe ninety days of continuous fighting. Díaz says he saw sixty-two Spanish prisoners being sacrificed alive. He says he used to piss himself once or twice before every battle.

When it was finally over, when Montezuma was dead and the new emperor had been captured, the buildings nearly all destroyed, the few survivors fleeing the destruction, Díaz says you couldn't walk through the city without stepping on the bodies and heads of dead Indians.

That's what's now Mexico City. From the ashes and dead bodies, it grew up again. Now it has, oh, I dunno, if we're counting the whole population that comes there during the week maybe . . . twenty million people?

Lost on La Condesa's Racetrack

I n Mexico City, what I did was: walk around.

That's all I did, all day. On my Big Southern Trip, I stayed for three days and nights and spent all of them walking around.

A good place to walk around in Mexico City is the Museo Nacional de Antropología. There's room after room of astounding objects and gigantic sculptures and whole pieces of buildings hauled back from the ancient cities of Mexico, from Zaachila and Desconocida and Cacaxtla and the shaft tombs of Jalisco, things carved and painted and formed by the Aztecs and the Maya and the Olmec. You could easily walk the halls of this enormous museum for a distance you'd have to measure in miles, and not see even a fraction of it.

But it's also good to walk in the park that's across the street, the Bosque de Chapultepec, where you can stroll in the shade and children are playing and women and men are selling all kinds of delicious or amusing things. Fresh water from nearby springs was brought down to the markets and temples of Tenochtitlán. On the hill there now is Chapultepec Castle, where the Niños Héroes, the Hero Children, fought to the death against the invading American army in 1847.

Not sure about the park, but the best time to walk the streets of Mexico City, for my money, is in the early evening or on Saturday night.

I stayed at the Condesa DF hotel, which is spectacular. Traditional on the outside, hypermodern on the inside. Tasteful, intelligent people are there, and as far as I could tell, they're who run the place. It's great. As I was writing this I wondered, *How did I hear about that place again?* and I checked my e-mails and I see I heard about it from a friend of mine who I don't think would mind being described as excellent, elegant, and *definitively* gay.

So maybe they thought I was gay. There were plenty of straight people there, too, though, in fact straight people who looked like they were skilled and robust and fortunate in their sexual lives, attractive and energized.

In my room, now that I think of it, there was a video playing when I arrived and each time I came back, with soothing music and images of the naked flesh of a beautiful woman and a strong, wet man. You saw the woman's nips for a prolonged point.

It made me feel a bit stupid that I was traveling alone. But sometimes that's the sacrifice of the explorer. Like the Mayan proverb says, if you try to see the world, better go alone.

One way to take in Mexico City in a burst is to go see Diego Rivera's mural *Dream of a Sunday Afternoon in Alameda Central Park*. It's a great wide painting of characters from the whole history of Mexico crammed together for a kind of trippy group portrait. If you can identify everybody in this portrait, I think they give you an honorary PhD in Mexican history.

But if paintings aren't your thing, you can walk the streets and see a living mural.

Mostly, I walked around my neighborhood, the Condesa. That's a famously beautiful neighborhood. Some of the buildings around it are old, old enough to have ghosts in them, but they all look healthy and alive, and the new buildings look interesting and alive, too. Neighborhoods change, and Mexico City neighborhoods change extra fast. Somewhere around here used to be Montezuma's clown neighborhood, and now maybe it's all motorcycle shops and tire places. On March 15, 2014, the Condesa was full of people and alive and fantastic. I walked pretty far that night, but I came back to the Condesa very late, and kept walking around.

I got lost for longer than I should have on Avenida Amsterdam. It seemed like I was going in circles. I didn't know then but know now that there was a good reason why it seemed that way. Avenida Amsterdam forms an oval, because when it was laid out, it followed the course of a horse racing track, the track of the course of the Jockey Club on land owned by the Countess of Miravalle—the *condesa* herself who gave the neighborhood its name.

That story I got from the writer Francisco Goldman, who wrote an incredible book called *The Interior Circuit*. If you want to read 300 pages about Mexico City, read that. I barely saw my own neighborhood—*colonia* is the word. Francisco Goldman tells us that the index of the *Guía Roji*, an atlas to Mexico City, lists some 6,400 *colonias*. There're 259 different streets called Calle Morelos, Goldman says. That's just the *calles*, not the *avenidas*, *cerradas*, and so on.

For expertise I can't top Goldman, or Daniel Hernandez, who wrote *Down and Delirious in Mexico City*. The guy I really can't top is Roberto Bolaño, who summons up the special and mysterious and troubling magic of Mexico City nights in his novel *The Savage Detectives*. Let alone the hundreds or thousands of writers born and raised in Mexico City.

But those guys and gals were residents. When you live somewhere, it doesn't take long until the astounding becomes familiar. You learn the place, become part of it. Almost no one can see themselves clearly, or describe with any distance places they're absorbed in. Maybe an open-eyed observer traveling through can't do much better, but at least he can report on what he found amazing.

If you've never been to Mexico City, and you want to hear it from someone who's just had flashes of short but intense experiences there, here are some impressions:

In some neighborhoods the way electric lights are strung makes it feel **like a carnival.** There is carnival energy, absolutely, in some places very strong. Just like at a carnival, there are some alleys you may not want to wander down, because what's down there might be upsetting or fucked up.

If you like **wild unplanned color combinations**, you will like Mexico City. Blues on reds, yellow and black against brick, pinks and turquoises and stripes of spray-painted fluorescence—if you're tidy in your color schemes, you won't like it.

There're also some chunks of Mexico City that're boring, let's be real, to the walker especially. You might find yourself having to walk under a pretty long concrete underpass. Or for a ways along, say, the Paseo de la Reforma, which is a very nice shady street, but so wide that it's dehumanizing. A totalitarian kind of idea. We're lucky the whole place isn't like that. Most of its neighborhoods were put up by people who aren't trying to redesign the whole thing in one stroke. They're just livin' life.

I don't want to say anything about Mexico City being dangerous. It may be, it maybe was, it maybe will be again, it probably is in some places and isn't in others. Nowhere I walked seemed stabby. From what I read, Mexico City's murder rate is something like 8.4 per 100,000, lower than Washington, DC's. But that's just murders. There're all kindsa crimes, and who knows where these numbers come from? Who's to say, really? I'm like six foot three, a giant, a gentle giant but still a giant, but there were no problems from me, on my patrols.

The **food is good**. On one trip, I ate at some restaurants I read about, but they all seemed off, kind of fancy but fancy in weird ways that I didn't understand or care about. So after that, I ate my food from stands on the street. I'd just find one that seemed to have people at it, and point to what somebody else was having, and have it. Almost always tacos. They were all at least okay and some were delicious. Some were greasier-meated or blander than others, but the gamble was half the game.

Drinking is good. I drank a lot. Any juices that looked good. Coffee, from any places that made coffee with obvious care. And bars of every kind. Any bar that caught my eye, and let me assure you that this was a fair trial: Any bar I passed got a chance to catch my eye. Victoria beer, in the bottle, ice-cold, that is what you want, and it is easy to get. Mexico City is an overwhelming place, the streets are intense, even a short walk will take it out of you. You must refresh yourself well and as often as possible.

The impenetrable night. In the night in Mexico City, there is everything that makes a night sexy. The heat is burning off from the flat roofs, but cool air comes in from the mountains, and it is crowded and there's a steady din some places, music live and recorded playing across a lot of it. There are big families piled together and feuding families living next to each other and a woman scootering to a political meeting and students congesting, every kind of dance place, and the way the lights work better in some places than in others means you can keep your night light or take it as dark as you want. Or jump back and forth.

Weaving and intersecting across Mexico City, there are groups of cool and sexy and sophisticated and dangerous young people. That's true in any city, of course, but it's especially true in Mexico City. Walking in the Condesa, drinking the homemade batch at some cantina where the owners are re-creating some old formula for pulque, a beer made from maguey sap, you can feel that, something sensual and ecstatic and fantastic is going on in the Mexico City night.

Believe me, I tried to join in. But just when I'd get close to the magic of a night out in Mexico City, it would seem to shimmer away, dissipate. I could never quite become a part of it.

Recommended Walk

Start at the Casa Azul, at Londres and Ignacio Allende, at, say, five p.m. That's what I did, getting out of a taxi juuuuust when it was closed. You'll forgive me if I was a *little* relieved. This was Frida Kahlo's house. I bet Frida Kahlo had terrific stuff on her walls and shelves. But do you really think she would've wanted me to wait in line, and buy a little ticket, and look at a brochure or listen to the audio guide? Fuck that. She would've agreed. I saw it from the outside, paid my respects, and walked on.

Whichever way looks good to you, that's what I recommend. I have no idea what's out there in several of the directions, to be honest, but the one I took was awesome. I walked, by accident, past the fortified monastery of Nuestra Señora de los Ángeles de Churubusco, where in Montezuma's day there'd been a temple. The invading Americans in 1847 and some Mexican diehards shot it out here. It was dark, but I could see bullet holes in the walls, and around it was now a park, empty. If I'd known what I was looking for, I could've found the house where Leon Trotsky got killed with a mountaineering axe by one of Stalin's agents.

Instead, I found a subway station, got on a train, went back to my hotel. The next morning, I had some chilaquiles and papaya juice and thick coffee with thick cream and these tasty little sausages. There was a car waiting for me, and the driver took me to the airport. Off an overpass I could see a small statue of Charlie Chaplin.

That afternoon, I flew over the dry scruff of southern central Mexico, and a few hours later I got off the plane in the heat and sun at the small airport in Oaxaca.

Under the Oaxacan Sun

The city—or town, let us say town, it's more a town—of Oaxaca is on a hillside along a valley. Fresh tomatoes, church bells, the afternoon sun beaming off roof tile and old glass: Oaxaca can seem like, well, like a Mexican version of an Italian town, some fantasy Italian town from a spaghetti sauce commercial. No one moves too fast on the cobblestones. Why would you? At night, the thin phosphorescent lights of a few stores don't do much to illuminate the pavement, though they buzz up the mountain air.

In Oaxaca, in the daytime, I drank beer. Late afternoon, the day I arrived, on the roof of my hotel I drank a cold Sol beer while across the street and over an alley, on a rooftop beyond, an old woman shook out dry laundry.

Never once did I think, *Man, I could really help that old lady.* Instead, I pulled rich sips of my beer and smacked my lips and said, "Ah, Oaxaca."

In Oaxaca I also drank mezcal, the clear liquor of the agave plant. It comes in four ages: *joven, resposado, añejo, dorado.* I drank them all. I am a *joven* man. I think fermented cactus water doesn't exactly age that great, or else they haven't figured out the tricks of aging, the way the Scotch guys have. But, hey, just about any mezcal is worth trying.

At the market in Oaxaca, you can buy grasshoppers, *chapulines.* Not totally sure how much the Oaxacan people eat them, but there're barrels of them. The guides sometimes make a point of saying they're grasshoppers, not crickets, but if you can tell me the difference between a grasshopper and a cricket without looking it up, I'll be impressed.

You can even, across from the old church of Santo Domingo, get grasshopper ice cream. As I ate some, a woman, a black woman of maybe sixty-four, walked up to me and watched.

"Some of your grasshoppers fell on the ground," she said, and pointed.

It was true, but to be honest, it didn't bum me out too much to lose a few grasshoppers.

"I could never eat those. Are they good?"

"Umm, they're okay," I lied.

We talked for a while longer. I told her I was on my way to the bottom of South America.

"Well, that's a long way." She said it without any judgment or surprise or really any emotion.

We said our good-byes and I went on my way.

The city of Oaxaca is a wonder. But I also wanted to see what was out in the hilly, cactus-spotted countryside. Ten miles out of town, there's a ranch where for three hundred pesos they'll let you ride horseback, see their operations, and they'll cook you lunch. There were three Yelp reviews of the place, two of them bad. The least happy reviewer was upset, most of all, when the rancher showed her his fighting roosters. She considered cockfighting a cruelty.

This did sound worth seeing, though, so the next day I went.

There were three roosters, their cages in order of rank, and in each cage with each rooster were two or three hens. The fighter's reward.

"They have to train," said the rancher, "just like any athlete."

"How do you train them?

"They train theyselves, mostly."

The last cage held a rooster that was one of the most hideous monsters I've ever seen. His featherless skin was like a vulture's, scabbed into a leathern armor.

"That's a five-time champion right there," the rancher said. "After a fight they need a year. I don't fight 'em for nothing. I won't take a fight for less than thirty thousand pesos."

He pointed at his horrible champion. "To kill him now, you'd have to get him right in his heart."

Before this, we'd been riding horses, the rancher and I. Across the road, a few miles away, there was a high ridgeline. I asked the rancher if anyone lived up there.

"Oh, yeah," he said, "strange people. They speak Zapotec."

"Zapotec."

"Hell, some of 'em are three and a half feet tall. There's a village up there that's just twelve of 'em. They span the century in ages."

"How long would it take to get up there, if you took me?"

"Six days," he said. Too long.

On the way back to town the rancher took me to see the world's widest tree.

The world's widest tree has a trunk that's around forty feet across. At a VERY leisurely pace, it took me four minutes to walk around it.

No one can say how old it is. A thousand years old? There's been some dispute about whether it might actually be three trees, and not just one. In his wonderful book *Remarkable Trees of the World*, Thomas Pakenham says about that (I'm quoting him exactly), "Who cares?" To me, it looked like three trees.

We left El Tule. On our way back to the center of Oaxaca, we passed through its fringe towns, which looked pretty rough and poor.

"These other towns aren't doing as good as El Tule," the rancher said. "El Tule's got the tree."

Up in the Hills of Chiapas
(with Marco of Croozy Scooters)

After an overnight bus ride, I got to San Cristóbal at maybe five in the morning, early enough to see a bit of darkness, and then to see the sun come up over it. San Cristóbal is in Chiapas, which in the mid-nineties, when as a civic-minded high schooler I used to read the newspapers, was sometimes in the newspapers.

There was a kind of open, running, scattershot uprising in Chiapas, something between a political movement and a revolt. At its center, or at least the most dramatic character from it, was a man (or men) (or: a woman?) who went by the moniker Subcomandante Marcos. Read for yourself about Subcomandante Marcos. Try to, and see if you can figure out what was going on—what happened when he himself (maybe?) announced that sometimes he had been a hologram.*

I cannot speak to this, or to the recent history of Chiapas, with anything helpful at all to offer. As a student of it, I am still in my own stages of bafflement. It is political to say anything about Subcomandante Marcos, it took me a while to realize. Nobody I talked to was interested in continuing the line of conversation if I brought up the name. So I stopped doing it, and I don't know anything about it. I can describe only things I saw with my own eyes, and what I myself heard and experienced.

What I actually saw, myself, of Chiapas was so pastoral and magical it was like falling into some bonkers fairy tale.

To say that some special and remote but beautiful place in Latin America seems half-magical is the oldest trick in the book. Literally, it is in the

---

*See "Mexican Rebel Leader Subcomandante Marcos Retires, Changes Name" by Dudley Althaus in *The Wall Street Journal*, May 27, 2014, which quotes a statement allegedly from the subcomandante himself: "Those who loved and hated Subcomandante Marcos now know that they hated and loved a hologram."

oldest cloth codices inked by the Maya and it's in the accounts of the conquistadors, in sixteenth-century books printed in Toledo and Salamanca, and then it's been reinvented, many times over—"magical realism." Places where the familiar and the fantastical cross paths.

Well, maybe this cliché is a cliché because it's true. There are places in Latin America that are like that, that are half-magical. The villages in the valleys and mountains around San Cristóbal are like that.

I'm not the first person to discover this. In the 1960s and '70s, a whole parade of anthropologists came to this part of the world to study this magic and try to write it down.

I'm holding one of their books here in my hand: *The Black-man of Zinacantan: A Central American Legend.* The book is a collection of sometimes sexually explicit tales collected and categorized by Sarah C. Blaffer, who on the jacket of the original 1972 edition looks like a very sweet young woman. I say that at the risk of being horribly patronizing, and if so, I retract it, but before you get mad at me, take a look for yourself and just be honest and ask, *Does this look like the kind of girl you'd expect to be camping out in Mexico or in a hut writing down dirty stories the old men tell?*

Because that is what she was doing, let's be clear, even if her book includes eighteen tables charting and categorizing types of "spook identities" (her words).

I am only teasing Sarah C. Blaffer. I admire her, obviously, and the other anthropologists who came here. There weren't roads then, let alone TV and Internet.

These places are changing, fast. Zinacantan has big long greenhouses now, where they grow flowers that can be shipped, fast, on paved roads.

"The monster," Marco said, pointing these out. "Globalization."

Marco was the guy who ran Croozy Scooters. We were on scooters. I'd wanted a fast way to see some of the towns in the hills in a single day, and next thing I knew, we were on scooters, winding up through the pines on steep mountain ridges. It was good times.

In these towns, the people don't speak Spanish at home. The languages spoken are Tzotzil Mayan, Tzetzal Mayan, and Ch'ol Mayan.

If you think I'm gonna get involved in sorting out the insanely byzantine world of Mayan languages—if you think I'm that fucking crazy, to involve myself in *that* whole thing—then you are right, I am, but not until the next chapter.

For now the point is that in the villages in the hills outside of San Cristóbal, we are in another country. We are in the expanse of the Maya. All this world was the world of the Maya. Across this area at one time was something like a single language, a shared religion, and a shared culture. There were towns and cities. The different cities and their ruling families were sometimes, like the city-states and ruling families of Italy during the Middle Ages and the Renaissance, at war with each other.

Chiapas is hills on hills on hills on mountains, thick forest in some places, down into jungle near the riverbeds. Even a thousand years ago in the middle ages and the renaissance of the Maya, it was remote. Remote places can keep their old character for a long time.

The air was clear, up in the mountains. You could see down across the pines and the places in the valleys. After Zinacantan we followed the winding road, nothing else on it but a farm truck or two, up and up and up to the town of San Juan Chamula.

I was in luck, then, because it was a feast day. When I got back to San Cristóbal that night, I'd call my mother, who knew it was St. Joseph's Day in the Catholic Church. I'd never heard of anyone making much of a fuss over that one. In Chamula, St. Joseph isn't even the number one guy. John the Baptist is the number one guy.

Well, man, then I'd like to see what they do in Chamula for John the Baptist, because on this day, which was just a Wednesday, by the way, a regular old day of the week, a lot of folks had turned up at the church. The church was bright white, intense green and turquoise in trim around the edges. It looked like a wild frosted cake, a white cake with thick but precise lines of frosting from some extreme berry. They do not paint churches like this where I'm from.

Around the wide square laid out with gray stone bricks, there were men in white costumes preparing for ceremonies around and inside the church.

In the guides to these towns, you are told to take no pictures of anyone, especially children, unless they've given you permission. Inside the church no pictures. That was just as well for me, because if taking pictures was fine, that's what I would've done. All across the floor were spread fresh pine needles. In some patches they were spread thin and you could feel the floor. In other patches it was like walking on a rug. The whole place smelled like pine. The roof of the church was high, it felt open, like a great big meetinghouse. In a way, you could say the meeting was already happening. All around the walls of the church, and across the front, too, were painted statues of saints. Famous saints, and folk saints of Spain and Mexico, I guess, many saints I'd never heard of during many hours of being lectured about saints in my Catholic boyhood. These saints were terrific, obviously. Their eyes and hair and clothes popped with color, and they looked ready for action. They'd spring to life if you asked them.

Many people *were* asking. Most saints had people there, at that minute, asking for things. Some silently but many in whispers, and some talking and confiding and asking more or less out loud. To see this was incredible to me. In the churches I knew, you talked only a little bit to statues, and you were meant to understand that the statue itself was a nice thing but maybe wasn't that important. But in the church in San Juan Chamula, another style was practiced, a direct style, as though you should treat the statue like it was the guy himself, right there. Sure enough, didn't it look like it might come to life? The Spanish monks, the Franciscan missionaries, thought this was idol worship. They complain about it in their letters home, they're frustrated, nothing they can do will stop it. Finally they just gave up. The smart ones had long ago shrugged their shoulders about it and moved on.

The saint I liked best was a giant bald guy and his little friend. San Cristóbal carrying Boy Jesus? Perhaps. The sketch I have here in my notebook is not detailed enough for me to glean much more, and it is labeled only *the bald saint and his friend.* But those are my guys now. I invoke their help to make this a good and true book.

That's what it was like inside the church.

Outside the church, there was the wide plaza again, under the clear sky and the sun, and the gray stone bricks cut narrow and set in the ground. Across the plaza, outside the Tribunal Superior de Justicia del Estado Juzgado de Paz y Conciliación Indígena, a few men and a few women slouched against the wall or sat against it in the streak of shade, waiting for whatever.

Gringolandia

In the grass in the hills by a running stream, almost a river, that ran so fast you could tell there was a waterfall around the bend, we found half lying, half sitting in the grass some shepherds. They were wearing clothes that were colorful and looked homemade. The scene was familiar to me but not from anything I'd ever seen in real life. I knew it from scenes in old pastoral paintings of shepherds and farmers at rest.

They greeted my guide in a friendly way, like maybe they didn't know him but they knew his deal and what he was up to, that he was a good guy. My impression, too, by the way. They asked him, in Spanish, something like "Where is this guy from?"

"Gringolandia," he said.

I understood what Marco was saying, but the shepherds didn't. Somehow they understood this to be "Iceland." They discussed Iceland briefly and without much curiosity or energy. It did not seem like they'd be interested if I corrected them, so I said nothing, and on we went, up the trail, to a place the guide showed me where the water cut a cavern through deep rock.

Karst

There are many caves in Chiapas, because the landscape is what is called karst. Karst landscapes are made of soft rock like limestone and dolomite and gypsum that dissolves fast, for rock. Water mixed with carbon dioxide can become, in geological terms, "aggressive water" that eats cracks into the rock. As the soluble rock washes away, holes are formed. There are sinkholes and caverns, underground rivers. Caves.

Strange and interesting cultures come from places where there's karst. That's my idea, anyway. Florida is karst. Appalachia, Kentucky, Tennessee are pockmarked with karst. Vietnam has karst. In Ireland, there's a famous haunted karstscape, the Burren. The cave paintings of France are in an area of karst. There is karst in Papua New Guinea, and the Heavenly Pit, a stupefying example of karst, in a hidden valley in central China. Spain has much karst.

The Maya were all about karst. Some of their cities are in places that seem to sit like islands in a sea of dissolving karst. Their greatest stories are all about the underworld. Caverns kept them up at night.

Wherever you find karst, you find odd and fascinating people, is my point. Gaping holes in the earth wonk us out.

Idiots and Heroes

I f you tell or write the stories of your travels, there's great danger of two traps, on opposite sides of a narrow road.

You can try to make yourself out to be more of a hero than you were. Few are dopes enough to do this bluntly. But you can do it with backhands, just by suggesting that the places were sketchy, danger lurked, but you kept your cool. That's an easy trap to fall into, because sometimes danger does lurk, and you will keep your cool. Most people do.

If you fall into this trap, you're done. People can sense fast when you're stretching to make yourself seem heroic, and they won't believe it.

The other trap is making yourself out to be more of an idiot and a fool than you were. To play your dumbness for laughs. That's an easy trap to fall into, too, because if you venture far from your home, to some other part of the world, you absolutely will be a dummy half the time. You're in some new place, you have no idea how it works, you're discombobulated, you'll make one dumb mistake after another as series of patient strangers bop you gently forward. That's just what'll happen.

If you make yourself more dumb than you were, you're also being dishonest and that's bad, but nobody will suspect you. People will believe you're that dumb.

Anyway, this is a true story about me being dumb: Somehow, I dropped the keys to both our scooters into a creek.

How I did this I don't know. We were on a bridge. The keys fell into the creek and disappeared.

Marco stared at me. How had I done something so dumb, and what was I going to do about it?

Shamed, I stripped down to my underwear and waded into the creek. But precious minutes were lost because I was reluctant to dunk my head into what I assumed was a river of invisible Mexican diseases. Marco continued staring as I fished around uselessly. Finally, it dawned on me that this *looked*, at least, like a beautiful and pure mountain stream. It might be freer of toxins than the tap water in Los Angeles. Maybe there was some horrific pesticide, but most likely the worst that was in it was cow and sheep shit and piss. If that's what I had to dunk my head into to get the keys back, it was my duty, to Marco and to myself. So I dunked my head many times and fumbled underwater with my eyes closed and at last I found them.

Letting the sun cook off the wetness of my victory, we scootered down the road until *brrrp*, my engine stopped working. This one I don't think was my fault. When we'd pulled to the side of the road and taken stock of the situation, Marco said it was something to do with the battery. He could fix it, but we were twelve kilometers up the mountain from town.

"Okay," said Marco. From the hatch of his scooter he took out some rope. He explained to me what we would do. Attach the two scooters and coast one a few feet behind the other. He thought it over and decided he'd better be coaster, presumably because coastee could more easily fuck everything up and he didn't trust me to do it.

That's how we coasted, back down the mountain, into the center of town, the narrow streets now blocked up with cars, all the way back to the door of Croozy Scooters. When we were done, we had garlic fish and cold Victoria beers.

Night Ride

My second day in San Cristóbal, Marco invited me to come with his friends who ride bikes around the city every month or so in the dark. At around nine I walked down to his shop, he loaned me a bike, and we met up with maybe thirty people in a little square, young people. When we were drinking beers the day before at lunch, he had told me some of the friendship and sexual dynamics that were most vexing to his life, specifically one woman who was both erotic and fearsome. It was not hard to guess which one she was.

There were many small but intriguing dynamics of women and men and friends and strangers on this ride. We took off and rode like a herd down dark streets, the bravest and best shouting and out front. A few people had a struggle on their hands. They hadn't realized exactly what speed and intensity and distance would be expected, nor the challenge of the roads. The scouts at front, when they came to a bump or a fall, would shout out "*TOOOPES*." The call would be picked up and passed on with enthusiasm as it spread down the herd. It's the word that I'm most sure of in Spanish. It means "a bumpy thing like a speed bump or any kind of bump you should be careful about on a bike, or debris. Also a ditch sometimes."

Getting a crowd of energetic people together, even if it's just to ride bikes around the city, is still getting people together, so I guess it's a kind of politics. The message is we're gonna go out here and ride our bikes around and have fun doing it. That is a positive political message, one I was happy to get behind. If that's a political message young people are strong for in Chiapas right now, it sounds like good news to me. Marco and the ferocious woman were leaders I could get behind.

Waterfalls to Palenque

Where I wanted to go was the ruins of the city of Palenque, some 130 miles from San Cristóbal.

The way I got there was in a twelve-passenger van. I'm not sure it was really an official twelve-passenger van, but there were twelve passengers in it, twelve Spanish and Mexican tourists and a driver and a teenage boy who if he had a job didn't do it. The van was not air-conditioned, that became very clear, and vocally lamented histrionically by the woman sitting next to me, who made it known to me in Spanish that she and those with her were from Spain, not Mexico, and this was outrageous to them. Several of the other people in the van, being Mexican, took offense at this. Her friends did not spring to her defense. She took vigorous charge of her case herself, however, and said many things quickly that I did not understand. By the end of them, it seemed to me, she had made herself much less popular but believed herself to have been pretty much elected president of the van, permitted to speak dramatically and imperiously to the driver on behalf of all of us. Including me. She several times referred to me as though I was one of the most wronged victims here, fortunate only in that I had her as an advocate. Her goal, it seemed, was getting the air conditioner turned on. The driver's counterpoint was that this was impossible as the air conditioner was broken, broken far beyond his and, he seemed to suspect, anyone's power to repair.

This answer was not accepted. She insisted her case until it became clear her arguments were not making it easier for the bus driver to navigate the absurd curves of the road we were taking, down from the mountain country into deep jungle-bedded river bends, often then back up a mountainside before coming down twice as far again. She was making it more likely we would topple off the side and die was the point. I do not think she ever agreed to this point, but she did stop her case, for a while, before we came to the waterfall Agua Azul, a local attraction included on our van tour.

Agua Azul. Blue water, and that's what it is, a stretch of cascades and rapids over and around and through rounded rocks. In both the cartoon-ish color and the worn, soft shape of the rocks, it looks less "real" than like something from an amusement park, something Disney.

There's not much to do with it, though, other than stare at it. You could swim in a certain roped-off pool, but the two old women who were trying it didn't appear to be having a blast.

Two Australian guys, eighteen maybe, walked up to an outdoor taco stand where I sat drinking a beer and considering the waterfall. They identified the movie playing on the TV as *Dragon Ball Z,* and stared at that for a while as the water ran behind them.

Rounded back onto the bus, we had two more stops, both karst-related natural water wonders of southern Mexico, neither disappointing, both worth a stop but both just little pauses between what was becoming a camaraderie of the insane aboard our sweatbox van. Many of the passengers had half fainted into zonked-out sleep, and my shirt was soaked by around four thirty p.m., when we finally came to Palenque.

Ancient Writing of Central America

From their earliest days in the Yucatán, the Spanish knew there were written books around. Some were very old and were hidden away like treasures among people who could no longer read them.

These books were made on bark paper, stitched together. Just by looking at them, you could tell the thinking recorded was complex. They were dense with mysterious writing, full of charts and vivid illustrations.

How many of these books were there? Thousands?

By the time the Spanish showed up, the golden age of Mayan writers and bookmakers had been over for two or three hundred years. Very possibly the age ended violently, in something like a revolution.

Maybe hundreds or thousands of books (and bookmakers) were destroyed.

Centuries later, in the 1500s, when the Spanish set up shop, there were still lots of books to be found. At least fifty, maybe a hundred. At Tenochtitlán, before it was destroyed, there must've been a library of them.

Diego de Landa arrived in Mérida in the year 1541. Of the Maya he encountered he said:

These people also used certain characters or letters, with which they wrote in their books about the antiquities and their sciences; with these, and with figures, and certain signs in the figures, they understood their matter, made them known, and taught them. We found a great number of books in these letters.

So: What did he do next?

Did you guess: *He put together a fantastic collection of these amazing books for posterity?*

Nope! The answer is:

Since they contained nothing but superstitions and falsehoods of the devil we burned them all, which they took most grievously, and which gave them great pain.

What kind of jackass shows up in a place and the first thing he does is burn all the books? Even fellow missionaries thought de Landa was too much of a hard-ass.

To look at it from his perspective, though? Just for one second? In his mind, he was in a jungle where every single person was an idol and demon worshipper, maybe even full-on Devil worshipper, and they were all bound shortly for a fiery Hell unless he could by a miracle save them.

Supposedly—who knows if this is true, but this is a story—on, like, his first day in the Yucatán, de Landa was walking out in the sticks when he interrupted a human sacrifice, and the whole thing freaked him out.

Anyway: The total number of Mayan books that survived—*codices* is the more accurate word, I'm told, because they're not bound like books exactly—the total number of Mayan codices that we have today is three.

Maybe four.

Dresden, Madrid, Paris, named for the city that had the dusty library where each was found, or "found" most recently by the people who comb dusty libraries. Maybe *Grolier* is authentic, too, I refuse to weigh in. *Grolier* is named for a private club of book collectors in Manhattan, where it was exhibited after it was, allegedly, found in a cave in the 1970s.

So, three books, full of dense writing.

The only reason we can read those books, in a bit of an ironic twist, is because of de Landa. Because he described how he burned all these Maya books in his *Relación de las cosas de Yucatán*, which he wrote when he got back to Spain. In this not-very-long book, he wrote down page after page explaining the Mayan calendar, and their cosmology of gods. And he also transcribed a Mayan alphabet.

Why did he take the time to write down a whole calendar, and the stories of different gods, and a whole alphabet? Did he feel bad about burning all the books before? Who knows? Probably he intended to understand the Mayans in the hopes that knowledge of their wicked ways might be useful in converting them to Catholicism. As for the local

Mayan man who taught him all this, it's said that after he died and was buried de Landa had his bones scattered into the fields because he suspected him of backsliding into his old religion.

As it turned out, nobody who was trying to read the mysterious Mayan writing could use de Landa's alphabet anyway, not for a long time. His *Relación* got filed away someplace, and everybody forgot about it for three hundred years.

That was just when people started getting curious. In 1822, a thirty-two-year-old French hypergenius named Jean-François Champollion announced he could read the hieroglyphics of the ancient Egyptians. He had the advantage of the Rosetta Stone, hauled from Egypt by Napoleon's invading troops. Carved into the Rosetta Stone was the same inscription written in three languages: ancient Greek; Demotic, or medium ancient Egyptian; and Egyptian hieroglyphics. With this clue, Champollion worked his way to deciphering hieroglyphics.

Champollion's discovery blew the minds of every intellectually interested person anywhere in Europe or in the United States. It was like *Oh, wow, this brilliant weirdo figured out how to read writing from four thousand years ago, which is Bible times, basically.*

People truly lost their marbles over this reading the writing of the ancients. Some of them turned their attention to the hieroglyphics of the Maya, and lost their marbles over that.

But the first amateurs and scholars to try Mayan hieroglyphics had nothing like the Rosetta Stone. They didn't even have de Landa's alphabet, lost in the library. Instead, they followed their wild imagination.

For example, Edward King, Viscount Kingsborough. He put two and two together—pyramids, hieroglyphs—and came to the obvious conclusion that the Yucatán must've been settled by the ancient Israelites. Since he had a comfortable family fortune, Kingsborough spent an enormous chunk of money publishing *Antiquities of Mexico: Comprising Fac-similes of Ancient Mexican Paintings and Hieroglyphics, Preserved in the Royal Libraries of Paris, Berlin and Dresden, in the Imperial Library of Vienna, in the Vatican Library; in the Borgian Museum at Rome; in the Library of the*

Institute at Bologna; and in the Bodleian Library at Oxford. Together with the Monuments of New Spain, by M. Dupaix: With Their Respective Scales of Measurement and Accompanying Descriptions. The Whole Illustrated by Many Valuable Inedited Manuscripts, by Augustine Aglio.

Nine volumes. Two of the Big Three codices plus a bunch of Aztec and Mixtec writings or at least detailed illuminations. This is a serious book. A copy weighs something like thirty pounds.

Demand for it was not off the charts. Also it was insanely expensive to print. There were only nine copies ever, but that was enough to put a dent in any family's finances.

On top of that, it turns out Kingsborough didn't actually *have* the family fortune he thought he did. For sure he didn't have it after what he blew publishing his thirty-pound book. He died in Sheriffs' Prison in Dublin. On the plus side, he got a Nahuatl codex named after himself.

How Mayan glyphs were decoded is a great story. *A bunch of wacky geniuses take on the world's hardest crossword puzzle, where the clues are hidden in the jungle* might be the logline. There're excellent twists, unlikely heroes. Nineteenth-century pornographers, amateur scientists, expeditions, the surprising impact of a new fad for chewing gum, adventure in the creepy-crawly ruins, and mysterious deaths and mind-blowing leaps made in dusty libraries by maniacs—all played a role in translating Mayan.

Take, for example, de Landa's alphabet. It was rediscovered in the Royal Library in Madrid in the 1860s by Charles Étienne Brasseur de Bourbourg, who was convinced of his own theory: that the Maya came from the lost continent of Atlantis. Most scholars now do not agree with this idea.

De Landa's alphabet is pretty simple: For every letter of the Spanish alphabet, he wrote down the corresponding letter or glyph in the Mayan alphabet. Simple, right? Except: Mayan writing doesn't have twenty-six letters. It has, I dunno, three to five hundred?

So what the hell had de Landa recorded? What use can be made of it? For years, students of Mayan were lost in baffled, confused argument that led them nowhere.

Whether Yuri Knorosov really did find a rare reproduction of the three existing Mayan codices in the burning ruins of the National Library of Berlin as the Red Army invaded in April 1945, I can't say. Somehow, this legend emerged. One way or another, he'd gotten his hands on reproductions of Mayan writing, and he set himself to work trying to read the hieroglyphics.

Knorosov (please, do yourself a favor and Google up a picture of him, the one with him holding his cat) probably figured reading this centuries-old language from another hemisphere, of which only three books existed, wouldn't be too hard. He already knew Russian and Chinese and Arabic, Egyptian hieroglyphics obviously, probably Uzbek, and he'd been messing around with ancient Indian scripts. Why not crack Mayan? So, first, he taught himself Spanish and read de Landa.

Knorosov suggested that maybe what happened was a Mayan scribe wrote down for de Landa the Mayan glyphs that sounded like the sounds de Landa said. Like de Landa would say "bay" (Spanish *b*) and the Mayan guy would write down whatever sounded the most like that in his system. Some of the glyphs might be whole words, and some of them might be pieces of words.

That wasn't much, but it was a start. Knorosov and other geniuses started to crack Mayan down, breaking it into its smallest pieces, sorting it out, squabbling with each other in articles and journals and letters and sometimes in person. Meanwhile, in the jungles of Central America, new sites were discovered, with new hieroglyphs carved into stone, giving new clues, adding new riddles.

It seems surprising how long a time it took for it to dawn on anyone that maybe the languages the people spoke in the highlands of Guatemala and the Yucatán might have something to do with this writing. This wasn't Knorosov's fault. He was stuck in the library in Moscow, rarely allowed to leave. But in tiny increments, Mayan writing started to crack.

The story of how they broke it open is excellently told in Michael D. Coe's book *Breaking the Maya Code*. I recommend this one. Michael D. Coe is so gentlemanly and enthusiastic, careful to include you in his clear excitement over decipherment. Best of all, Coe is opinionated. He writes with feeling. He knew half the people involved, and he's always trying to be fair to them while also admitting that most of them were, in one way or another, bonkers. His book has a few tricky passages about things like "preferred" transitive sentence order, whether verb-object-subject or subject-verb-object and so on. It's not easy to describe the rules of one language in another language. But that just reminds you how hard it must've been to work some meaning out of these symbols. Coe's a kind of intellectual hero, in my opinion, not just for his work on this project but also for trying to tell the story of how it all happened.

I read the book twice I enjoyed it so much. But I must confess to you, Reader, that despite that, I myself cannot read Mayan.

This is a shame, especially as I'm pretty sure I'm above-average interested in ancient and bizarre languages. If I'm not gonna read Mayan, who is? Well, luckily, the answer is "some people." They're at work on it even as we speak, and what they discover is amazing.

Guatemala Pam in the Lacandon Jungle

In the jungle or the forest northeast of the ruins of Palenque, there's a stream, and along the stream is a ruin that's called the Queen's Bath. Whether this was truly some kind of stone bathhouse for the royal elite, I don't know. Archaeological fights get shockingly intense—I'm staying out of it. All I know is, there's this ruin by the stream, and it's out a ways from the ruins of the main squares of the city. If you go there first thing in the morning, you can be the only person around.

In the forest around the edges of the former city, there are ruins that might have been something like apartments. Whether they were more like a slum or a royal guesthouse is the kind of thing archaeologists spend years of their careers digging in the heat trying to work out. Is it any wonder that once, exhausted, they make a guess, they spend the rest of their careers quarreling at conferences with anyone who disagrees?

At the edge of the forest, there's grass. Whether it's some local grass, or what, I don't know, but it looks almost like you're stepping onto a golf course. I can't imagine that Palenque ever looked like that in its heyday. I bet in fact in the year AD 700, all this was earth pounded hard by thousands of people.

Either way, then or now, there are buildings that tower over you. One is pretty much exactly that, a tower. Perhaps it was used by astrologers, maybe it was a royal penthouse. The Mayans were very into the movement of objects in the sky, that is undisputed. Michael Coe tells us that astronomers in the Mayan city of Copán worked out the lunar cycle so exactly that their estimate is .33 seconds off ours. The tower is four stories tall and has a simple, pleasing style like a pagoda. It's part of a complex called the palace, but maybe it was something more like a university or an academy or the Vatican.

Across the grass, there are also staggered pyramids and temples. Whether the pyramids were sometimes tombs as well was a very explosive argument for a while in Mayan studies. Now we know they were both, because dead kings were found buried in chambers inside them.

The most amazing tomb, found in the Temple of the Inscriptions, is the tomb of Pakal, or K'inich Janaab' Pakal. Lord Shield. Undisputed, all-time greatest ruler of Palenque. Hard even to compare him to anybody. People just don't dominate the way he did. He practically built Palenque, or bossed the slaves and crews who did, and he ruled until he was eighty (probably). Whether this is really his grave or not is another fight. There's some concern about dating the age of the teeth in the skeleton—they seem like the teeth of a younger man. You can poke your head into the shaft where Lord Shield or Not Lord Shield was put down and from where he was removed 1,270 years later.

The carved lid of Pakal's tomb is an incredible, trippy work of art. It is hard not to look at it and at least *consider* the possibility that Pakal is flying a rocket ship. A German hotel manager slash petty criminal named Erich von Däniken claimed in his book *Chariots of the Gods?* that this is exactly what was happening. This book was wildly popular after it came out in 1968. Whether or not Erich von Däniken was just a talented con artist, and yes, that's definitely what he was, he fired up a lot of people about all kinds of ancient sites in Central and South America. Sometime in my boyhood I got my hands on a copy and read it in shocked amazement that these secrets had been kept from me.

I myself no longer believe visits from space aliens were a part of Mayan development. The thing is, there's no need to add weirdness to the mysteries of the Maya to make them any more interesting. Whatever they were up to is plenty baffling on its own. Take the ball court. Palenque has one. Most Mayan cities do. We know the Mayans played some kind of ball game with a rubber ball. It seems like you couldn't hit the ball with your hands. Oh, and also the losers or possibly the winners were human sacrificed.

One theory says that if you got captured by the warriors of Palenque, you might end up being forced to play Ball Game against the hometown heroes, and if you lost, you'd get your heart cut out, etc., on top of one of the nearby temples. Very doubtful your captors spent too much time, either, answering your questions about the rules or letting you practice.

There's all this stuff to examine and ponder at Palenque. An enriching experience, surely, to ponder Palenque. But you're in the jungle: By ten a.m. or so, it was unpleasantly hot. There was only so much pondering I could do.

Luckily, I'd set up base at a wonderful magical place, just down the road from the ruins, called Mayabell, where there's a clearing in the forest, with a campground and some cottages. A few trailers belonging to benevolent-seeming wanderers from all over the continent and beyond were parked there. There's an abandoned pool, drained for it looked like a long time, but that didn't stop me from sitting by it. In the early evening you could hear what you'd swear is the loudest animal howl you've ever heard. If you're me, you'll assume it's a jaguar until someone explains to you it's a howler monkey. You'll try to act real casual about thinking it was a jaguar and wondering about jaguar procedures.

The howler monkeys came down to the edge of the pool while I was there, a rare occurrence, I'm told. Perhaps they came because I'm well-known in monkey communities for my friendliness.

At Mayabell, there's a bar with a thatched roof, and plenty of people drink at it. There's a restaurant, where your food might take an hour or more from the point at which they remember you ordered it, but it's pretty good.

If you are interested in the kinds of women and men who travel alone and sit at the end of the day and write in little notebooks, you will find them here.

That's how I met Guatemala Pam.

It was around noon, just when I was considering that my goal of observing and studying Palenque might best be served if I stayed right here, at the bar, all afternoon, and rather than exert myself physically, in the sweaty heat, perhaps I could reflect on the glories of the lost civilization while transporting myself to a mystical open state by drinking five or so beers.

When I saw her, Guatemala Pam was being held captive by a shirtless French hippie.

Conversationally, anyway. He was across from her at her table and holding forth unbroken on traditional hippie themes like Fukushima radiation, the extraterrestrial origin of magic mushrooms, and how *his* body was made of healthy protein.

I'd seen her the day before, actually, at Agua Azul, a small Asian girl in a ridiculous sun hat, chattering in an unembarrassed and giggly American voice to two Israeli guys. At the time, I'd been jealous of their situation, young people having fun while I was stuck with the imperious Spanish woman and my middle-aged, heat-wilted van mates.

Now here she was, and she seemed to have no idea how to get out of her present situation. She was pinned. The shirtless Frenchman was complaining disingenuously about the "ceremony" he was supposed to attend that night, and how he hates when ceremonies go on too long, and how the combinations of various hallucinogens don't affect him in negative ways as they do less-evolved people stifled by their pathetic societal hang-ups. Pam was responding with politeness, as if for instance she was talking to one of her mother's friends she'd run into at the grocery store.

The shirtless Frenchman showed no sign of relenting. In fact, he was making himself more and more comfortable contorting his body into yoga poses of (I suspect) his own invention while looking at Pam as if to suggest, "Oh, do my lithe and sinewy limbs impress you? I forget so easily the laws of this crude physical plane, that of course my stretched proteins are alluring to you."

She was helpless. I could never forgive myself if I let this go on, or worse yet, walked away. It was clear the honorable thing was to fall on a hippie-babble grenade and rescue her. With a pull on my beer for courage, I got up, walked over, introduced myself, asked if I hadn't seen her the day before, and sat down.

If you travel, sooner or later you will talk to a hippie. Be prepared, know how to handle it. When you talk to a hippie, you must practice judo. Agree with everything they say. Even suggest they're not going far enough. This defeats them. For example, when the shirtless French hippie says that the world's leaders held a secret conference at which they agreed to suppress the fact that all vegetables and milk on Earth have become hopelessly irradiated, look back with slight confusion, as if you don't want to be rude, but you're not sure why you're being told something so well-known if not obvious.

Like all male hippies, the shirtless Frenchman's prattle was just poor and obvious cover for his actual goal: to pleasure himself sexually. On Pam's body in this case. Now that I was there, this had become a more difficult puzzle, a problem beyond his mushroom-addled calculation ability. So, huffily, he declared, "This isn't the real Mexico."

He stared at me as if daring me to disagree. *They're all the real Mexico, dumbass* was what I thought. Instead of saying it, though, I just stared back at him with doubled condescension.

"That's why I'm thinking of going back to India," he said. The ultimate card for any hippie to play. Now his hand was empty.

"Well," he said. He got up and retreated to his tent, leaving me and Pam alone there. For the next three days, we traveled together.

I was surprised when I learned, later, that Pam was thirty. She had a precocious-child quality, like a girl detective in a chapter book. She was plucky and relentless but oddly innocent. She laughed loudly at unpredictable times, which was very jarring, especially because she *never* laughed at the many hilarious jokes I made. Those seemed to baffle her. We were a pretty odd pair, but she was fascinating.

Her story was crazy. Her parents were Korean immigrants who ran a store in Wisconsin. She'd gotten a master's degree in marine biology but burned out on it. At random she'd picked New Orleans as a city to move to, a crazy choice because she was morally upright and didn't drink. She worked as a waitress in a restaurant where (she said this as if I, too, would be shocked) all her coworkers were doing drugs and sleeping with each other. The amazing part of her story was that because her mother would consider it a disgrace for her to be a waitress, she had constructed an elaborate lie that she worked as a researcher for the Louisiana Department of Wildlife and Fisheries. She had invented an impressive and supportive boss, filled a whole imaginary office with fictional colleagues, and described large-scale, well-funded, made-up research projects. Whenever she got enough money together, she took a trip, traveling rough for a few dollars a day in pretty out-there places, while telling her mother she was on research trips under the careful supervision of her made-up bosses. In December she'd spent a month in Nicaragua, for example. She described this as a majestic adventure, though the actual facts of it, once stripped of her gloss, sounded a bit grim. In her tale of her magical Christmas, for instance, the basic story was that some impoverished children took pity on her.

She told me all this while we walked through the modern-day town of Palenque, which sucks. About eight kilometers down the road from the ruins of the seventh-century city, it's just a bust of a town, not even terrible enough to be interesting. The best neighborhood in it is the cemetery, where the aboveground tombs are colorful and wackily, cheerily decorated, and there's no traffic. The cemeteries in southern Mexico are pretty great, generally, the one in San Cristóbal terrific, but there the town of the living can compete with the town of the dead. In Palenque it's an easy win for the ghosts. We walked through a grassy park that was okay, except for the guy on the bench who stared at us with a fiendish smile and obvious intent to rape and dismember one or both of us. Pam seemed oblivious to this, and it was a wonder to me no harm had come to her yet, although maybe her pie-eyed quality somehow kept a bubble of safety around her. She could speak Spanish better than me, that was for sure, but even that she did with a giddy enthusiasm.

She was headed, like I was, to Guatemala. For me, it was the next country to pass through on the wonder trail south—for her, it was where she planned to spend the next month.

Together we found a tour operator to take us to some remote Mayan ruins along the Usumacinta River. Up until the mid-2000s, this was wild country. Bandits robbed rafters, the Guatemalan side was held by rebel guerrillas, and the Mexican side was occupied by army units that might've been into various criminal activities in their off-hours. Illegal immigration and logging is still a problem along the Usumacinta. The country's pretty rugged, the river cuts through thick jungle, but I gotta say I had a pretty pleasant day riding a motorized wooden canoe up it with Pam and a few young Mexican tourists. There was a crocodile laid out on a sandbar along the banks. The ruins of Yaxchilán, a riverfront city that hit its peak around the year AD 800, are worth the visit, real Indiana Jones stuff, overgrown. In the dark stone temples, you can shine your flashlight up and see hundreds of bats. Palm-size spiders scurry away along the damp walls. In the 1880s, the English explorer Alfred Maudslay, who had family money from an ancestor who helped invent the screw-cutting lathe, hacked his way down here, cut out one of the best carvings of Yaxchilán, lintel 24, and shipped it back to the British Museum, where it remains. We now know from reading its inscription that lintel 24 depicts Lord Shield Jaguar, "captor of Ah-Ahaual," and his wife, Lady Xoc, who is pulling a barbed rope through her tongue. Lord Shield Jaguar was into that, I guess. In the carving he's standing over her. He has something attached to his headband, which might be a shrunken head, maybe Ah-Ahaual's head.

The next day, I planned to cross the river into Guatemala. So in the late afternoon the van dropped me off at a dirt crossroads where there was a place that rented cabins. Pam got off, too. We were in the Lacandon Jungle now, where the indigenous people wear a tunic called a *xikul* and leave their hair long under a simple bowl cut, like Gene Simmons. We walked down the road, where a strange Lacandon woman came up to us, chattered at us for a while in some indigenous language, and then walked on. She seemed crazy, but how could you tell?

The sound of singing and frantic preaching came from a painted wooden church. It didn't stop for a good three hours. Pam, ever frugal, was planning to just sling her hammock somewhere, but I told her to stay in my cabin, and we slept to the white noise of ten thousand or so insects.

In the morning she was gone. Down at the riverbank, I crossed into Guatemala in a motorized canoe for fifty centivos. In the wooden shop that doubled as a bus station in the border village on the Guatemala side, she was cheerfully waiting. Together we rode for four hours in a converted school bus to Flores, a cramped city on an island in Lake Petén Itzá that was once Nojpetén, the last holdout of the Maya, bombarded into submission by the Spanish in 1697. In a picture taken from a distance, Flores looks lovely, filling its little island with red-roofed houses with white plaster. When you're in it, though, it's nasty, smelly, and malevolent and full of mosquitoes. Pam, determined as usual to do the worst thing possible, planned to stay there, but I convinced her to come with me, and I hired a taxi to take us to El Remate, a chilled-out village on the remoter side of the lake.

The single best photograph I ever took traveling, the one I'd submit to a travel photo contest, I took in El Remate. It's of a motorbike, parked under a tree in shallow water, beyond the end of a worn gravel road that disappears into the lake. Light from the sunset reflects off the water, giving a pink tone. The kids who had the bike were barefoot in the water, catching minnows.

The next morning while it was still dark, Pam and I got on a bus that took us to Tikal, maybe the greatest Mayan city of them all, where the tops of the pyramids stand above the treetops of the jungle. Scholars have worked out a dynastic order of thirty or so rulers of Tikal, including two women. The last of these was dead more than a thousand years ago. On the top of one of the pyramids, I sat and watched child monkeys jump around and chitter and grab fruit from the branches of the trees.

Pam was spending three weeks in Guatemala. She had a long list of places to go. For instance, a remote mountainside village where they make a special kind of fermented cheese.

Well, Pam was an excellent person, truly interesting. But if I stopped at every remote cheese-making village in Central America, I'd never get to the bottom of the Western Hemisphere, so I wished her well and we parted ways.

If you're out there, Pam, I hope you're doing terrific.

The Murals at Bonampak

B efore researchers could read their inscriptions, imaginative specula-
tors could fill the silence left by the ancient Maya with anything they
wanted. You could believe the ancient Maya were mystical, harmonious,
and peaceful dwellers of the forest. Something like Smurfs.

But slowly, the glyphs revealed themselves. Many of the inscriptions
had to do with the complex Mayan calendar. Births, deaths, ascensions
to the throne. Then, too, there were glyphs like "he was captured," "he is
the captor of," "it was destroyed."

In 1946, Giles Healey,* who was exploring the jungles of far southern
Mexico on an assignment for the United Fruit Company, discovered or
was taken to the ancient Mayan site of Bonampak. He may have been
tipped off by Charles Frey, sometimes described as an impoverished draft
dodger, who drowned mysteriously a few years later. No matter. In spider-
and bat-filled stone rooms atop the overgrown pyramids at Bonampak,
Healey found and photographed murals that were painted in vivid color
sometime around the year AD 770, before the great cathedrals of medie-
val Europe had even been begun.

Professor Mary Miller of Yale, foremost expert on the Bonampak murals, and Professor Claudia Brittenham of the University of Chicago, describe them as "an artistic tour-de-force, outstanding in their sheer
quality and artistic conception . . . a powerful and sophisticated reflection
on the spectacle of courtly life and the nature of artistic practice, a work
that reaches beyond the confines of its time, a window onto a world that
could not know its doomed future."

That's all true. Cleaned up a bit by the time I stepped into the still-
spidery rooms and saw them, the murals at Bonampak have incredible,

---

*I am no relation to this superfluously voweled man.

vivid colors. Depicted on them are parades and processions, dancers, trumpets, parasols, cloaks made of jaguar pelts, smokers of pipes, a king ascending the throne.

Also depicted is a crazy intense battle, with bodies tumbling all over each other, people spearing each other and hacking away at each other. Plus: prisoners screaming as their fingernails are ripped out.

The Maya achieved all kinds of astronomical, mathematical, and calendrical wonders. They were also violent bullies who were capturing, torturing, and killing each other.

But, I guess, what civilization isn't?

Now, do me a favor: Take a look, you can find it online, at the mural from room 2 at Bonampak, the "battle mural."

Now take a look at any mural Diego Rivera painted. Any one will do, but try, say, the murals he did for the National Palace in Mexico City. He began these in 1929, more than a decade before Bonampak was, supposedly, discovered.

These murals were painted 1,200 years apart, but in the same country. Don't you think the artists who did each of them would understand each other?

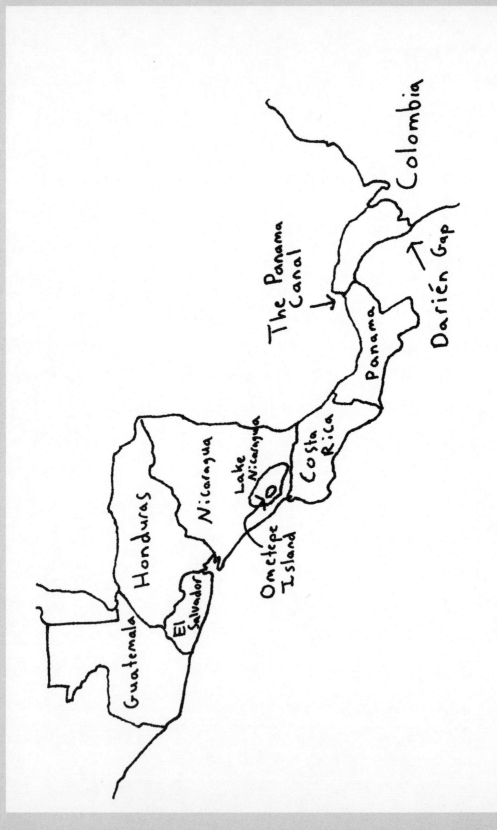

Central America—Guatemala, El Salvador, Nicaragua, Costa Rica, and Panama

Catherwood & Stephens

S ometimes the president of the United States has a problem: He doesn't know who's in charge somewhere. Who's he supposed to be dealing with?

I'd guess this is a problem every president could relate to. In 1839, President Martin Van Buren had this problem with Central America. So he asked John Lloyd Stephens to go down there and take a look.

John Stephens was a New York lawyer who also had a side career as a travel writer. In those days, sometimes if you got sick, what you did was take a trip, which seems counterproductive but maybe it worked. Stephens got a mysterious respiratory illness, maybe tuberculosis, so he went to the Middle East. When he got back, he published *Incidents of Travel in Egypt, Arabia Paetra, and the Holy Land* and then a sequel, *Incidents of Travel in Greece, Turkey, Russia, and Poland*. These books were "received with great favour," I'm told, and Stephens got a reputation as "an excellent and agreeable writer of Travel and Narrative," which is exactly the reputation I'm after.

I even look kinda like Stephens, at least according to the sketch in my copy of *Incidents of Travel in Central America, Chiapas, and Yucatan*, the third in the series. (Be careful, don't get this one confused with *Incidents of Travel in Yucatan*, book 4, recounting adventures from when Stephens went back for one more look). Not that I'm putting myself up there with Stephens, believe me. Despite his nerdy appearance and bemused writing style, the stuff Stephens went through was true adventure. Everywhere he went he was in danger of dying of disease, and his every moment, by my standards, was uncomfortable. I slept in beds most every night and was on edge if I went three days without WiFi. But then again, I doubt Stephens was that free of disease or mishap in 1839 Manhattan.

Anyway: Van Buren's first pick for this job died, and Stephens got the job. He sailed from New York City to Belize with his buddy, Frederick Catherwood, who was an English architect and draftsman.

Catherwood was a tremendous illustrator—just look:

I mean, the guy is fantastic. If you can look at Catherwood's illustrations and not be interested in the people who built these ruined cities of the jungle, then, man, you've looked at too much Internet. Imagine how interesting these illustrations looked in 1839, *when there was no Internet!*

Our two friends trekked around three thousand miles of southern Mexico, Guatemala, and what's now Honduras and El Salvador and Nicaragua. They went by mule and boat, dodging cholera epidemics and insurgents and criminals. Stephens describes weddings and funerals and fiestas and cockfights and bullfights. They got arrested, they slept out storms in leaking barns, they saw snakes and parrots and monkeys and jaguars. They climbed volcanoes, they witnessed revolutions, investigated oddities, forded rapids, crawled into caves. They hacked their way into ruins. Stephens loved ruins. He couldn't get enough of them. Nothing made him happier than sleeping under the stones of an abandoned Mayan palace. He tried to buy Palenque. The local authorities wouldn't let him unless he was married to a Mexican woman, so his immediate reaction was to check out and consider the local teenagers and widows, before deciding it probably wouldn't work out. His dream was to buy a whole Mayan city and somehow float it to New York.

Catherwood and Stephens explored forty-four ruined cities. Catherwood would draw the toppled statues and overgrown walls and inscriptions, sometimes while wearing gloves to protect his hands from all the mosquitoes. These guys went through the wringer. One day, Stephens says, some kind of tick hatched inside his foot, and he had to cut them out with his knife, and then his foot was so inflamed he couldn't get his shoe on, so he had to leave it hanging out for a day while black flies ate away at it, which he couldn't feel at the time but which left "marks like the punctures of a hundred pins." A few days later he finds Catherwood: "He was wan and gaunt; lame, like me, from the bites of insects; his face was swollen and his left arm hung with rheumatism as if paralyzed." Stephens sorta just moves on from that, assuming no doubt that Catherwood would shake it off. No doubt he did.

The one consolation for Stephens in his travels was his favorite thing: smoking. Waking up soaked one morning after sleeping in the ruins of Palenque, finding his tortillas all moldy, he says, "Blessed be the man who invented smoking, the soother and composer of a troubled spirit, allayer of angry passions, a comfort under the loss of breakfast, and to the roamer in desolate places, the solitary wayfarer through life, serving for 'wife, children, and friends.'" A strong stance, but I gotta say the more I traveled, the more I started to agree with him.

Catherwood and Stephens never did really figure out who was in charge in this part of the world. The problem, it seemed, was that nobody was. What had once been a kind of Federation of Central America had collapsed. Various gangs and warlords were fighting it out, things shifted, it was hard to say.

So they sailed back to New York and published their book, which was a big hit. Catherwood's fantastical illustrations sparked and kept alive curiosity about the Maya. They went back for another trip, and then they went their separate ways. Stephens became president of a company, a start-up, you might say, that aimed to put a railway across the Isthmus of Panama. But he caught some combination of tropical illnesses—"by long and incautious exposure in that deadly climate . . . brought on a disease which terminated fatally in the autumn of 1852," says Catherwood, in a fond reminiscence of his friend, reprinted in my copy of *Incidents of Travel in Central America*. Three years later, Catherwood himself was lost at sea and presumed drowned when the steamship *Arctic* crashed into the *Vesta*, off the coast of Newfoundland.

Disasters of Guatemala

Guatemala is literally unstable. Like: The ground, the very earth underneath it is unsteady. Volcanoes pock the earth like acne on an unfortunate teen. The active volcano Pacaya gurgles to this day. I toasted a marshmallow in a hot and sulfury crack in its rock. You can see Pacaya from the capital, it's less than twenty miles away. There are plenty more. You could walk the length of the country from her northwestern border with Mexico to the southeastern border with El Salvador on volcanic ridges (but why would you?).

The old city of Antigua used to be the capital, back when Guatemala was a Spanish kingdom. But it got destroyed too many times in earthquakes. For forty quetzals you can climb all over the collapsed stones of the Iglesia y Convento de la Recolección. On the other side of town, you can stare up at the wide blue sky from between the open arches of the old Catedral de Santiago. The place couldn't stop getting ruined. So they moved the capital to Guatemala City, which isn't very far away, where the earthquake and volcano problems continued.

I can't read Spanish well enough to go truly deep into the history of Guatemala. What I've read in English tells me a story of misfortune and misadventure and catastrophe.

Beyond the earth shaking and sporadically spitting rock and fire on everyone, it's a tough country to get around. The mountains are big, the jungle vegetation grows thick, the rivers plummet and roar and aren't easy to paddle along. The devastation that followed the Spanish left Guatemala even more isolated. When the Spanish were done destroying Tenochtitlán, they'd also destroyed a social, economic, cultural, and political network of trade and exchange that rippled out around it. Destruction continued as Spanish adventurers hacked their way outward on expeditions that ended in disappointment for the adventurers and disaster for everyone they encountered. Compounding all this, maybe many times over, were new diseases hitting vulnerable populations that'd never been exposed to them before.

Our old friend, Cortés's guy, Bernal Díaz ended up in Guatemala, where he'd been awarded a plantation. But he didn't get rich there. There wasn't enough of anything anybody wanted to put much effort into connecting Guatemala to the wider world of trade and money. Missionaries from the various Catholic orders came, souls are souls and they wanted those. But Guatemala's rugged country, it's hard to get around on foot and mule. By the time some dusty and ragged missionary showed up in a mountain village, he might not find it all that easy to convince people to worship his sacrificed god whose pronouncements were written in an incomprehensible book and who had commanded this missionary to lead a bizarre and sexless lifestyle. Mayan languages and village traditions hung on in the valleys and hilltops of Guatemala. No new order replaced all that, for hundreds of years in some places, to this day in some places.

People *tried* imposing new orders. Dictators, revolutionaries, executives for fruit conglomerates, CIA operatives, communists, criminals, all kinds of missionaries, lunatics, bullies. Local uprisings, violent oppressions, ragtag armies hacking and shooting each other, people getting their heads put on spikes.

This became kind of a pattern in Central America.

When John L. Stephens was in Guatemala City, he said you had to be careful walking around at night or you'd get shot by "sentinels" working for somebody or another. He had dinner with a young widow whose husband "had been shot in a private revolution of his own getting up."

Private revolutions of somebody's own getting up seemed to happen a lot in Guatemala. Take the United Fruit Company. This conglomerate emerged out of companies started by sailors bringing bananas home to Boston. By the early 1900s, United Fruit was enormous, well financed, powerful, and could do more or less whatever it wanted.

Take their land deals, for instance, which were negotiated with whoever seemed like the friendliest strongman by the New York law firm

Sullivan & Cromwell. A partner from Sullivan & Cromwell, John Foster Dulles, became our secretary of state. His brother, Allen, who was on the board of directors of the United Fruit Company, was head of the CIA for a while. It's not even a secret that the CIA was behind a 1954 coup that overthrew an elected president of Guatemala. Dwight Eisenhower discusses it calmly, even with a little pride, in his memoirs.

But CIA-funded coups never seem to lead to happy endings in the long run. So it was in Guatemala. By 1960, the country was in a full-on, multi-sided civil war. It wouldn't end until 1996. Maybe 200,000 people died. There were massacres and roundings up, bombings and assassinations. When the Catholic archbishop tried to put together a report about the civil war, *he* got killed. Smack in the middle of the wars, in 1976, was a tremendous earthquake, which didn't make things easier for anybody.

Things are getting better in Guatemala. If you're looking for a turn-around guy, you might pick Alfonso Portillo, who became president in 2000. But, on the other hand, Portillo ain't exactly Dudley Do-Right. As a young man, Portillo shot and killed two people. This is while he was a lecturer in political science. After he was out of office, Portillo ended up getting extradited to the US and charged with laundering money he'd been given as a bribe by the government of Taiwan. He spent some time in federal prison in Colorado before being shipped back to Guatemala.

Not great behavior, sure, but it's a little rich for the United States to come down too hard on somebody for crookedly enriching himself in Guatemala. And is he really the only foreign leader to launder his money here? The whole thing seems fishy to me.

Guatemala's had a tough time is the short story. An unfair deal.

My cleaning lady comes from Guatemala. She's from Chichicaste-nango. I've never thought it would be great for us to have a conversation about the absurd outcomes of luck and geoeconomics and history. When I told her I was going to be in Guatemala, she looked at me, as she so often does, with great worry, as I'm quite slow, mentally, and not really capable of living on my own.

"Don't go there," she said. "Go to Costa Rica. It's nice."

Wonders of Guatemala

Guatemala is also beautiful. There are, for example, Pam's remote mountainside cheese villages, which I cannot personally vouch for but which I believe in.

A place I saw with my own eyes and can report is a world-level wonder is Lake Atitlán. Even Stephens was impressed by this one. He said it was "the most magnificent spectacle we ever saw. We stopped and watched the fleecy clouds of vapour rising from the bottom, moving up the mountains and the sides of the volcanoes."

I would've liked to watch the fleecy clouds of vapor for a while, too. But the bus I was on was careening down the mountains and the sides of the volcanoes to the shore of the lake. No problem: The rising lake vapor was still impressive from the window.

Fifty square miles of silver lake set in a ring of volcanoes. Around it is a ring of villages: Panajachel, Tzununá, San Pedro La Laguna, Santiago Atitlán, Santa Catarina Palopó.

The villages range in degree of what we might call "hippie-ness" and "hostel-ization" and "indigenous authenticity," but in a given day, every one of them probably has both an ancient woman in traditional Kaqchikel Mayan dress carrying a basket of chickens on her head and an Israeli backpacker. Being raised on 8-bit RPG video games, I couldn't help but take the lake and its villages, and the boats that'll ferry you from one to the other, as a challenge. I tried to visit as many villages as I could, fueling myself with coffee or hot chocolates in each one. The boys who loaded and tied up and shoved off the boats from the dock were skilled and fast and competed with each other. Just watching them was good for a couple of minutes. On a ride across, a pretty girl with a guitar got in the back, asked permission in Spanish to play some songs, and did. The Mayan women riding looked indifferent, but when they arrived, more of them than not reached into the pockets of their dresses and gave her coins.

At lunchtime I was in San Marcos La Laguna, where trails and dirt roads lead to meditation lodges and Reiki retreats. There was a restaurant there called Blind Lemon's, called that because the owner loves Mississippi Delta blues, and that's where I ate. I was the only customer. While I ate, a Guatemalan boy who was either the brother or the son of the girl cooking tried on my hat and sunglasses, did a very good if somewhat mean impression of me, and played with my phone.

Lake Atitlán wasn't safe from the violence that tore up Guatemala. In Santiago Atitlán, for instance, you can see the church of Stanley Rother, a Catholic priest from Oklahoma, who translated the New Testament into Tzutujil Mayan. He founded a hospital in nearby Panabaj. In July 1981, he was shot twice in the head in his church by gunmen. Thirty people from his village had already been killed.

Rother's hospital was destroyed in a mudslide, in 2005. If you go looking for sites of massacres and disasters in Central America, you'll find them. You'll find no end of them. In going on this trip, and writing it, I don't want you to think I'm looking away from that. This book could be filled with stories of tragedies. But there are plenty of books about Central America that are already anthologies of violence and misfortune. What good would one more do? It's important work, to chronicle the terrible things that have happened, to remember them. Brave people take that job, tough people, but I'm not the guy for it. I prefer pretty girls singing songs in boats, like most people do. Believing that's what most people prefer makes me an optimist, because those people so far outnumber gunmen who'd shoot priests in the head that they can't help but win out. The gunmen can make things ugly, but I don't think they can make them ugly forever. The morning I was on the lake was clear and terrific. There weren't any guns, as far as I could see. It used to be believed that Lake Atitlán was bottomless. John L. Stephens didn't believe it, and neither now does science, and neither do I. But you can see how they believed it. If I'd never heard of science, I'd believe it, too.

If someday I am forced to become a fugitive, hide out someplace where no one knows my name, no one will ask too many questions, and no one will think to look for me, a little house up on the hilly shore of Lake Atitlán might be the spot. Although of course now I've given that away. And while I know I can trust you, Reader, I can't trust everybody, so maybe I've just blown it. Or maybe this is part of my game. I'm just trying to throw you off my trail. Lake Atitlán is exactly where I'll be. Except I won't be. Don't look for me there.

On this trip I'd find plenty of good spots to disappear.

Over El Salvador

I flew from Guatemala City to San Salvador, which was a real knuckle-head move. For the price of a plane ticket, I probably could've found somebody to drive me across the border and right to the door of where I was going. For a whole lot less, I could've taken buses and vans, and maybe I would've learned something, too. But that would've taken time, the thing we have least of. So I flew.

Flying, I learned a few things anyway. For one thing, I learned that southern Guatemala and northern El Salvador are bumpy. All but the best topographical maps have the problem of revealing only two dimensions. You forget that the earth rises up, too, and falls down again, in unruly ways sometimes. Getting across a colored square of map might not be so easy on the ground. In San Francisco this lesson has been pounded into me, many times, when I assume I can walk from Union Square to Fisherman's Wharf in twenty minutes, and I could maybe, if I could stay level and walk through hills. From the plane over El Salvador I could see lakes in the craters of volcanoes, incredible silver lakes it must take days to get to.

These days, El Salvador is more violent than Guatemala. Not that it's a contest. You can tire yourself out reading more history where an arch-bishop who calls on soldiers to be decent gets assassinated during Mass and a torturer called Blowtorch Bob runs for president and almost wins.

There was a truce declared in the civil war, and amnesty declared for everything that happened in it, but El Salvador is still not exactly a para-dise. In January 2015, there were fifteen murders a day,* in a country that has about as many people as Massachusetts, where there are .37 murders a day. That makes El Salvador a pretty good contender for the most

---

*That's from *The Economist*, "Crime in El Salvador: The Broken-Truce Theory," January 31, 2015.

murdery country in the world, with neighbor Honduras also putting in a strong show.

On the plane behind me were two Salvadoran Americans, strangers to each other, who made friends and spoke to each other in English. One of them was from Los Angeles. He said that when he was back home and met a Salvadoran who could speak English pretty well, it always made him nervous, because he figured that was a guy who'd gotten kicked back out of the United States for doing something real bad.

You can, on YouTube, watch an infinite number of documentaries about MS-13, or Mara Salvatrucha, a violent gang whose members do an excellent job of being terrifying, with their face tattoos and reputation for doing things like killing twenty-eight passengers on a bus* as revenge for something or another.

But like I said, I didn't come to Central America to come back with horror stories. I came for wonders and curiosities, for the spectacular and the terrific. So when I got to San Salvador, I set off for a place I guessed might be the best spot in the entire country.

---

*"Gang Linked to Honduras Massacre," BBC News, December 24, 2004.

Surf Pioneers

*S*urfers come first. So said a friend of mine who does aid work down in El Salvador. I'm not sure what he does, exactly: builds schools or hands out soccer balls or something. Partly, I suspect, he's down there to go surfing. I think he meant surfers are first to arrive in some beautiful, remote, as yet unexploited coastal spot. But like a lot of surfer sayings, the more you contemplate it, the more possible meanings are revealed to you.

Down on the west coast of El Salvador, the Pacific side, near a fishing village called Playa El Esteron, there is a hotel called La Tortuga Verde. It's near the surf spot called Las Flores.

Here is how La Tortuga Verde describes itself on its website: *a hostel/hotel, restaurant, health spa, turtle sanctuary, yoga center, pelican retreat, coconut plantation, sustainable practicing, student educational facility, and marina . . . dedicated to the idea of recycling, composting, lessening one's carbon footprint, and living a cleaner greener lifestyle in harmony with sea turtles and all marine life.*

Well, that sounded great. A lot better than strolling around the world's murder capital, nodding somberly at the sites of notable bombings and assassinations. Next to that description is a picture of a hand (a young female hand) with a baby sea turtle flopped on it.

Off I went, in a car from San Salvador. A guy drove me, we crossed half the country.

El Salvador doesn't even bother to have its own currency, they use US dollars, so at a gas station by the road, I could buy a bag of M&M'S and a Coke and end up with nine Sacajawea dollars in change jangling in my pocket. Ten minutes away from the airport and you're in true country. The countryside of El Salvador looks like it was first settled by humans maybe six months ago. The stands and houses by the side of the road look makeshift, just a few notches above camping. Natural enough, I guess.

Why knock yourself out when all history suggests storms and murder gangs and earthquakes will most likely destroy it all again soon enough? The vegetation's thick and wet and unstoppable. You could hack at it all day and be nowhere by tomorrow, maybe even end up moving backward, given how fast it grows. But on the other hand, enormous fruits are everywhere, mangoes and pineapples and annona, which look outside like green alien spores and have inside pink fibrous sugar spheres like balls of cotton candy. Beyond the road were folds of hills and green valleys, and on the road we passed pickup trucks with eight or twelve people standing, bouncing along on the bed, whole families sometimes. It was Saturday.

When I got to La Tortuga Verde, it was late in the afternoon. The outdoor tables in the courtyard were filled up with families, big Salvadoran families having picnics, and beyond them, framed like a picture by big palm trees, was the beach and the ocean.

This was great. I flopped my bag down in my room, walked outside, and sat down on the sand. A teenage girl sitting nearby was smiling at me. She said hello.

"What should I do here?" I asked her.

She shrugged. "Do nothing."

The owner of the property has been surfing since the age of 12 and so the La Tortuga Verde connection with the ocean and having a positive impact on it is more than a focus . . . it's a lifestyle. So, too, read the website. In the night after the sun went down and the local families left and I was eating fish and drinking cold bottles of Pilsener beer, I met this owner.

His name was Tom. I have to tell you I didn't like him. That's because when he asked me what I did and I told him I was a TV writer, he interrupted me and said, "Well, it's pablum for the masses, but you know, everybody has to make a living." He wasn't wearing a shirt, obviously—people who are having a positive impact on the ocean as a lifestyle don't wear shirts. He had wild hair and was maybe forty-five, well sunned, the obvious lazy king of his backpacker kingdom. I also didn't like him because the teenage girl who'd smiled and told me to do nothing turned out to be his girlfriend—I dunno, maybe she wasn't a teenager but she looked like it, and he tossed off some instructions to her in a tone like he was so far beyond her in worldly experience, it was adorably tiresome to speak to her.

Just because I didn't like him doesn't mean he was uninteresting, or even a bad guy. He had, after all, built this place, on the wild shore of Central America, a lot of it with his own hands, and the local families and the tripped-out Germans and Americans and Canadians washed up and lounging in bliss there all seemed to find it a happy place. I did, too. It was terrific. It's just that, okay, first of all, we are in *a golden age of television* and I don't think *The Office* and *30 Rock* and *American Dad* (fifteenth-longest-running TV comedy of all time) are quote pablum unquote, and second of all, decent pablum is *very* hard to make. Pablum should be much more appreciated. If you don't believe me, *you* try making pablum the masses enjoy. It's a lot harder than running a friggin' turtle sanctuary slash pelican retreat, believe me.

Anyway. Tom told me that he'd been surfing breaks in Costa Rica for years, but he knew from the geography of the coastline there must be good breaks in El Salvador. So he got out a nautical chart and a map and he deduced the best break of all might be at Las Flores. He came up here, saw he was right, and bought the place.

Surfers had followed. At the bar that night, I drank with three American kids. One had been down there for it was not clear how long. When asked how long he planned to stay, he could only smile at the question. He was in some kind of apprentice- or disciple-like relationship with Tom, though he would no doubt not use such words, suggestive as they are of hierarchy. His eyes were glazed over with pure surfer bliss. I would maybe believe that he *had* transcended human concerns to some higher level if he wasn't trying to suggest all the time exactly that. He ate food as if he wanted you to see the deep and tactile way he enjoyed it. I liked him anyway, though. I liked the way he described how in the battles in the fantasy novel he was reading, while the warriors hacked away at each other and the archers shot their arrows, the magicians stood apart and did battle with their minds.

The other two Americans were a kid named Miah and his girlfriend.

They were so genuine and kind, it came off of them. They'd been volunteering at an orphanage in Nicaragua, but it had turned sour somehow, not in any terrible way but in a way that they were disappointed, and had to leave. They'd gone and worked on coffee farms, and then at a hostel in Costa Rica, where they swam in hot springs and floated on rivers, but now those days seemed over to them, their money was up, there was a wedding to go to, back in the United States. She didn't surf, but she liked sitting on the beach while he did, so for now they were saving the last of their money to surf a big swell that was due to come in from a storm out on the Pacific.

The surf the next day was already gonna be pretty good. I asked Miah if he'd take me out and teach me if I paid the fifteen bucks to rent him a surfboard—deal.

The Excellence of Surfing

Everyone can agree that surfing is cool. It takes grace and skill and courage and timing and you do it outside with your shirt off. Balancing yourself while riding the manifested force of the impartial universe—I mean, what else is there? What else is life but a ceaseless ride forward where the best you can hope for is to keep some composure, some control of yourself, express your will in shifting tensions and harmonies with the overpowering, indifferent momentum until you're knocked off or deposited and the whole experience vanishes, erasing itself behind you as the wave collapses, absorbed back into the formless spirit that gave it rise?

I mean, right?

How can you not admire surfers, testing the ageless heroic qualities of man, not against each other or even against anything as crude as a mountain, but against dissolving judgeless pulses of energy as they pass in and out of infinity in beauty that can only exist beyond consciousness? Waves appear and pass over you like breath blowing forth the veil that hides the true face of the universe and then are gone forever, unpreservable.

Well, maybe you can preserve them in videos. Like on YouTube maybe.

"I tried to teach a friend of mine who's a great swimmer, real strong, but he couldn't catch anything," Miah told me. "Then I went out with a friend of my sister's who's not a real good athlete at all but she's *fearless*," said Miah as we paddled out. The way he said it made it clear what quality he admired, who had proved more excellent surfing. Surfing, like anything worth doing, is scary and takes effort. I used to work with a guy, the great writer Brent Forrester, who grew up in Malibu and went to Malibu High. Every day before school he went surfing.

"Man," I once said to him, "you must've really loved surfing."

"No, I *hated* it," he said. "It was cold and terrifying and exhausting and there was great risk of bodily injury, getting yourself knocked around."

"So why'd you do it?"

"Because if you wanted to be *anything* at Malibu High, you had to be a surfer, and if you were a surfer, then you went surfing *every day*."

For me, out on a Sunday afternoon, off an El Salvador beach, there was nothing terrible at all. Miah and the glassy-eyed apprentice coasted by, joyous and effortless, like God's favored children, while I mostly wore myself out paddling, lying beyond the waves for a while, then from time to time buckling in for a ride that would never get me higher than my knees before my board would shoot out like a rocket and I'd go spiraling around under the warm waves. The beach was nearly empty, here and there a wooden boat pulled up and left to sit, beyond it the deep green vegetation. When I was good and tired and the sun started to set, I rode on in as best I could, fired off belly-down on my board on a good wave, ending up rocked over into froth and soft sand and hauling myself into the open courtyard of La Tortuga Verde, hosing myself down and flopping into a hammock.

That night at the outdoor bar, there was a gang of cheery Canadian teachers on holiday, their clear leader a winning guy with a solid accent who pounded beers happily and unaffected. He told me the five of them were "old friends" while one of the old friends, a woman who was clearly in deep love with him, maybe had been for a decade, stared at him wistfully. I told him I'd flown with the Mounties from Yellowknife up to Iqaluit.

"Oh, yeah?" he said. "That's pretty far up there now."

There was an American guy, too, who was on his honeymoon, though his wife was nowhere to be seen and he was too drunk to properly land the punch lines of the many jokes he remembered half of—the Canadian teacher kept having to help him out. Nearby was a gang of twelve or so young and boisterous Europeans, mixed up from all over, it seemed. They went from French to Italian to German, often dropping into English to punch in some phrases from aged hip-hop, like "doing the nasty," but they were all having a great time. The rumor from the glassy-eyed apprentice was that he and Tom were heading up to a village in the mountains the next day to check out a circus, a literal family circus. The vagabond circuses of El Salvador are an old tradition. I would've liked to see that.

Man, a vagabond circus, I thought. *That's* just *the kind of thing I'd like to see.*

(Reader, as you might realize by now, my interests are tough for me to corral.)

No, no, I decided. Gotta stay on point. If I stopped to see every vagabond circus in Central America, I'd never get to the bottom of the Western Hemisphere.

Turns out there was a boat you could take to the next country, Nicaragua. Who doesn't love an international boat ride?

Me and Kelly Slater on the
Gulf of Fonseca

He wasn't the real Kelly Slater, though, my God, he coulda been. The Europeans just nicknamed him that. Not even because he looked like the real Kelly Slater. He didn't, not really. He looked like what you might *think* Kelly Slater looked like if you knew Kelly Slater was a professional surfer, maybe the best ever, but you didn't know what he looked like.

He looked like *he could be* named Kelly Slater. I actually forget his real name now. I seem to have never written it down. Presumably, at the time, I assumed I'd remember it forever. That's what you'd think, too, when he looked you in the eyes.

Big wide shoulders, chiseled cheekbones, the first time I saw him he was shirtless and holding a surfboard with one strong hand and folding his wet hair back with the other. He could've been a professional surfer. Maybe. If that one picture was all you needed. I also didn't see him surf, and he did say he was bad at it, but if all you needed was the look? Goddamn, he had it.

He wasn't a professional surfer. He was a Swiss German technical representative or something at a telecommunications company. We'd cross the Gulf of Fonseca together.

The Gulf of Fonseca, that was just the kind of thing I was looking for, some crooked corner on the map that you'd never heard of anybody going that *must* be interesting. Reader, feel free to consult a map at this point. You'll see the Gulf of Fonseca is a bay that's shaped like the head of a giraffe. This giraffe has three ears, but other than that, you must agree it's very giraffelike. There's even a thin tongue sticking out in the southeast, the Estero Real, licking into Nicaragua.

We crossed this in a narrow motorized *launcha*. Going this way, you can see, allowed me to skip Honduras. Kelly Slater had been to Honduras, he'd been robbed at gunpoint there, though he seemed to shake it off as almost fair play, since he'd been riding a scooter on a remote road. I'd have to skip some stuff on this trip, and Honduras, though interesting and supposedly beautiful and full of good ruins, is not easy to travel around. I made the executive decision to go by sea and bypass it. Next time, Honduras, no insult to you, just in a hurry.

First, though, we had to have breakfast.

Pupusas

We had pupusas, Kelly Slater and I, at a table on the road down to the pier in La Unión, El Salvador. Pupusas are like the national food there, and with good cause: They are delicious.

Say what you will about El Salvador: In a contest of number one national food against any other country's number one, I think pupusas can hold their own.

They are handmade corn tortillas, always handmade, and they're folded over cheese and whatever other deliciousness is on hand and you want in there, and then they're fried on a grill, and then you can put more sauce or whatever on top. Two big ones cost a dollar, a bargain. Kelly Slater ate three, and considered a fourth. He was a great man, Kelly Slater.

To the Sunny Isle of Meanguera

J ust off the dock, there were a few boats loading. None of them loaded as though they were on any kind of strict schedule.

Ours went when it was full. We helped launch it, Kelly Slater and I, wading out up to our waists because it was loaded so heavy it was stuck in the mud. The mud felt pretty good, sucking my bare feet half off. Shoeless is the right choice sometimes. Once we hopped in, it was easy enough to dry off in the sun. A clear day, a choppy ride from the boat, but the water was unthreatening. Just a beautiful day, on the Gulf of Fonseca, with my new friend Kelly Slater. Tremendous guy. He could speak French and Italian and German, of course. He was working on Spanish, but we spoke in English, which he spoke in succinct and clear sentences full of calm positivity.

Halfway across, we stopped over at an island: Meanguera del Golfo. About this island I can tell you almost nothing. I was surprised we stopped, to be honest. I hadn't even thought about the islands of the Gulf of Fonseca. This one, I can tell you, belongs to El Salvador. There was a dispute about it, until an international peace commission sorted it out and awarded two islands to El Salvador and one to Honduras.

The island felt to me like its own republic. We went ashore at a little town carved into a steep valley on the mountain that was most of the island. The few streets climbed up, so from the dock they looked like they were each on top of another. Only a few of them, and they spiraled off or ended or disappeared into the mountain. There was a small store, where I'd guess the inventory is not that predictable, but on the other hand I bet the guy behind the counter could get you anything if you gave him time. I had a bottle of Coke and some cookies.

Kelly Slater and I sat on the dock for a while. It didn't seem like much was happening. Maybe lots of exciting stuff happens there, but I doubt it.

It looked like nothing had happened there for a very long time, and nothing was scheduled to happen for a long time into the future.

Teenage guys sat along the water. There were boats tied up, fishing boats and boats that were maybe going back and forth and boats that looked unused. The guys were skinny and shirtless. They all had phones they fiddled with, texting or playing games, I guess. If texting, then texting who? Maybe each other.

"Everywhere in the world, people are checking their phones," Kelly Slater said to me. With a smile, no judgment. He drank a Coke and ate some cookies, too. I knew he probably wouldn't care, but there was some small chance he would think less of me if I smoked a cigarette, so I did not.

We watched the small waves caress the boats as they came in. The boys on the dock weren't interested in me. They weren't interested in Kelly Slater, either, which was crazy. *Didn't they see how handsome he was?*

One thing Kelly Slater was interested in was efficiency. Excellence. Good planning. There was humor to him, for sure, but nonsense was uninteresting to him. He couldn't even understand it, when people did things in some way that didn't seem transparent or efficient or guided toward some obvious improvement in condition.

In Central America, this was often, as had become clear to him. He was a worldly man, and the reservoir tank of his patience was deep-draft and full. He didn't come to El Salvador and Nicaragua to bring judgment on efficiency, he knew that. He was here to surf and improve his Spanish and investigate a few interesting towns, and then he was proceeding on to meet some friends at surf camp in Costa Rica on a certain date. This was vacation and he made the most of it.

But at the border station in Nicaragua, he finally encountered a situation his patience could not tolerate.

After passing close along a dense mangrove-y coast, our boat shot in to a sandy beach. We waded in, hauled it up, took our bags, and helped shove the boat off again. Left on the shore were three Nicaraguans: an old woman, an old man, and a young guy with shades on, built hefty but strong like a college football lineman, and us.

The Nicaraguans carried their bags up a dirt road from the beach and we followed them. There was a concrete building, a box, up the trail, with the Nicaraguan flag.

The front of the box was open like a booth. Inside were two men and a woman in government uniforms, an ancient copy machine, and two computers.

When Kelly Slater and I caught up with the Nicaraguans, they were waiting. Inside the box, no one was moving.

Then, very slowly the woman started to move. She moved across the office, one end to the other. Slowly. As if there were no purpose to her movements but to see how slowly she could move.

When she got to the other side, she took her time. Like a lethargic house cat she eased into a few positions leaning against the wall, slowly feeling which might be best. Then she eased into a good, comfortable sit, and stayed there.

Now, slowly, the two men at their computers began to move.

If you'd seen, at an experimental theater, the slowness with which they moved, you would have been exhilarated by the dancers, the control of how slowly they moved. The choreographer, too, you would've admired, who staged such a bold and expressive satire on the tedium of bureaucracy, the suffocating effects of oppression, whether from politics or the tropical heat or society, the human condition. *A dance of slowness*, you might say, admiring the choice.

Kelly Slater stared at this. If he had one flaw, perhaps it's that he might not be as appreciative a dance critic as me, but I bet he would be great at even that if that were a task assigned by an appropriate supervisor. This was a border station after all, not the strangely colorful set of a black-box theater.

It probably took them an hour to give us the stamps we needed, and file away some meaningless papers in such a way that they'd obviously never be anywhere where anybody looking for them could find them.

The slowness wasn't just for us. The Nicaraguans waited first. It took longer for them, actually. There was no extra aid offered out to the old woman or the old man either. When they were done, the hefty guy went through. That took forever, too.

Kelly Slater watched all this with increasing incomprehension. The hefty Nicaraguan in the sunglasses could feel him watching. When they at last stamped him in, he looked over at Kelly and said, in Southern California English,

"Yeah. Welcome to Nicaragua."

When we were finally through, and out of earshot of the border station, where I assume like puppets in a box the officers were put back to motionless rest, Kelly Slater said, "That cannot be the best way of doing things."

I had to agree.

"But perhaps they do not send their best people here," he said then, by way of forgiveness.

Another two hours or so waiting under a tree before a packed, converted yellow American school bus took us all to Chinandega, where Kelly Slater and I just barely had time to buy some fruit before a van took us on to the town of León. We got there at sunset. We agreed to split a room, and we found one at a funked-out hostel where French Canadians were rolling cigarettes by the hammocks in the vine-covered courtyard. We had dinner together, Kelly Slater and I, steaks at a mysterious restaurant with a fountain in the middle of it, where a large group of seemingly unrelated people were drunk and laughing and eating a noisy banquet. That night it was steamy hot in our room. The rickety fan offered little relief from the sweaty evening. I promise you, Reader, if there were one night on this trip when I was going to have a passionate experiment in male-on-male lovemaking, it would've been this night. A first for me. I'd thought I wasn't interested in that kind of thing, but I tell you, if Kelly Slater had suggested it, I can't promise what I would've done. He didn't, though. He just lay atop his sheet in bed and studied his guidebook for a while, then he smiled and turned out the light. The next morning, blissful and relaxed, we had coffee and fruits and walked the main street of León to see the gory painted statues at the old church, where the sufferings of

Jesus were carved to be as vivid as if they happened yesterday. We strolled back down again, joking a little about it. We each had an ice-cream bar. Kelly asked if I wanted to climb the volcano. He wanted to see red lava at night. No, I said sadly, I had to keep going. There we parted ways.

Women, or perhaps gay men, I don't know what Kelly Slater is into, but I apologize because while a magical night and morning, it feels like I robbed Kelly Slater from somebody who might've enjoyed him in even more passionate ways. I know I'll never forget him.

Like I said, though: I can't remember his actual name.

Bizarre Mural at the Hotel Gran Francia

*M**ural* is probably not even the right word for it: It was a rectangular stretch of painted shag. The colors used were red, blue, green, brown, and black. The whole thing was maybe ten feet across. A tapestry? A dyed wall rug? I can't claim to be expert on Nicaraguan shag art. Perhaps this is even a famous example.

Depicted, from left to right, on this artwork, were:

- a faceless peasant/soldier carrying a rifle,
- a wounded man, also faceless, slumped on the ground,
- a man (faceless, they were all faceless, although in fairness, it might be hard to do faces in shag) hanging dead from the branch of a tree,
- three men in hats, shooting at each other,
- a leader commanding two rifle shooters, and
- a man bayoneting another man.

The green ground beneath them was already strewn with bodies.

I was the only customer in the bar. The bartender dried glasses. On the TV was an American baseball game. The bartender and I said a few words about Everth Cabrera, then of the Padres, and Erasmo Ramírez, then of the Mariners, the two best Nicaraguan baseball players. I didn't know anything about either one of them, but I tried to say "I admire them," which is true. He didn't care about the game much, though. I drank cold bottles of Toña beer, and enjoyed them very much. It'd been hot all day and still was, even though the sun was almost down.

This was in the city of Granada, Nicaragua, on the shores of forty-four-mile-wide Lake Nicaragua. By sailing up rivers and then across the lake, you can reach Granada from the Atlantic Ocean, and it had been a city for a hundred years by the time the *Mayflower* reached Massachusetts. By the first year of the American Revolution, Granada had already been sacked three times by pirates, once by Captain Morgan himself, the guy on the rum, who in real life was not always as jolly.

When she was barely twenty, a woman named Rafaela Herrera led the defense of Granada from yet another pirate attack, in 1762. In the depiction of her on the Nicaraguan five-córdoba note she is very hot, wearing a low-cut dress as she fires a cannon.

Granada is terrific, colorful, and relaxed. Just the right distance from the pretty main square the streets meander down to the shore of the lake. I walked around all day. Tourists drank happily in bars on the Calle La Libertad. I had a couple myself at Reilly's Tavern, maybe the best Irish pub in Nicaragua.

On benches around Parque Central, there were Nicaraguan men sitting with nothing to do. They talked to me, friendly and without any agenda, until my Spanish ran out and they shrugged. Sitting on a bench by the park is something I never do at home. Whenever I do it abroad, I'm surprised by how great it is. Just sitting there, staring, maybe drinking some water or a coffee. It makes me think I will enjoy being an old man.

Down by the lake, I leaned over the water and watched the waves change color as the sun set, until tiny insects got the word to start feasting on me and went to town. That's when I retreated to the bar of the Hotel Gran Francia, and stared at the painted rug.

About the history of Nicaragua: The rug's a pretty eloquent summary.

The latest round in a long recitation of shootings and massacres was a revolution that turned into a civil war. Here is my quick summary: From the 1930s until 1979, Nicaragua was ruled by a US-supported father-and-sons bandit team called the Somozas. In the late 1970s, a liberal newspaper editor got killed by agents of these guys, there were riots, then a kidnapping campaign, and then open revolution. The last Somoza fled to Paraguay, where he eventually got killed. The Sandinistas took over the country and started redistributing land. They weren't always gentlemen princes, but at their best they were trying to spread literacy and reduce poverty in a country that was a total mess. All that land redistributing seemed awful Communist, though, and a right-wing group called the Contras tried to overthrow them.

Ronald Reagan once said that the Contras were "the moral equivalent of our Founding Fathers," which they weren't, even when you remember that many of our Founding Fathers owned human slaves. The Contras were a bad-news bunch, assassinating people and shooting up the countryside, just generally doing anything to overthrow a government that had, after all, won a more or less fair election.

The United States had not been successful or a positive force in its messings-around in Nicaragua up until the Contras. So, in a case of perhaps rare wisdom, in the early 1980s the US Congress declared that the CIA and the Department of Defense had to stop helping the Contras. Fervent anti-Communists in the Reagan White House, namely a Marine lieutenant colonel named Oliver North, concocted a way to work around all that by selling weapons to Iran (another thing we weren't supposed to do) and then sending the money to the Contras.

That was the Iran-Contra Affair, which I remember Tom Brokaw telling me and my mom about during the nightly news when I was a kid. Oliver North testified before Congress in his Marine uniform and was pretty unabashed about the whole thing. After all, shouldn't the president conduct foreign policy, not Congress?

If you try to learn about all this, as I did from old books and archived articles and stuff, you come across all kinds of twists and convoluted motives and lies and excuses and weaselings and ever-deepening confusions folding on top of each other. Also interesting trivia, like the fact that the never-married Edward Boland of Springfield, Massachusetts, after whom the congressional "no money for Contras" resolutions were named, fell in love at age sixty-two with a woman thirty years younger than him, fathered four kids, and quit Congress to raise them.

Your darker conspiracy theorists can find in the thicket of Iran-Contra evidence that the CIA was also funding the Contras by selling crack cocaine in America's inner cities, fulfilling a double-secret agenda of destroying black communities. This seems implausible to me, because a scheme that sinister would require a lot of competence. Even the much simpler double-secret scheme of funding the Contras with Iran weapons got found out. One thing that is true is that the lines between "good guys" and "bad guys" became pretty much indecipherable.

One thing the Iran-Contra scheme didn't do is work. The Contras lost. The current president of Nicaragua, Daniel Ortega, was on the Sandinista side. He ran things for most of the 1980s, and he's been officially back in charge since 2007. What a life you go through as a Central American politician: If you're on the road to the presidential palace, you'll definitely detour into prison somewhere along the way. I'm no expert on Nicaraguan politics, and don't want to offer a strong opinion on Ortega. I can say with confidence that while much of his rhetoric is about uplifting impoverished people, he is not 100 percent purehearted in the way he has run the country.

As crazy as Iran-Contra was, it is dwarfed in hubris by *another* American intervention in Nicaragua.

Walker, Nicaraguan Ranger

In 1856, William Walker, of Tennessee, Louisiana, and California, went down to Nicaragua with about sixty guys and declared himself president. Walker was amazing. He'd graduated the University of Nashville at age fourteen; graduated medical school at nineteen; been a doctor, a lawyer, and a newspaper editor; fought in a duel; and been engaged to a beautiful deaf girl who died. He'd already tried to create a republic in Baja, California, and Sonora, Mexico, but that didn't work. He got driven out and was lucky to be alive. Back in California, age thirty, he was put on trial for violating the Neutrality Acts, but his fellow Americans liked his gumption and he was acquitted. His plan wasn't *that* crazy, after all. This is sort of how Texas was created. Two years later, Walker went down to Nicaragua and tried again.

He succeeded for a while, before an army from Costa Rica came in and drove him and his guys out. In the chaos, old Granada was burned to the ground. In the smoking ash that remained, one of Walker's guys put up a sign he'd written in charcoal: AQUI SE GRANADA—here was Granada.

Incredibly, after he'd been hauled back to New Orleans by the US Navy, put on trial again, and acquitted, again, Walker went *back* to Central America. They'd had it with this guy, though. A firing squad of Hondurans shot him to death on the beach, and they buried his body in the sand.

This story is told in a few places, perhaps best of all by Walker himself in his memoir *The War in Nicaragua*, written and published sometime before his death, which is not included.

The story is also told in the 1987 Acid Western *Walker*, starring Ed Harris, a movie whose "poverty of imagination has to be seen to be believed," according to Roger Ebert. It's true, it's not a good movie. Peter Boyle, who played the dad on *Everybody Loves Raymond*, plays Cornelius Vanderbilt. He's great in it. At one point he declares that Nicaragua is a "fucked-up little country somewhere south of here."

The Perfect Cup of Coffee

O n the island of Ometepe, at Ojo de Agua, I sat half in the sun and half in the shade, my feet splashing in volcanic water. *Eye of water?* Something like that. This place is a natural pool. A spring, cool and clear. There's something special or healing about its waters. They bubble up from the volcano, the ancient peoples worshipped here—something like that, who cares. You can't learn the story of everything.

A crazily pleasant, wonderful place. I mean it. Just in terms of pure good, relaxed feeling washing over me, Ojo de Agua might've been the best place in Central America. You swam if you wanted, sat there if you wanted, dangled your feet. There was a girl who would chop a straw into a coconut for you, if you felt like drinking a coconut, which I did. There were birds and you felt like you were in the jungle but only in the best ways. Everybody I talked to seemed nice, but maybe their best quality was how little they cared about talking to me. Just: Lemme know if you need a coconut, until then let's both relax.

Near me were four Americans, three girls and a guy. Average age maybe thirty, from North Carolina. The guy was shirtless, obviously. It was unclear his relationship to these women. My guess, later confirmed, was that these were women who were up for an awful lot. They took pride in being wild.

"I just don't give off that vibe, you know? To girls? That I'm threatening," said the guy. "Even though I am very sexual, you know?"

This is terrific, I thought as I leaned back in comfort. *Now on top of everything, I have entertainment.*

What I had been doing was reading *One Hundred Years of Solitude* by Gabriel García Márquez. You can't really show your face in Colombia if you haven't read this book, and Colombia was coming up, and it's not a short book. Marquez tells the story of a village over the course of a hundred years. You follow a family, there are revolutions, the railroad. *Magical realism* is a term to describe the genre of which it is the most famed example. Surreal and beautifully strange things happen to the people in the book, time bends and repeats. Their world perplexes and folds in on our world, and thus reminds us of the true weirdness and cruelty and wonder of our world that so often gets left out of descriptions of reality. Only by getting a bit magical, you might say, can you truly evoke the strangeness of reality.

Look, man, it's a great book, but just at this minute? At Ojo de Agua as I drank my coconut, dried off from a swim, and cooled my feet? Listening to my countrymen chat was more compelling.

Of course, it's not right to eavesdrop on your fellow Americans. That's an obvious truth, and it's rude of our federal government to keep forgetting it. Though I guess I had, too. The truth was I liked these people. Maybe I'd meet up with them down the road. I dried off my feet and went back to my motorbike.

Ometepe is in the middle of the lake. It's made out of two volcanoes, it's about twenty miles across, and there's really only one road to speak of that goes around the whole place. Perfect place for a motorbike.

Before leaving California, I got my motorcycle license. It wasn't easy. I failed the test the first time, which should've told me something. It should've told me that if you're nervous on a motorcycle, which of course you should be, you will die. To ride a motorcycle well, you need to be both focused and brave. While I've been both, I'm neither consistently.

In this way riding a motorcycle is not unlike surfing, I guess. Except instead of waves, you'll land on skull-smashing pavement. To be effective, you must be fearless when you should be fearful. This is the lesson I was trying to teach myself by riding around Ometepe.

Great place to learn. Get five hundred meters out of the town and you're on a country road, with big wide vistas up to the volcano, and you're the only thing in sight. Maybe a cow or something. You can cut loose and it feels amazing and thrilling.

Tiring maybe, whipping around those curves with the waves of the lake crashing below you. But a good kind of tiring. Maybe that's why at Ojo de Agua I felt so great. I'd ridden a while, but I still had a while to go, to a coffee plantation, the Finca Magdalena.

My mission was to have the world's best cup of coffee.

Before I left Los Angeles I did some investigating into coffee. Research. Believe me, if you start trying to learn about coffee—its geography, its nature—you will never run out of passionate opinions. Many people have gone far deep into the world of coffee.

Look, I barely peered in. It was too dangerous. You can get lost in learning about coffee.

The best idea I learned is the theory that caffeine developed because it killed insects. That it was like an evolutionary pesticide that grew within coffee plants. Beyond that, I learned some basics and some place names.

In El Salvador at the bar of Tortuga Verde, I shared what I'd read with Miah, who'd worked on a coffee plantation for three months and was able to correct me on some practicalities and offer things he'd learned. Like that anywhere there's shade on a volcano, there grows good coffee.

With this knowledge I studied my maps, read what scraps I could on precious minutes of WiFi, and determined:

The best coffee in the world will be at Finca Magdalena, Ometepe.

About four in the afternoon I got to the trail. It was at the far end of the island, the south end, on the slope of Volcán Maderas. Road, trail: It wasn't good anyway. There were huge rocks sticking out of it as it ran steep uphill. There were logs and stuff along the way, holes dug by what must've been frequent floods.

Well, there was nothing to do but rev my motorbike and attack it.

An hour later, maybe a third of the way up, half a kilometer at most, I had to give up.

When I was a boy, I'd read somewhere that a *well-executed retreat is the most difficult of military maneuvers to perform.* I've taken a lot of comfort in that quote, though I forget who said it. Whenever I've had to retreat, which is often, I've taken comfort in the idea that what I was doing was *deciding to accept a serious challenge* rather than *quitting*. It helps.

My retreat was imperfect but honorable. I just shut the bike off, put it in neutral, and rode down, bumping my ass off along the way. Bruised but unharmed, I shook it off. *Finca Magdalena is best visited in the morning, after all,* I declared to myself. Bravely I resolved to come back in the morning, when the coffee would be all the more delicious.

As I mounted my bike to find a place to sleep, a whizzing sound came upon me. It was a middle-aged man, I'm guessing French, with a slender woman of about the same age gripping him tight from behind as he blasted, with sureness and confidence, up over the rocks and around the logs, steady up the road I'd just quit on.

Sir, I salute you, I said, again to myself, and off I went.

With night ready to come in, the wind picking up on the lake, I went back along the coast road. Those Americans I'd seen earlier—well, maybe we'd end up at the same place and drink beers together, and then they wouldn't mind me writing up the funny things they said, because we'd all be friends. There was a place I'd passed, a rickety painted hotel right on the water, where I guessed they'd be. That's where I went.

The other Americans didn't turn up before the sun went down, and they didn't come after. Alone in the restaurant, I drank bottles of beer and ate spaghetti. I ate spaghetti a lot in Central America because it's hard to screw up. Anytime I was in a place that looked like it screwed everything up, that's what I ordered.

This place looked like it screwed things up. There were both too many people working there and not enough. Two employees, men, smoked and whispered in a dark corner of the place. A fat, gloomy teenager was at the desk, unhelpful, distant. A storm was brewing on the lake. Not a serious storm, but gray and windy. A lot windier than I like it on a tropical isle. Spooky wind, eerie wind. It rattled the shutters. I left half the spaghetti and asked if I could take some beers back to my room.

My room was across the road, now pitch-dark. You couldn't see the lake. Why had they put me back here? Was this worse? I tried to read *One Hundred Years of Solitude* but couldn't concentrate. A fan rattled away, co-echoing with the clattering from the wind. Guatemala Pam had told me that you have to watch out on Ometepe, that thieves swim over from the shore in the night and rob tourists. That seemed crazy to me. The swim must be five miles at the narrowest. But who knew out here? I was alone in the cabin, behind me was forest, across the road the black lake. When I fell asleep, I don't know.

In the morning it was the most perfect day ever.

So: I hopped on my motorbike and went back down the road around the south volcano to the trail to Finca Magdalena.

This time I walked up it, and I gotta say it wasn't even easy to walk with all the rocks and stuff. I don't know how the other motorbike got up it. Maybe halfway up the one-and-a-half-kilometer trail, the trees sprouted pink and red and orange cherries, in narrow bunches. Coffee cherries. Like you could pop them in your mouth and they'd have delicious coffee juice inside.

The trail bent, chickens squawked and hopped across the path, and there was the big house of the Finca Magdalena. An old wooden house, wide porch all around it, aged and falling apart in just the charming ways.

On the porch at a table a black-haired girl who looked intensely hippie'd out read a hippie'd-out tract of some kind. Two Danish (maybe?) women ate French toast in silence. Below me the slope of the volcano rolled down, a clearing first and then thick with green trees, down to the road and the shore of the lake beyond.

At an open window to the kitchen, a girl asked me what I wanted.

Café, por favor. I ambled to an old wooden chair at an old wooden table to await the best coffee in the world.

Ten minutes later it came.

It was okay.

Wait a Second

W ait a second," said my coworker Bobby months later, when I told him this story of the Finca Magdalena and the perfect cup of coffee. "You told me the exact same story about tea."

He was right. I had.

Three years before, I'd been in Darjeeling, India, where they grow tea on the mountainsides. *Man*, I thought to myself, *in Darjeeling I'm gonna have the perfect cup of tea.* So I went a few kilometers out of town to a tea plantation. Women with wide hats and huge baskets on their backs worked their way down the side of a mountain, in the steep green foothills of the Himalayas.

At the plantation house, the old woman had lectured me about the highest excellence in tea, demonstrating each step in a slow and meticulous preparation as she asserted that what she was making for me was the freshest, finest kind of tea in the world, made only from the tip of Silver Darling Darjeeling tea leaves, the water prepared exactly properly. She presented it to me with reverence, like a sacred gift, as though I should be very honored just to try it.

She locked eyes with me as I took a gentle sip.

It tasted . . . fine? Like . . . tea?

Don't get me wrong. This was a beautiful place. I was lucky to get to go there. Same with the Finca Magdalena: spectacular place, a dream of travel. Going to these places were two of the best experiences of my life.

The point, I guess, is it might not matter how good the tea is, how great the coffee. The experience you get isn't always the experience you went looking for. What you were after sometimes turns out not to be the point. But who cares? What matters is the trip you took to get there.

*   *   *

On the boat back to the mainland, I saw the North Carolinians again. The ferry was crowded, tourists and Nicaraguans both, and most people were keeping to themselves. There was a radio playing and a few of the crew guys stood around it, watching a spectacle: The brassiest of the North Carolina women was, lustily and imperfectly, performing along to "Black Velvet" as recorded by Alannah Myles. Our brassy North Carolinian didn't know the words exactly, but she didn't care. She positioned herself in a doorway, arched her spine backward like a cat, and belted it out, projecting her voice and using her space like she was the second-to-last song before closing time at a karaoke bar. It was maybe ten in the morning.

The crew guys weren't *un*interested with this. She was being plenty sultry. She definitely thought so, at least. But these guys were from the tropics. The average Nicaraguan woman is sexier washing her shoes off than the average American is at having sex. I tell you honestly that a raisined old Nicaraguan woman projects more sexuality as she hobbles along the cobblestones than many much lither and younger women doing yoga in Los Angeles.

She bent herself against the steel staircase and smiled at them as she lip-synced. They watched, but they weren't impressed. They looked like they'd seen stranger performances.

A Nicaraguan Canal

There are plans, put forward by entrepreneur Wang Jing, CEO of the Hong Kong Nicaragua Canal Development Group, to build a canal across Nicaragua, spilling into and out of the lake.

Based on my estimate of how things go in Nicaragua, completion of this canal will take roughly ten thousand years.

Costa Rica: These Guys Are Awesome

"These guys are awesome," the guide said, in adorably accented English and a voice like a cartoon animal. "I love them." She was talking about a species of tiny tree frog. One was illuminated in the beam of her flashlight, just off a nature trail. The frog sat in the darkness on a wet leaf. His eyes made up a fifth of his body.

I was in El Silencio de Los Angeles Cloud Forest in the Central Highlands of Costa Rica, taking a night hike. With me were some American parents and their children. So far I was crushing them all at frog spotting, and would continue to do so. Don't think the guide didn't notice.

You might not need me to tell you that Costa Rica is fantastic. Close to a million Americans visited Costa Rica last year, and I bet most of them had a tremendous time. When you enter Costa Rica from Nicaragua, you are struck by, for instance, the pavement on the highway (that it's good) and the streetlights (that there are some) and the cars (they're less likely to be smoking). You might also be struck by the people. At least I was. They seemed happier. Calmer. Less burdened by the crushing weight of oppression and war and cruel history and poverty.

That was my impression, anyway. When it comes to poverty we can measure it. The per capita GDP of Costa Rica is $10,184. (This is from the World Bank.) The per capita GDP of Nicaragua is $1,851.11.* Costa Rica is ten times richer. Why is that?

GDP doesn't measure everything, of course. It doesn't measure happiness and culture and the smiles of children and so on. Some sociologist somewhere is probably measuring the smiles of children right now. I hope so, that'd be interesting. By my amateur glance, the numbers between

---

*If you're wondering what ours is in the United States, it's $53,042. We're tenth in the world, getting smoked by Luxembourg with $110,664.80. When you compare that to dead-last Malawi ($226.50), can you not be a little 1) relieved, 2) grateful, 3) disgusted, 4) embarrassed?

Costa Rica and Nicaragua on that would be a lot closer. But Costa Rica would still win, I'd bet. Why is that?

You can ask a Costa Rican that, like I did, and they might give you a thoughtful and nuanced answer. More likely they will shrug and say something like *"Pura vida."*

This is a phrase you will see and hear many times if you go to Costa Rica. "Pure life" is what it means. You may not have needed me to translate that one. There's more meaning in it. *Good life, real life, honest life, unworried life, unstressed life.*

Now, this is a great idea to tell people who are on vacation. If I ran a resort in Costa Rica, you can be damn sure you'd hear about *"pura vida,* pure life, our national way of living in Costa Rica, and our philosophy at Villa Hely" every damn day. But as far as I can tell, they really mean it.

The first morning I was in Costa Rica, I went zip-lining. This is something you can do in Costa Rica: get hooked into a system of wires and ropes across the rain forest canopy and zip around. On the way there, I rode in a van with a happy family of English bird-watchers. At least the dad was a bird-watcher. The children seemed to be humoring him. His wife, without really trying, glanced out the window.

"There! Chestnut-sided warbler!"

The dad whipped his head around, binoculars already to his eyes.

"Well *done*, Mrs. Thichett!" he declared, proud anew in his sensible choice of spouse. As excited as he was about bird-watching, Mr. Thichett was a bit trepidatious about zip-lining. The Costa Rican kids, half of them girls, who ran the place teased him. They wanted to strap him in facedown and let him zip seventy meters across like Superman.

"I have quite severe vertigo," he told them, "and I don't care to go facedown. I'll go faceup." So he did, and his children congratulated him. It wasn't easy for him, and he was proud he'd done it. On the ride back he was exhilarated. He asked me where I'd come from, and I listed off the countries I'd been through.

"Well. I'm quite taken with Costa Rica."

*   *   *

Guatemala, El Salvador, Nicaragua: These countries are all, to be blunt, fucked up. Costa Rica has plenty of problems, but compare it to its neighbors and it's a paradise. Why?

Because they don't have an army is one answer you hear. In 1948, Costa Rican president José Figueres symbolically sledgehammered a stone wall at the country's military headquarters. Then he handed the keys over to the minister of education. Since then, Costa Rica hasn't had an army, a navy, or an air force.

A smart move: If you're a Central American president, especially a reform-minded one like Figueres, there's a good chance the military will end up overthrowing you. He'd just come out of winning a civil war, and the military was not on his team. How he pulled it off without getting killed is impressive, and it lasted. In 1987, while neighboring Nicaragua was still fighting its civil war, Costa Rica's president Óscar Arias won the Nobel Peace Prize for working to end it.

Because they didn't piss off the United States. That's another answer. Figueres stayed friends with Allen Dulles and the CIA. He was friends with Castro for a while, too, but they had a falling-out. He wasn't a pushover, Figueres. In 1958, he testified before the US Congress, and gave them a pretty stern lecture that veered into discussing "the fragile virtue of female stars" in Hollywood. But he was skillful and cagey, and the phrase "CIA-sponsored" appears less in Costa Rica's history than it does in those of some other Central American countries.

Because José Figueres was a great man. Seems like it to me. Vain, maybe, but as far as I can tell, from 1948, when he brought the country out of civil war, to 1991, when he died, he navigated a very narrow path very dexterously. He credited himself with 834 reforms. He called his farm La Lucha Sin Fin, the struggle without end. He married two different American women, too. No doubt that helped, perhaps in ways we may never know.

Because Costa Rica protected its environment is another answer.

Twenty-five percent of Costa Rica is some kind of national park or biological reserve. In Costa Rica you can find something like 5 percent of the species in the world. But that might be an effect of being a great country, not a cause. I'm not sure.

Because Costa Rica's democratizing coalition redistributed elite property early and exercised effective political control of the countryside. That's an answer I'm paraphrasing from the back cover of Professor Deborah J. Yashar's book *Demanding Democracy: Reform and Reaction in Costa Rica and Guatemala, 1870s–1950s.* I read it when I got back and was still wondering about why Costa Rica seemed so much better off than its neighbors. A politcal scientist friend recommended Professor Yashar's book to me.

It's a little dry. There're a lot of sentences like "Yet, by focusing on individuals, the moment of change, and efforts to redirect conflict, these choice-oriented approaches theorize neither the source of political conflict that generates democracy's overthrow nor the conditions under which democratization is likely." But Professor Yashar certainly seems a lot smarter and better informed than me. She points out that, politically, Guatemala and Costa Rica were on pretty similar tracks until around 1950. After that, it's coups and civil wars for Guatemala, and tree frogs and *pura vida* for Costa Rica.

Professor Yashar discounts what she calls "agency-oriented approaches"—the idea that a few great people can make the difference at the right moment. She points out that Costa Rica had more equitable distribution of land than Guatemala. That makes sense. I bet she's right.

Or maybe they're just lucky.

Or maybe constant reminders to yourself and your countrymen to live *pura vida* might work.

Panama: Cut That Thing!

Look at Panama there, on your world map or globe: a taunting dangler clinging North and South America together. It's like one of those plastic thingies that keeps a price tag attached to a shirt: Don't you just want to pop it right off?

The temptation to cut through Panama has been around since the world map got filled in. Just that thin strip is gonna keep the Atlantic and Pacific apart? Really? C'mon, surely we can get through *that*.

The idea really got appealing in 1849, when it appeared California might be chock-full of gold, and the extra five thousand miles of sailing it took to go *all* the way around Cape Horn started to seem ridiculous. The more impatient gold rushers took to stopping at Colón, on the Panamanian Atlantic coast, and trying to walk across to Panama City, on the Pacific side. Lots of them, both humans and the mules they hired, died. One solution was a railroad across the country, which is what our boy John L. Stephens was working on when he, too, died. Something like six thousand people died building the railroad, which was finally finished in 1855, many of them Chinese or Caribbean workers. They died from malaria and cholera and yellow fever, some of them killing themselves during the depressive haze that can follow a case of malaria. There was a whole side business of putting the corpses of dead workers of the Panama Canal Railway into barrels of preservatives and selling them to medical schools. Supposedly, one of the doctors involved in the railroad bleached skeletons of dead, relation-less workers in the hopes of creating a museum of skeletons of every race in the world.

You can contemplate all this horrifying mortality in pleasant comfort as you take a ride on the Panama Canal Railway. On the porch of the Panama station, there's a parrot that says *"Hola!"* over and over again. Somehow it seemed like a true wonder to me that a parrot might speak in Spanish. But, duh, why would a parrot care? I wonder how many languages have a parrot speaking them. Is there a parrot that speaks Inuit? (Maybe I should train one? Job for another day, I guess.) There must be several polylingual parrots. I wonder which parrot in the world can speak the most languages?

Luckily, I didn't have WiFi or I might've watched videos of parrots all day instead of experiencing the Panama Canal Railway.

A one-way ticket on the Panama Canal Railway, Atlantic to Pacific, costs twenty-five dollars. That's what it cost back in 1855, too. Back then, that was an absurd amount of money for a forty-seven-mile ride. The alternative might be weeks at sea in the furious storms off Tierra del Fuego. William Mulholland, the badass who brought the water that made Los Angeles, couldn't afford a train ticket. He walked.

The train, for me, was easy. It's quite comfortable now, the seats have an antique glory, and so does the bar where you can buy Pringles and coffee and cold green cans of Panama beer. You rattle through jungle, and out the window sometimes you can see enormous ships, tankers and freighters ten stories tall, three hundred yards long, traveling right by your side like they're cars in the next lane, lining up to go through the locks that raise and lower them twenty-six meters up and back down again. You go through labyrinthine swamps of the Chagres River, and through the cut at Gold Hill, killer of hundreds, thousands maybe.

Man, I love a good train, and this is a great one, one of the best maybe, when you think about what an accomplishment it was, what Stephens did, the ambition, the stupefying cost in money and energy and lives.

"He's not enjoying the scenery."

That, whispered, by a French woman, bespectacled. My age or maybe younger, poised and thin and elegant, traveling alone. With a very subtle movement of her eyes, she indicated a Russian guy, one of four huddled into the tabletop seats across from us. I'd heard these guys come in. They were drinking and sunburned and sweaty already, first thing in the morning. They'd clearly been rolling hard. One of them was straight-up passed out, facedown on the table. His fist still held a beer erect. The others looked woozy, like they might soon be casualties, too.

We were on the Gatun causeway, which works its way across five miles of the fifty-mile lake. It's true, he didn't see anything. Me and the French woman looked at each other. We smiled, just enough, to let each other know we both agreed we were having a much more engaging experience of the Panama Canal Railway. Although I, at least, thought that the way the Russian dudes were rolling also ruled, in its own way.

Kidnapping

When I went to Central and South America, many Americans warned me I'd get kidnapped. I found this a little insulting, both to me and to Central and South America.

Sure, kidnapping got so bad as to become a way of life, in some times and some places like, say, Colombia in the 1980s and Venezuela now. People do go down the wrong road someplace south of the border and never turn up again. A friend of a friend of mine, Harry Devert, went riding his motorcycle across Mexico. Last time his girlfriend heard from him he was headed to Zihuatanejo, on the Pacific coast, and then he disappeared. Six months later they found pieces of him, and his motorbike, on the beach. He went missing right before and around the place where Mexican special forces captured cartel leader Joaquín Guzmán, "El Chapo," so who knows what was going on. My friend who knew him said Harry was a great guy who could charm anybody, and he had a real integrity to him, and he was very brave and knew how to handle himself, and he loved adventure.

He loved adventure more than me, for sure. The way I traveled, you'd have to be pretty lucky to kidnap me. I moved fast and didn't stick my nose anywhere that felt too kidnappy. Trust your feelings, that's the best kidnap-avoidance advice I heard, and I did.

The only time on the whole trip my kidnap alarm went off was in a car from Colón on the Atlantic coast back to Panama City, on the Pacific side. When the train brought us to Colón, I took one look around the place and decided not to wait all day for the train back. Instead, I was gonna turn around. From what I'd read, it was a bad-news situation in Colón, and it sure looked that way to me. The people I saw looked like they didn't want me anywhere near the place, and couldn't believe anyone would be stupid enough to come there voluntarily. The French woman appeared determined. I nodded her off and wished her well, and I went to the swarm of taxi guys hustling for business.

I've probably been in two thousand cabs or taxis in my life, in China and Mongolia and rural Australia and India and Cuba and New York and Vegas and plenty of odd towns in America, and this was the only time the hairs on the back of my neck stood up and it seemed real that this guy might do something truly crazy on purpose. Ominous mutters turned to shouts and then disappeared, all in some patois he must've known was incomprehensible to me. He'd snort like a dragon and then a minute later cry out and bare his teeth at me.

Guessing on it now, more experience under my belt, I'd say he was probably just high out of his mind on cocaine. He drove at ninety miles an hour down roads that didn't seem right at all. While I tried to seem cool, I felt around in my backpack for anything that might be heavy enough to hit him with. Best I could do was a seven-inch flashlight that wasn't gonna do much more than annoy. A cigarette lighter, maybe, aimed at the eyes?

He jerked the car over. He wiped sweat off his face. It was soaked. Fingering my lighter, I waited. If he was gonna make demands, let him do it.

But wiping the sweat: That was it, actually. He might've been fucked up, but he was trying at least to do something like his job and not perform any crimes on me. He jerked the car back into action. He made me understand he was gonna take me to see the locks at Lago Miraflores.

The Panama Canal Railway is impressive enough as a human accomplishment, a triumph of vision and grit and engineering.

Compared to the Canal, it's nothing.

How Did They Dig the Panama Canal?

The biggest problem was that Panama was a pesthole. That's not my word, that's the word the great historian David McCullough uses. His book *The Path Between the Seas* is the best book I know of about the building of the Panama Canal. What I say here comes from what I learned from him, or what I learned gaping at the actual thing, watching the informative movie, and asking questions.

The French tried to build a canal for twenty years. They were led and inspired by Ferdinand de Lesseps, who was everything magnificent and grand and ridiculous you'd want from a Versailles-born genius of the age of steam. He wasn't an engineer at all, he was a diplomat and a big-idea man. Through sheer willpower and promotion and trickery and enthusiasm, he brought the Suez Canal into existence, cutting right through Egypt. You could sail now from the Mediterranean to the Red Sea and on to the Indian Ocean. It cut the trip from Europe to India by something like four thousand miles. No one could believe what de Lesseps accomplished. He became an international hero. Everyone knew his name, they threw banquets for him, mobs cheered him on the streets of Paris, Queen Victoria of Great Britain gave him, a Frenchman, the Grand Cross of the Order of the Star of India.

Then he came to Panama.

Thousands of people died before the French gave up. Mudslides, explosions, collapses, but mostly disease: malaria and yellow fever. All medical people at the time agreed that digging up mucky earth caused pestilence in the air, but the French did it anyway. De Lesseps was determined to keep his canal at sea level the whole way across, no locks to raise or lower ships, so the amount of sheer digging involved was incredible.

Something like five thousand people died before they ran out of money. Five years in, the French Panama Canal Company went bankrupt in a haze of scandal, corruption, rumors of bribery. Years later, de Lesseps would be put on trial and found guilty for various financial wrongdoings brought on as he tried desperate ways to keep his scheme alive. He couldn't do it.

What the French couldn't finish, the Americans could.

So decided President Theodore Roosevelt. If you don't know by now that Theodore Roosevelt was an incredible, bear-killing, book-writing, shooting-surviving tower of manly strength, then I weep for our public schools. Theodore Roosevelt was the kind of guy who declared, confidently, THIS IS GOING TO *HAPPEN*.

And it did.

There were two keys to building the Panama Canal:

1. Figuring out that malaria and yellow fever were caused by mosquitoes

That was huge. The Americans pumped in clean water, they built sewage systems, they put up mosquito nets everywhere, they drained stagnant pools of water, and they sprayed the hell out of the place with experimental insecticides. They topped cisterns of water with layers of oil to kill mosquito larvae.

Still, almost six thousand people died, most of them workers recruited from the West Indies. On top of the diseases they were killed in accidents. Twenty-three of them were blown up in a dynamite explosion at the Bas Obispo Cut.

Digging was dangerous, and that's why the second American insight was so important:

2. Digging less

There were already tons of water across Panama, lakes and rivers and swampy marsh. Instead of hauling in smoky steampunk mechanical digger inventions, the Americans as much as possible strung together the lakes and rivers that were already there. They flooded thousands of acres of forest and jungle, and built the largest man-made lake anyone had ever seen.

The only problem was, now you'd have to raise and lower seventy-thousand-ton ships, up and down, to get them across the uneven terrain.

How do you do that? De Lesseps thought it was impossible.

It's not. You just lift and lower the ships, floating them, in five of the world's biggest bathtubs.

Detail from Diego Rivera's mural *Dream Of A Sunday Afternoon in Alameda Central Park*. That's a lot of Mexican history packed into one mural.

A Mayan church and graveyard in the hills outside San Cristóbal. Seemed like it could be a very cool start to a horror movie.

The waterfall at Agua Azul. Would you rather watch this or *Dragon Ball Z*?

Mural of a royal festival, Bonampak, Mexico. Not pictured: captives getting their fingernails ripped out.

Road, Guatemala, seen from the bus.

Motorbike parked under a tree in El Remate, Guatemala. This is the photo I would enter into a travel photography contest. If you're having one let me know.

Temple of the Cross, Palenque.

All the food groups, Guatemala.

Lake Atitlán, Guatemala.
Don't look for me here.

Guatemalan boy stealing my look.

Shag mural depicting the inspiring history of Nicaragua.

Volcano on Ometepe, Nicaragua, seen from the island's main (only?) road.

The Panama Canal Railway. Definitely Panama's #1 railway.

A ship squeezing its way through the locks of the Panama Canal. Not a ton of wiggle room.

The ruins of Old Panama. A crap UNESCO site, in my opinion.

Guna women waiting in the San Blas islands.

The crew of the *Jaqueline.* The girls are making lanyards, which was a fad aboard.

Cartagena. I don't think the theater is open.

Good Friday procession, Popayán. An angel and her skeleton-slave.

Soccer game, Iquitos, Peru.

High water on the Amazon.

The shaman's house.

A sloth, trying his best
to keep it together.

Llama, Machu Picchu

The author at Machu Picchu, smiling with altitude-related lightheadedness and delight at seeing a llama eat an apple.

León Dormido, or Sleeping Lion Rock, the Galápagos. (Doesn't look that much like a sleeping lion if you ask me.)

Blue-footed boobies doing their thing in the Galápagos.

Dried llama fetuses for sale in the witches' market of La Paz, Bolivia.

La Paz, Bolivia. Twelve thousand feet and climbing.

Roadside/seaside store, Chile.

Sixteenth-century church in the Atacama Desert.

I don't think the bus is running.

Desert lake in the Atacama. Chile is so cool even their deserts have lakes.

I feel you, pal. Santiago, Chile.

Colored houses and steep streets in Valparaiso, Chile.

New friends (guanacos) in Torres del Paine, Patagonia.

Punta Arenas, the bottom of the world.

The World's Biggest Bathtub

*P*anamax, that's a word for a ship that's at the exact hugeness limit to go through the Panama Canal. A Panamax ship can carry fifty-something thousand tons of cargo, it can be 965 feet long and 106 feet wide. The locks are only 110 feet wide. Ships are hauled in by a special train to a space so tight you'd think they might get squished, the metal doors close, and they flood the chamber with twenty-something million gallons of water, and up she goes. Or all that water rushes out, and down she goes.

To see it would excite the eight-year-old in anybody.

That's it, I decided. *I gotta get down in this thing.*

Fish the Panama Canal

*G*reat, I thought, *how can I get in the Panama Canal?*

I could swim it, I guess. That's what American travel writer and adventurer Richard Halliburton did, in 1928. He was charged a toll of thirty-six cents. So that's been done.

Well, there're expensive tour boats, I thought, *but that's no fun. I'm supposed to be getting close to the ground here, or in this case the water. Maybe somebody will take me fishing?*

There you go. I googled "Panama Canal Fishing," and that took me to www.panamacanalfishing.com. The next morning, I was down there in the thing in a motorboat, catching peacock bass as giant tankers and roll-on/roll-off car transporters passed by.

"Just a terrific morning for fishing," said Captain Rich, and I agreed with him. Captain Rich had been born in Panama, to American parents, and he loved it, he was proud of it, boyish about wanting to talk about the canal. He'd offer up little facts about it like they were cookies on a plate and he really wanted us to enjoy them. I ate up every one and asked for more.

The other guy who'd paid to come out fishing that day was an American, too, about my age, from Oklahoma. He lived in Colombia now, where he worked as a coal mine engineer. He several times described the women of Colombia as *muy bellísima*, that Spanish phrase always. Access to *muy bellísima* women seemed to him like the main perk of his job. He had big wide eyes and smoked Winston cigarettes. He'd done a lot of fishing in the lakes of Oklahoma and Texas. Though it wasn't yet ten in the morning, he and I were already reaching into the packed cooler of Panama beers the captain kept happily reminding us about.

Piloting the boat was a black Panamanian, Victor, a serious guy. He looked like he hadn't laughed in at least four years. Captain Rich spoke of Victor with awe and gratitude for the good fortune of finding him.

"He's the only man in Panama who doesn't drink," said the captain. Victor didn't even look up.

The pilot said nothing the whole trip except single words yelled when exasperation finally overtook him and he needed to jerk me out of my general haze of idiocy and wake me up to some obvious point, like I was fishing in exactly the wrong spot.

We were after peacock bass and, if we were lucky, enormous fighting tarpon in from the ocean. Peacock bass are native to the Amazon. They are yellow and green and the shape of the flying bird-fish in *Super Mario Bros. 3*. (They're called "Cheep Cheeps," don't think for one second I don't know their proper name.)

To catch them, we took the boat over what was once rain forest flooded to make the canal. The water level was low, a dry early spring in Panama. The pointed tips of old flooded trees spiked through the surface of the water like pylons from a rotted-away dock.

"Eerie, right?" said Captain Rich. "Eerie." Behind him an enormous tanker glided along, filling the horizon on its transit across Earth, moving with a steady intelligence though you couldn't see a person on it.

The peacock bass were easy enough to catch, especially with Victor pointing exactly where I should cast my line, like there were underwater bull's-eyes he was baffled I couldn't see. Since they're invasive and all, I didn't feel bad catching them, reeling them in, unhooking them, and tossing them in a cooler—just doing my bit to rid the canal of enemy agents. Who cared about the fishing anyway? Down on the waters of the canal, you could see the genius of it: that instead of digging a huge ditch, the Americans had strung together natural waterways and made a river that God surely meant to put here but he just forgot to finish off. Ingenious, really, and no less impressive for using what was already there. Bobbing on the water, drinking beers, watching international shipping come and go, feeling a tug on the line now and then? A terrific day, I was having a blast. From some vines near a bank, some monkeys came down. Captain Rich fed them Pringles. I wasn't sure monkeys were supposed to have Pringles, but these monkeys knew what they were and wanted them bad.

"Yup, these guys are old friends," he said as a mother monkey and the baby on her back begged for more chips with an almost scary urgency. "I don't know where Pop is today. Sometimes he runs off."

The coal engineer from Oklahoma, though, wasn't having as great a time.

"Look at this," I said, "we're in the Panama Canal! How great is this?"

"Be a whole lot greater if we tuck into a few more fish," he said. He hadn't come here to appreciate engineering marvels. He knew all about those. He came here to catch tarpon.

We nearly did, too, both of us. Trolling fast closer to the Pacific mouth, we both hooked into unseen fish that sent the line singing out with a jerk you could feel in your shoulders and the muscles of your back. Mine got away easy, to the unsurprise of Victor. *Just as well*, I figured. *What am I gonna do with a tarpon anyway?* But when the Oklahoman lost his, he was pissed. He sucked on his Winston with a new intensity, and his eyes stayed wide the rest of the afternoon.

"Man," said Captain Rich, "you're gonna be thinking about that tarpon all day." He smiled like "It's all part of the fun, right?" but the Oklahoman just smoked and looked off.

"Hey," I said, pointing to a giant Maersk container ship, "there's a gigantic container ship, *right there!*" The Oklahoman looked, but it didn't do much for him. Not everyone's as into container ships as me.

At a restaurant on the bank of the Chagres River, they fried up our peacock bass for us and served them to us with a spicy Cajun sauce and French fries. We were joined by a South African charter pilot, fat and in his fifties. He seemed to know Captain Rich well. The polite but unwelcoming way the captain spoke to him made me suspect there was something disreputable about this guy. Like if you let him even get a hint you two were friends, sooner or later he'd tell you a story you wouldn't want to hear.

The South African was on a mission, it seemed, to hunt and kill one of every species of fish in the world. He said the names of different fish from around the world, and the way he looked at us after he said them made it clear which ones he considered formidable opponents. He spoke of fly-fishing while standing on shallow coral reefs in the Caribbean for strong and vicious kinds of barracuda, crafty fish not easily fooled and that knew how to fight. There's a darkness to a man who travels the world looking for dangerous species to battle and kill. There was a solemnity, too, in the way he talked. A respect. Like the only thing he cared about, perhaps the only thing he enjoyed, was confirming his belief that the world was a ruthless place, all life carrying in its blood the true understanding that this life is an unending competition played by all, consenting or no, where the cost for the losers is death. Sharp as you are, you can never be sharp enough. Stack up your thousand victories and they could all be undone by the smallest slip tomorrow, and though you learn every trick and master every skill you, too, are doomed to vanish. Death alone will win in the end, as pitiless life consumes its own creations.

Dark wisdom this may be, but it's a little much at lunch. I spaced out, sipped my beer, and stared at the water and the butt of the waitress and enjoyed my peacock bass, fatty dummies that tasted delicious.

Thought That Just Occurred to Me

Geez, I hope that bespectacled Frenchwoman got home from Colón okay. Might've been chivalrous to keep an eye on her.
Meh, I'm sure she's fine.

The Ruins of Old Panama

Scattered across the world are 1,031 sites, natural and man-made, ancient and modern, designated by the United Nations Educational, Scientific and Cultural Organization to be of such outstanding value to humanity that they're declared World Heritage Sites.

The Parthian Fortresses of Nisa. The Sacred City of Anuradhapura, the Saloum Delta, the Tomb of Askia. Just reading the list makes me happy. Man, if I could I'd go to all of them.

Now, don't get me wrong: Some of them are better than others.

Some of them are astounding: Angkor Wat is one. So is the Redwood National Forest in Northern California.

Some of them, like the ruins of Panama, are . . . well, they are not amazing, let us say.

Look, how could they be? How could they all be equal? How could you even compare, really, the historic center of Gjirokastra in Albania to the Grand Canyon?

To be honest, it wouldn't shock me if UNESCO were slightly corrupt. If some kind of money didn't change hands to get, say, the Neolithic Flint Mines at Spiennes or the Struve Geodetic Arc on there. But hey: Having a list of the world's wonders is fun.

Already on this trip I'd seen six. Mostly, they were amazing. Tikal? Absolutely. Oaxaca? Yup, deserves it. The ruins of León Viejo? Well, the casual traveler could skip those, no problem. I myself didn't bother with the Pre-Columbian Chiefdom Settlements with Stone Spheres of the Diquís, in Costa Rica. Someday perhaps I'll regret it.

Oh, they're right there, I said, in a bar, to my map, *might as well go, then*, so I got a taxi and went.

Look. I'm not saying they should destroy the ruins of Old Panama or anything. Maybe, if someone lavished money and thought and time and design on them, they could look almost interesting. If this book makes more than a hundred million dollars, I promise to donate a generous portion to the project myself.

But for now? As a UNESCO site the ruins of Old Panama suck. They bring down the whole franchise.

What's there are the vacant shells of a few stone buildings—Old Panama. We can't blame the Old Panamanians for the fact that the ruins of their city suck. If they had their way, they wouldn't be ruins at all. Old Panama would still be there.

What happened was Captain Henry Morgan, he again of the rum and the destroying of Granada, managed to navigate and paddle a thousand pirates down the rivers and swamps from the Atlantic coast and attack Old Panama from the undefended jungle side. All the cannons and walls were pointed seaward, and while the Old Panamanians were turning them around, everything and everyone got destroyed and raped and killed and burned. The gunfire stores exploded and the whole place was wrecked.

So the ruins can't be expected to be that great.

Actually, it's kind of impressive they're still there at all.

No one was there at all. Just me. The buildings are far apart. Old Panama was big. Whatever adornment they may have had, though, had long ago been blasted off or otherwise extracted. They're hollow and empty. Birds roost in the empty windows and open roofs. There's no one around and it's lonely.

When is a ruin not a ruin? I wondered. When does it cross the threshold into, just, like, a pile of stones? A ruin has to have some kind of structure, right, some skeletal resemblance to what was once there? The ruins of Old Panama are so ruined they're barely even a ruin.

Outside the park, there's a highway, and then the city starts right back up again. In the travel guides and wikis and forums, it's said that the area around there is one of the most dangerous in Panama, but it looked fine to me. I could hear a brass band playing.

Fuck the ruins, I thought. *Lemme see what's up in Now Panama.* So I followed the sound of the brass band, and I stood there listening for a while.

Then it dawned on me that whether this street was dangerous or not, I was the creepy one, standing there outside a school smoking and listening to a kids' brass band, so I got out of there.

Wallet Stolen in Casco Viejo

On top of the ruins of Old Panama, there's also Casco Viejo, "Old Casco," which is still an old part of the city. The streets are narrow and the buildings are epic. It's a maze to walk through, and intriguing things are happening on every side of you. Stalls are selling coloring books, and women will sell you thick black stews and single cigarettes, and men are playing card games, and kids are doing all kinds of what might be normal Panamanian activities or just insane kid things, I'm not sure.

One afternoon I set out walking, watched the sun go down, had a cocktail, stopped at my hotel, and then walked on into the night. Saturday night. A street was blocked off for a film festival, and on the causeway in the distance, fireworks were going off and I could hear a concert. Heading that way, an old man recommended a diner to me, so I popped in and sat down. It looked like a drugstore counter from the 1950s, but the food was spicy and good and the beers were cold. But when I went to pay, my wallet was missing.

Goddammit, I thought, *Panamanians are a bunch of wretched thieves. Maybe that old man tricked me. Dammit, here I am trying to be an adventurous traveler and some bullshit like that overtakes me.*

I'm embarrassed now by how steamed I was.

To the woman behind the counter I explained the thing, she explained it (not pleased at all with me) to her boss, who waved it off. Off I went, fuming, back to my hotel room.

When I got there I found my wallet lying on the bed.

So off I went, back to the diner where I paid my bill, to the confusion of everyone, and then, by way of apology to the Panamanian people, I had a beer at three different bars.

They're a good people, the Panamanians. It's a damn shame the pirates burned down their city. That was an asshole move by Captain Morgan. I suspect he was an asshole, and from now on I won't be drinking his rum. I sure as hell didn't order it in Panama.

The pirate experience was about to become much more real to me. I was headed into a lawless region with lawless people who made the most of their lawless opportunity.

Cartagena
San Blas
Islands
Guna
Yala
Panama
Darién
Gap
Medellín
Bogotá
Popayán
Ecuador
Peru

Around the Darién Gap
and Colombia

On the Beach in Guna Yala

"WE ARE IN THE GUNA YALA! THERE ARE NO TAXIS HERE!" The German man wasn't wearing a shirt. He hadn't earned that right through physical beauty. His Gorgonic corpulence was heaped on top of itself in fleshy rolls. He was yelling into a cell phone to some lost party of Australians who were trying to make their way to his boat.

We were indeed in the Guna Yala, a kind of autonomous state within Panama where the Guna people live. The Guna people have coffee-ice-cream-colored skin, they fish from dugout canoes, their women weave outlandish depictions of birds and fish and plants into colored cloths called *molas*. They wear bright patterned dresses made of these *molas*. I saw no Guna man or woman who was taller than five feet or so. The Guna are somewhat famous, medically, for having low average blood pressure and low rates of cardiovascular disease—perhaps, goes one theory, because of how much hot chocolate they drink, or perhaps because they spend their lives on the undeveloped coast of their own land or paddling between the many islands of the San Blas, surrounded by shallow fish-filled reefs and dotted with coconut trees. Still, though they live in what looks like paradise, I can't imagine their lives are easy. A Guna woman in her *mola* dress and blouse and head scarf, face wrinkled and weathered by unidentifiable age, held a baby on her hip, waiting on the beach, for a boat, I guess, taking her to or from who knows what errand.

It wasn't a great day for sailing, the sky was gray and gloomy. I was on the beach for a boat, too, the German's boat, a catamaran that would hold eighteen travelers who were looking to sail around the Darién Gap.

The Darién Gap

You could drive all the way from California to Chile, and on paved road, too—well, mostly paved road. I read reports that it gives out a bit in Honduras. But there's road, all the way from North America to the very bottom of South America.

Except for one big gap.

The Darién Gap, it's called. About 150 kilometers of mountainous, lawless jungle between Panama and Colombia where the road disappears. The landscape is too rugged, and no country wants the responsibility. All authority dissolves away into the wild. Drug cartels, tribal people, guerrilla fighters, ants and snakes and jaguars—who controls the Darién Gap? Nobody knows.

People have crossed it before. Noted Canadian travel writer, historian, ethnobotanist, and overall brilliant badass Wade Davis walked across it in 1973. He was twenty. He went along with Sebastian Snow, the "Rucksack Man," an English adventurer, an Eton alum and bearded maniac who ended up walking from Patagonia to Costa Rica.

In 2000, two Englishmen, Tom Hart Dyke and Paul Winder, went into the Darién Gap. They ended up getting kidnapped for nine months by Colombian FARC guerrillas, a story told in their bestselling book, *The Cloud Garden.*

"Yeah, we used to run a trip into the Darién," Captain Rich told me, back on the Canal. I wanted to hear all about it. "Lately some new guys came in there," he said. "They wouldn't be too excited about us taking people in there, Americans especially," he said ominously. "You get lost in there, and nobody's coming after you. Not Panamanians, not Colombians—I mean *nobody.*"

Gaps are interesting. For a while now I'd been fascinated with this one. I bought the best map I could find of it, the National Geographic

Panama Adventure Travel Map. Even on there, the trails drift off and disappear.

The best firsthand account I found from anyone who crossed it is a book called *Crossing the Darién Gap: A Daring Journey Through a Forbidding and Enchanting and Roadless Jungle That Is the Only Link by Land Between North America and South America*, by Andrew Niall Egan, self-published by the author.

Let me highly, highly recommend this book to you. Andrew Niall Egan now works as a real estate agent in Florida, but when he was an eighteen-year-old kid in Canada, he went off on a three-month adventure from Mexico to the Darién Gap, determined to walk across it. So he does, and his adventures are amazing. He slept among tribes who had no idea what country they lived in, or how many people might be in the world. Many thousands? He encounters an incredible man, "The Prophet." Let him tell you. He tells his story in a brisk and clear and compelling way.

When I finished his book, I wrote to Andrew Niall Egan to congratulate him on it and thank him for writing it. I said I was maybe thinking of trying the Gap myself. He wrote back and said he thought it "too risky to cross the Darién Gap overland right now, due to the risk of kidnapping."

Fine with me, I thought, glad to be let off the hook. Andrew Niall Egan knew his shit and was a lot tougher than me, judging from his book. Anyway, he's a great guy.*

But for me: I'd take a boat.

That's how I got to Guna Yala, about to board a boat for a three-day sail to Colombia.

---

*He wrote a five-star Amazon review of my last book.

Pirates of the Caribbean

There were two Swedish girls, who were eighteen. "WHERE IS THE FUCKING DAMN SUN?!" one of them would yell, poking her head through the porthole, when she saw the sky was still gray. There was a German woman, maybe twenty-five, who sat in her bikini absorbed in an English book called *An Irish Country Christmas*. There was another German woman, maybe twenty-two, who spoke no English and kept to herself and read Anne Morrow Lindbergh's *Gift from the Sea* in German (*Muscheln in meiner Hand*). The two German girls didn't seem to like each other. I didn't know why. They never said a word to each other in German.

There were two other Americans, Katie and Lucas. Katie was like a beautiful girl from a catalog for some clothing line with positive values. She was half-Asian and had a huge smile and she looked like a camp counselor your kids would fall in love with. Lucas was not super handsome. He was balding, even though he couldn't've been older than twenty-two, but he was just pure winner, charm oozed off him, he was so comfortable in himself and so happy to help you feel comfortable. A great man, Lucas, I'm enjoying just remembering him now.

There was another American, too, a sweet-hearted guy, but he had brought his guitar aboard. This was an error. No one wanted to hear him play it, that was made clear to him with increasing clarity and force until he got the picture. He would get so seasick on the last days of the sail that he just folded himself into a ball and knocked himself out every six hours with Dramamine and rum. In Cartagena at last, it would seem to me that the girl who spoke only German was game to have sex with him, but he missed his moment and she disappeared.

Lena was a Dutch woman, my age and laughably tough. She would offer to beat any man on the boat in arm wrestling and did. She was the manager of a bar somewhere, but when she got giggling, it was hilarious, a very funny time indeed if you got her to laugh, which was hard but not that hard.

Then there was the captain, a Colombian, who spoke no English but projected calmness and competence. "He doesn't drink, and he is all the time reading the Bible," the shirtless German Gorgonic shipowner said on the beach in Guna Yala. He said it with scorn, as though this wasn't exactly the kind of guy you'd want as your captain. He apparently didn't have the wisdom of the Panama Canal's Captain Rich, who knew the rarity and value of a nondrunk sailor.

The captain handled himself on the whole voyage with tremendous coolness. He was aided by a mate and cook, a black Panamanian, skilled at darting around the boat and checking lines and cooking on bad seas. He was skilled, too, in turning a blind eye to unbelievable acts of idiocy.

That was important because the other eight people on the boat were Australians.

Australians Abroad

By my calculations, there are no people age eighteen to twenty-five in Australia. How could there be? There aren't that many people in Australia, but everywhere you go in the world, there're Australians.

Australians are special. The first event that happened in Australian history was a drunken debaucherous beach party. This is a fact. It happened on February 6, 1788, as the first shipment of female prostitutes and convicts arrived at Port Jackson, near where the Sydney Opera House stands. Let me quote from Robert Hughes's *The Fatal Shore: The Epic of Australia's Founding*, as he describes what happened when the sailors were given an extra ration of rum and set loose on the beach: "As the couples rutted between the rocks, guts burning from the harsh Brazilian *aquardiente*, their clothes slimy with red clay, the sexual history of colonial Australia may fairly be said to have begun." One of the officers later wrote, "It is beyond my abilities to give a just description of the scene of debauchery and riot that ensued during the night." That's how Australia starts, and they haven't stopped.

That's white Australian history, anyway. The aboriginal peoples of Australia didn't write their history down, though they keep long strings of it in oral tradition that maybe they're still keeping secret. They must've reached Australia in boats, but then they forgot or quit boats forever.

Australians respect nothing except the epic and ridiculous, because that is the nature of the native animals of their homeland. Wherever you go in the world, you will find Australians being preposterous. I love them.

I've always gotten along with Australians. I visited their country once, for four days. I was invited to hug their television host, Julia Zemiro. This is a great honor in their land, they insisted. She won *Australia's Brainiest TV Star*. Out in the bush I saw a koala asleep, balled up in a tree, and many kangaroos. The butter in Australia is fantastic.

But I like Australians best when I meet them abroad, because they seem to share with me, the ones I run into, anyway, a sense or a hope that the world is wonderful and ridiculous and to be enjoyed as much as possible.

A group of lions is called a pride, a bunch of birds is a flock. What is a bunch of Australians called? A party.

On this boat the Australians were:

- a primary school teacher named Emma who got so high on cocaine and so drunk she was sputter-giggling with lascivious joy, pounding the table for hours. If her third graders could've seen that!

- two dopes who I will call Bill and Ted because they resembled the good-hearted time-traveling simpletons of the 1989 film. These were the very same dopes I'd seen turn their backs on the waterfall at Agua Azul, settling in instead to watch the movie *Dragon Ball Z* on a tiny TV in a taqueria back in Chiapas. I call them dopes, which they were, but I will admit they were handsome dopes. They tried without success to have sex with the Swedish girls on the boat. It was a bit pitiful to watch. Their art at pretending to listen to girls was unskilled. But God bless them for trying. I hope they found pliable and equally dopey women somewhere farther down the trail.

and:

- the A-Team. These people, four dudes and a beautiful half-Venezuelan girl who was their leader's girlfriend, had quit or taken leave of their jobs, then flown to Mexico City, where they bought a used Dodge minivan, which they drove down the coast of Central America for three months, surfing at every remote and legendary local spot they could find their way to, and then they'd sold their minivan in Panama City and now they were on the boat with me.

The Dread Ship *Jacqueline*

The *Jacqueline* was a fifty-six-foot boat, and with the captain and the mate, there were nineteen of us on it, two to a bed belowdecks, narrow bunks above, or you could sleep out in a hammock under the stars.

The food wasn't bad, but it wasn't good, either—flapjacks with honey one night, fish when we caught some.

The people aboard were age twenty, I'd say, on average, all skinny, far from home, looking for adventure, and getting drunk from wake-up until late at night. Every free space had cans of beer stuffed into it. I had two huge bottles of Abuelo rum and I'd run out by night two.

By the end of the first day, everyone had smoked all the weed they had, which was a lot. Cigarettes were in desperate demand. One advantage age and maturity gave me was I'd anticipated that, I'd known the idiots who'd be on this boat would get desperate for cigarettes, and my backpack was stuffed with them. Regular Marlboros and Pielrojas, a brand of Panamanian loose-tobacco deals Captain Rich had recommended I sample. They were hard to find, a cigarette for the poor and old-fashioned, but I bought up every pack I could, and by this devilish means or impressive gift of foresight and logistics I became at least the fourth- or fifth-ranking officer on the boat. The stretch of water we were in, between indigenous islands of Panama and Colombia, on the wild southern fringe of the Caribbean, was and is lawless ocean.

Stoned and drunk, it dawned on me that this is what a pirate ship would've been like. The crew would've smelled much worse. Their teeth would've been nastier, everyone would've been more plague-ridden, there would've been way less in the way of swimsuits. Also fewer hot blond women from Northern Europe. No women at all, probably. And maybe sociopathically violent. But still I bet they would've been skinny kids, about our age. Perhaps lured in by some shady procurer. Setting out for adventure at sea in jovial chaos until it got out of control and bloody and psychotic or the ship sank or was blown to splinters by cannons.

Skinny kids, drunk and out for adventure—that's who I bet Captain Morgan had with him when he canoed and marched across the swampy isthmus and destroyed Panama. His trip got real dark real fast, I bet.

Luckily, on this boat, everyone seemed more into chillin' and swimming around than raping and murdering and burning cities to the ground. So it was all good times.

Islands in the Stream and the Drug Canoe

There are something like three hundred fifty, three hundred sixty San Blas islands. Some of them are no bigger than a table. Some of them have five or six shacks on them. Some of them have one palm tree, like the desert island in a cartoon.

Anchored off one, we snorkeled and swam through the sunken wreck of an old boat, from the 1930s maybe, or the '50s, or the '70s, who knows? Hold your breath and you could dive down to the rusting hulk of its engine. On the shore, Guna women sat and smoked and chatted with each other in their language, next to woven *molas* of psychedelic sea life and plants and pan-eyed birds laid out in the sand. We swam and kicked a ball around on the beach, dove off the side of the ship, lay in the netting slung between the hulls of the catamaran.* We swam underneath it and climbed back on up to drink cans of Panama beer and eat bananas and chips.

By the second day, there was some antsiness, at first semiprivate but soon a shared discussion among passengers that we were out of drugs. Attempts to communicate this to the Guna island residents, seeking remedy, were optimistic but led nowhere.

In the waters between Panama and Colombia, lack of drugs is not a problem you won't be able to solve. Under sail from one island to another, a wooden dugout canoe paddled by two Guna men waved to us and were hailed over. They were selling fish, and sure, yeah, we'd take some of those. It fell to Katie the multiracial sweetheart from a catalog to suggest in the Spanish she'd learned volunteering in an orphanage that maybe they might also sell . . . other things?

Yes, in fact, they had that, too. Under their pile of fish was a package in

---

*I believe this netting on a catamaran is technically called the trampoline, but captains don't really lean in to calling it that so you don't get the wrong idea about jumping up and down on it.

a Ziploc bag. It was told to me that these men had seen many bags thrown from a speedboat under pursuit by the Colombian coast guard. Once the chase passed out of sight, the Guna fishermen dove down and hauled up one of the bags and here it was, packed with marijuana and cocaine. A collection was hastily gathered and the *Jacqueline* passengers bought the whole thing. The afternoon, evening, and following day and night out on the open sea in a storm were thus much enlivened.

The A-Team

Everyone on the boat was pretty agreeable to me. I liked them all.
What I was up to seemed confusing to the younger ones. I can't
blame them. I wasn't totally sure what I was doing here myself, but it was
good times and I was happy to keep going with it. *Maybe the whole point
of this trip was to find myself at sea partying with these strangers*, I
thought.

My favorites were the A-Team, the four Australians with their gorgeous half-Venezuelan translator and guide and den mother. I called
them the A-Team because 1) they traveled together for months in a van
and 2) they each had some special skill. Pyle, for instance, their most
hippie-ish member, tripped out and shaggy, was a skilled fisherman who
hauled in thin but tasty bonefish, trawling over the side with a thin line
and hook he'd brought himself. Gale was their jovial accountant, he kept
the books on this expedition, and while this might not seem like the sex-
iest job, he was respected by them for it. Their leader, James, was a Greek
Australian. At night on watch he sat perched by the open deck chair,
holding the starboard rigging wire, shirtless. *Goddammit*, I thought,
again stoned and drunk, *that must've been what Odysseus looked like*.
And sure enough he could tell a tale and wax on in near poetry. He told
of trips out to council land, empty stretches of wild Australian coastline
where friends camped and built great bonfires and took hallucinogens
and fucked each other and reveled in the glory of life. Meanwhile, sure-
handed Mitch rolled joints, skilled hands working precisely even as the
seas bucked and rolled us and storms passed over.

On the last night we were way out on the open sea, international waters, no land for miles, tossing all over the place in a storm in the soaked
darkness. The Australian dopes blasted the Avalanches from their speakers and ripped lines of coke off the wobbling table and we smoked weed

and cigarettes and thumped the table with drinking games. Late late in the night, the dopes and I were the last ones standing, having a dance party.

When I went to sleep I'm not sure, but when I woke the sun was up and glistening off the glass of hotels. We were anchored in the harbor in Cartagena.

Port of Call: Cartagena

S ince its founding, in 1533, a whole lot of money has passed through Cartagena. The Zenú people who lived around there before they vanished from the Earth buried their noble dead with all kinds of gold things. When the tombs were found, they were plundered, and word got out that if you could find secret tombs and rob them, there was gold to get in Cartagena. Slaves were brought to the port of Cartagena, some of them fated for the mines of Peru and Bolivia. Silver and gold were hauled on mule trains to Cartagena, and from there Spanish treasure fleets sailed to Havana and onward.

Now, all that treasure sailing along the wild coast tempted every pirate and semi-pirate on the sea. Sir Francis Drake, Jean-François Roberval, Martin Cole, Sir John Hawkins, Bernard Desjean, Laurens de Graaf, Nicholas van Hoorn—they were partners until the one killed the other—all the great pirates and privateers took a try at Cartagena. The history of the city is like a listing of raids and sieges. Some absurd amount of money was invested by the very wealthy Spanish in defending it. Engineers and masters of geometry and artillery were brought over from Spain and Italy to devise bastions and barbicans and fortifications.

By the time the War of Jenkins's Ear broke out—you remember that, had to do with a sailor named Jenkins getting his ear cut off, which he displayed in a bottle, but deeper down, it had to do with the English wanting to continue to profit off selling slaves to Spanish America—Cartagena was shut up like a lock behind a fortress of stone walls.

Still, Admiral Edward Vernon of the British navy decided to attack. He was such a cocky bastard, this Admiral Vernon, that early in the attack, feeling like *I got this*, he sent word back to England that he'd already conquered the city. Fuck no. He lost fifty ships and eighteen thousand men and never took Cartagena.*

On April 10, a Thursday, sunset, walking the old walls, watching the waves break, everything looked peaceful. The morning before we'd landed, we'd been sailing for four days and nights and were disgusting. After a dragging-on tropical sit in the comically languid, grand but decrepit customs and immigration office, we scattered off to hostels to shower and stuff. I followed the A-Team, because they obviously knew what they were doing, and indeed they did. Within an hour or two I was clean and changed and drinking a beer in the courtyard of the El Viajero Hostel. This place was good times. All around were teenagers and twenty-year-olds having passionate and earnest conversations with strangers they'd just met from around the world. My thinking was, I was thirty-four years old. One more year and I'd absolutely be the creepy guy if I stayed in a Cartagena hostel, but I think this last spring I could sneak in, the last second. Nobody seemed to look at me strange at all 'til the last night I was there, when I gave half a bottle of rum and some weed to two Canadian kids sitting outside my door. "You want this?" I said. "I'm leaving and I don't want to carry it."

Then they looked at me strange all right. They looked at me like I was a glorious god of incomprehensible benevolence.

When a pirate ship, or any ship really, got to Cartagena, what they wanted to do to celebrate being alive ashore was drink and party. That's what my shipmates wanted to do, and the first night we were there, that's what we did.

We partied. Some of us partied harder than others, like Emma, the Australian schoolteacher, who partied so hard that her eyes became like flaming embers of pure party fire and she laughed like a crazed goddess-queen of the sea witches. But everyone partied hard. People ran into old friends they'd met up the backpacker trail of Central America, and

---

*George Washington's brother Lawrence (*was he ever called Larry? Larry Washington?*) was there with Admiral Vernon. He admired him so much he called the family farm Mount Vernon.

strangers from the same parts of Australia as them, or just strangers al-together who fell in on the roving party, became best friends for several drinks, then vanished forever in Cartagena, perhaps someday to reappear on Facebook.

Around noon the next morning, pulling myself together, I thought, *Well, good job, well partied, but maybe today I will just take it easy.* Stroll-ing the streets of Cartagena on a gorgeous April evening is one of the pleasantest things I've ever done. There are old squares and leaning churches, rows of houses with fading paint in tropical colors, kids kicking soccer balls around, dogs of independent spirit, people selling all kinds of delicious treats, empanadas and sweet pastries and also here and there drugs. There are statues of forgotten admirals and drummer boys, and you can walk for miles above the shore on the old city walls.

See, I said, *this is pleasant. It is possible to enjoy life in ways that aren't just drinking and partying.* And then I ran into the A-Team, and we started partying again.

The next day, resolved, I was about to go to Cartagena's famed Museo de Arte Moderno to experience firsthand the works of Darío Morales, famed for his bronze female nudes, when the A-Team asked me if I wanted to go with them to the beach.

I can't tell you anything about Darío Morales. I can tell you that on the beach in Cartagena, men push ice carts through the sand and sell the most delicious ceviche you've ever had. Sooner or later somebody will come along offering to sell you just about anything you might want, like beers or sex with a voluptuous prostitute. The water feels nice on your toes.

We drank beers and joked around until the sun went down. I got along great with the A-Team. They were all hilarious and good storytellers and had good ideas like we should get another beer. What I liked best about them, though, was that they liked the TV shows I'd worked on. They did *not* think sitcoms were pablum for the masses, hell no, or if they did, at least they thought it was wonderful pablum. These guys wanted to talk about TV for hours. They'd seen all the best stuff. Their three-month surf odyssey halted often for marathons of pirated shows.

They were all terrific. I loved them. I was sorry I'd have to leave them tomorrow.

"Yeah?" said Mitch, maybe the most intense of them all, funny and a great man but unrelenting and uncompromising in his drive toward good times.

"Yeah, I'm going to Medellín."

"Yeah? We're going to Medellín."

"Well, that's fantastic," I said, realizing by my flush of joy how much I'd missed having friends around. "What're you gonna do in Medellín?"

"What are we gonna do in Medellín?" Mitch looked at me like there'd been some deep miscommunication or else I'd revealed with this communication some unseen imbecility. "We're gonna *party*."

And that's what we did.

One Last Word About the A-Team

For all their own intensity, there was a friend of theirs they spoke of, a legendary man. When this man's name was mentioned, they all paused in awe and delight. Perhaps fear as well, just a bit. He was said to be the best surfer any of them knew, though I'd seen three members of the A-Team spot a break from an underwater rock or reef at least half a mile out from anything like a coast or a beach and grab boards without hesitation to discuss or consider danger and paddle out to it and try to surf it.

This man's name was James McAfee, and I print it here with the A-Team's permission because the name of such a legend should be recorded.

"All you need to do to understand James McAfee," Mitch told me, "is that all he is trying to do, ever, all he's after, is a *sick time*."

Sick Times in Medellín

Colombia was violent before there was cocaine. Extreme and desperate and ferocious fortune seekers from a Spanish kingdom emerging from centuries of racial and religious war with Moorish invaders hacked into the countryside, sometimes annihilating the native people they met, sometimes evaporating forever into the jungle, sometimes claiming some portion of the land for themselves and then fighting each other over it while meanwhile fighting whoever kept emerging from the wild mountainsides.

That's for a start.

Before the Spanish were even exhausted of this, there were people born in Colombia who no longer considered themselves Spanish. Creole people—choice of word here could land me in treacherous ground, but *Creole* seems fair, agreed upon—like Simón Bolívar, born in Venezuela but you won't cross Colombia without passing a statue of him. "The Liberator." But he liberated what from who exactly, it's not clear or settled. Colombia's stories are full of people saying "You didn't liberate *us*, motherfucker, we gotta do that ourselves, liberate from your sorry ass" as they start firing.

That's my understanding, anyway. I'm sure as hell no expert on Colombian history. No way, dude, that's a tough and thankless job. I'm not walking into that tricky thicket with *my* bad Spanish.

On top of history (underneath it, maybe?) there's geography. Colombia is mountainous. Maybe the second-most mountainous country on Earth, after Nepal. I dunno, how would you measure mountainousness, really? A very beautiful Colombian woman claimed that "second-most, after Nepal" fact to me and I'll take her word for it.

Countries are all the same flatness on a map, but they aren't all in life. If you haven't figured that out, plan a bus trip across Colombia and discover why it might take you twelve hours to get from Medellín to Bogotá, even though it's only two hundred and fifty miles.

The green valleys of Colombia are lush and heavenly. Millennia of degenerating plant life leaves behind a rich, loamy topsoil that's said to be a hundred feet deep in some places. But there's not much of it. Only about 5 percent of the country is suitable for farming. The people who ended up with these lands wanted to keep them, while people who would like to live in them, maybe people who used to have them and were now driven up into the mountains, were sometimes pretty pissed about how land was given out. That, more or less, is what a ten-year period (1948–1958) in Colombian history called *La Violencia* was about.

The mountainsides of Colombia are perfect for some things, though. Like growing coffee beans, and coca trees.

Medellín shares its name with the village in Spain where Hernán Cortés is from. If Cortés could see Medellín, Colombia, maybe his head would explode. Four million people. In the valley, there's a dense downtown with skyscrapers, while up the sides of steep mountains there are slums that climb so high you reach them by cable car.

Or maybe Cortés would see all that and shrug and say sure, what else could be expected?

I'll tell you this: Cortés and Pablo Escobar, that would be an interesting meeting. The conquistador and the cocaine kingpin. They might understand each other perfectly, or at least have the thrill of meeting an interesting rival.

You can grow coca maybe even better in mountainous (third-most mountainous?) Bolivia, or in Peru. But Bolivia's landlocked and Peru's so far away, on the Pacific. Colombia's got those Atlantic ports, right on the old pirate coast, just across from the islands that've always been good for hiding your money.

Others can tell you the story of Pablo Escobar when he ran Medellín. *The Two Escobars* is a terrific documentary about him and soccer and the city and Colombia. Eventually, US Special Forces helped trap Escobar and kill him, as told by the great Mark Bowden in his book *Killing Pablo*.

Now you can play paintball in Pablo Escobar's house. One of his houses, anyway. He had, like, twenty, including the mansion he lived in while he was in "jail."

A friend of mine lived in Bogotá in 1993, the year Pablo Escobar got killed. He said in those days, you could get someone killed for a thousand pesos—about seven dollars. For that money, you could hire a gas-huffing gamin to shoot somebody.

"How come no one killed you?" I asked.

"Not that many people had a thousand pesos."

Cocaine

Some people try cocaine, not that much happens, and they don't bother with it again. Some people try cocaine, and their immediate reaction is to want to do all the cocaine in the world that very night. That demand is why cocaine was, at its peak, perhaps a five-hundred-billion-dollar economy, despite an aggressive complex of prisons and surveillance and ships and helicopters and paramilitaries trying to stop it.

Some people try cocaine and die. That happened to Len Bias, who was gonna be the future of the Boston Celtics, in 1986, when I was seven and the Boston Celtics meant a lot to me. That made an impression on me. I'm against cocaine.

I'm also, as a person and a writer, curious and borderline insane in my hunger for experience, so I've tried cocaine. You have to reckon with the fact that you're consuming something produced in an unregulated, exploitive business that lots of people get killed in. But maybe that's true of everything. In our hyperglobal system, who can trace what crimes we're all implicit in? Trace back my morning orange juice and I'm sure there's something awful along the chain.

Cocaine isn't for me. That's lucky. In my experience of people who keep using cocaine, dramatic problems and disasters enter their lives with a frequency that doesn't happen to people who don't use cocaine. Many people smart and crazy have lots to say about cocaine, but that's all I have to say about it.

Center of Innovation (and Partying)

Medellín, today, is like a famous urban turnaround story. *The Wall Street Journal* and Citi named it Innovative City of the Year in 2013. I walked around the downtown parts of Medellín, and it was beautiful and peaceful. There was a cool-looking park for kids, good food, on the street and in good restaurants, and pleasant places to sip coffee and try to read the newspaper.

With the A-Team, I rode a cable car up to San Javier. The view below to the improvised streets of vertical neighborhoods was like floating over a living maze, and I could've stared at everything that was happening and rigged up and tottering for days. Veronica, the half-Venezuelan girl, suggested it wasn't a wise or even really polite thing to go wandering on foot and gawk-eyed around a community like this, so when we reached the top, we turned around and rode back down.

They hadn't forgotten why they'd come to Medellín, the A-Team. They'd come to party.

In that they succeeded. We had a sick time.

A Story of a Kidnapping

Late that night, in fact early the next morning, the A-Team and I were sitting on a balcony overlooking the downtown valley of Medellín, drinking cold bottles of Aguila beer that'd been brought to us on an enormous platter.

The A-Team's ultimate destination was Venezuela, to see Veronica's mother. Venezuela is a fucked-up scene. Hugo Chávez, their maniac president/strongman, had died after rigging the system so the functioning of the nation depended on him. No one had really taken his place. Former vice president Nicolás Maduro was in charge, maybe. It was widely believed that to shore up himself and his authority, Chávez had invited in Cuban troops, but now who knew who they answered to. They were a bunch of foreign mercenaries running around on top of every other kind of chaos.

Getting into and around Venezuela would not be easy. The A-Team's menfolk were a little nervous.

Veronica figured they could do it. She'd spent time in Venezuela as a teenager, and had maybe a cynical or maybe a very accurate sense of it.

Almost casually, by way of example, she told a story about the time she got kidnapped. Here, with her permission, I'll try to retell it.

She and her friends were in an SUV, driving to a party. Her friend wanted to stop to make a call or put on lipstick or something, so they pulled over. Veronica got a bad feeling right away. Wherever they were, it was not where you should pull over.

Sure enough, a guy with a gun ran out from around a corner, put the gun to the window, opened the door, screamed at the girls to get down on the floor of the SUV, and drove off. He was crazy high on cocaine, was Veronica's guess, and as he drove he made the girls pass up their cell phones and he tried, as he drove, to call their parents. But it was very late, no one picked up, maybe luckily.

From the floor of the passenger seat where she was sitting, Veronica saw a sign: GUARENAS. As soon as she saw it, she thought to herself, *I'm fucked*, because this was a place you only heard of in stories about dumped bodies.

"Why are you doing this?" she said to the kidnapper. "Don't you have kids?"

"Shut the fuck up," he said. "You don't know fuck all about my life. You're a rich girl driving around our neighborhood, flashing yourself, rubbing our faces in it."

He was crazy and high and pissed off.

Veronica didn't know what, but something on the road to Guarenas startled him. He pulled over. He got out, kicked them out of the SUV, and drove off.

The girls were still miles from anyplace they knew. They still had to get back home. That was a whole other story, Veronica said. She shrugged and got another beer.

Weeks later I'd hear from the A-Team. They'd made it to Venezuela, spent a week in Caracas, and flew back to Australia.

They said it was crazy.

Good Friday in Popayán

W hat the fuck was I doing down here in South America?
That was what I thought when I got to Popayán.

It was Good Friday, two days before Easter. Holy Week, Semana Santa, is a big deal in Latin America. There are strange and colorful and idiosyncratic festivals and processions and parades of all kinds, in remote Mayan villages and in bursting cities. They are expressions of mixed-up and mingled traditions that evolved over centuries. I knew I'd be down here at Easter, I knew I ought to experience one. Popayán's was the one I'd settled on, in "the white city" in the western hills of Colombia, once a colonial outpost, small and hard to get to and said to be preserved in time. Their Easter celebration is on UNESCO's list of Intangible Cultural Heritage of Humanity, so you know I'm down.

Good Catholic boy that I am, Good Friday made me take a somber look at myself. What was I doing, exactly? I'd set out for the bottom of South America, and I was determined to get there. But why? Just to say I'd done it? To write it up and sell it? To gather stories?

Then what? Much as I fancy myself a wandering adventurer, the most fun I'd had was with people, partying on a boat and on the beach and in bars with my Australian friends, and when our trails split off, I was sorry to see them go. The existential questions that swirled around in my head as I meandered Popayán in the late afternoon were way less delightful as company.

This wasn't a new or original feeling. I bet most travelers on most long journeys, from vacation to business trip to pilgrimage, find themselves asking, trying to remember, why exactly they'd come in the first place. Maybe the greatest travel writer of all time, Bruce Chatwin, collected a bunch of his dispatches from places as far away as Benin and Nepal and Russia into a book called *What Am I Doing Here?*

Ain't that the simplest way to put it? That's the question I came here to answer, and it was bigger than Popayán or South America or the whole Western Hemisphere. The question was what am I doing here, like, on Earth? In the universe? Aren't we all just travelers on a trip where the purpose, if there is one, is mysterious to us? A journey of uncertain duration to and from points unknown to us?

The answers, if there were any, weren't made clear to me by the other guests at the ParkLife Hostel Popayán. There was a teenage Japanese girl who stayed in the bunk bed across from me all day and all night. Whatever she had experienced or was experiencing had overwhelmed her, or else she was just really tired. I wondered if I should offer to help her, but I doubted that would do much good except to exhaust her further.

The ParkLife Hostel Popayán is a sleepy-making place. Wonderful light comes through the windows, it's in the loft and attic of one of the tallest buildings in town, five stories up the wooden stairs. There are pillows everywhere. You can look out the window and see, as I did, the gentlest kind of afternoon rain falling on the red tiles and the cupola of the white Catedral Basílica de Nuestra Señora de la Asunción, and up the streets of the town to the green rolls of hill that rose beyond, and say drowsily to yourself, *Yes, I am come here to some magical valley as if from the dream of a child. Tomorrow I will explore but now I will nap.* In the nooks of the cathedral roof cooing pigeons roosted themselves out of the rain.

Two English girls (I think they were English) whispered and giggled to each other, cradling each other under a blanket. They watched the movie *27 Dresses* on a DVD in the airy attic and when it ended, they didn't get up, they just let it start all over again as they cuddled.

In the kitchen a female gym teacher from Belgium danced around as she chopped and prepared all sorts of fresh fruits and vegetables. I bet she was a good gym teacher. At no time did her improvised squats and aerobics let up as she described to me a relationship with a Costa Rican man that perhaps had come to an end. She was sad, she said, but she shrugged and danced on.

Slumped down on a pile of pillows in the common room, I read the obituaries of Gabriel García Márquez. Top dog and number one by a mile, most famous Colombian writer of all time, winner of the Nobel Prize in Literature, *Love in the Time of Cholera*, *One Hundred Years of Solitude*, *News of a Kidnapping*, *Chronicle of a Death Foretold*—he wins for all time on titles alone. News of his death had reached me by Twitter on my phone in an enormous supermarket in Medellín, where I was exploring the section devoted to little frosted cakes while James from the A-Team studied the grill workers of the burger bar across the floor with absorption that stemmed from his career as a mechanical engineer and his passion as a burger enthusiast.

"Hello. Excuse me."

I and the few others lounging on pillows and benches looked up to see a striking German woman with a practical but elegant cut of short black hair, six feet tall at least, and trim.

"Who would like to climb the volcano tomorrow? I'm looking to form a group, three or more, and hiring a guide. Sixty thousand each."

An amount of money, I knew, but dispensed with the idea of doing the conversion math. The command with which she said it made clear this was a fair price for a climb up the volcano.

Lifetime, I'd already climbed two full and several fractions of volcanoes. I'm for it, generally, but it's hot and dusty work, very dry climbing unless it's raining, in which case it's cold and soaking. If the volcano's alive enough to be worth climbing at all, your shoes will be covered with black soot and your clothes heavy with sweat and dusted with gray ash before you're done. There are destination restaurants in Popayán. To stroll to one of those and have a boozed-up lunch, poking my head into a cathedral or something for cultural credit beforehand, that'd been my plan.

Honestly, unless I was gonna see fire beasts swimming in a spuming lake of lava, fuck climbing the volcano.

I didn't use those words to the German woman, who now looked to me, the others in the room having either stared back at her in stupefied bafflement or muttered declines. I smiled a shade and shook my head.

"Why didn't you climb the volcano with her?!" was my mom's appalled reaction some months later, when I absently mentioned this story (we were on the topic of volcanoes or Germans or something). Her shock was so real and so full of true disappointment in my character that it threw me. She was right. Lesson learned, and I set it down for myself as at least one solid rule for life:

If a striking German woman wants to climb the volcano, go with her.

Well, anyway, here I was, might as well enjoy it. Not hard at all. On Friday night was the opening procession of the weekend. The streets of Popayán were packed with families, some in from the country, kids and parents and grandparents crammed into doorways and pressed to the old white walls along the narrow sidewalk of Calle 4. The kids try desperately to contain themselves somehow, because the Good Friday procession is slow. Almost like they're entering it in a contest for slowest parade in the world. The military marching band plays very slow.

The stars of the parade, the equivalent of floats, are wooden platforms carrying painted statues. Jesus, Judas, the Virgin Mary, a skeleton—all the heroes of Easter. They're compelling statues. The processions of Holy Week in Popayán are not on UNESCO's list of the Intangible Cultural Heritage of Humanity for no reason. But I did get bored before it was over.

The next morning the air and the sky were clear, people were feeling festive, just a great Saturday in Popayán. There was a llama tied to a scooter in Parque Caldas.

"It is very nice, your llama," I said in Spanish to a man in a beret who appeared to be its guardian. He nodded with dignity but gave me no further information about it.

"Why is it, this llama?" I inquired further.

"Oh, it is not my llama," said the man. "I'm only watching it for a friend."

"Of course," I said, "*claro.*" We stood there for a moment, and then I walked on.

A few hours later, when I was walking back into town from a hike up to the statue of Simón Bolívar, two university students, one chubby and with glasses and the other skinny with eyes that just hinted serial killer, stopped me in the parque and asked me in English where I was from.

California, I told them, and they got excited and asked me if I could help them with their assignment. They were students studying tourism and business at the University of Cauca and for a class they needed to interview three foreigners.

This sounded suspicious, an all-too-clean setup for a twisted con game, but sure, I said. They debated with each other whether they could each count me as one of their three foreigners, and then they took worn folders and pens and Xeroxed assignment sheets out of their backpacks.

If they were con artists, their commitment to mundane detail was impressive. The questions were things like asking me to rate Popayán on a scale of one to five in various categories such as historical interest (four) and beauty (five, really a four, four and a half, but I said five) and cleanliness (three and a half, but I said four).

"Would you consider returning to Popayán?"

"I don't know, sure—I mean, I'm still in the first time."

That wasn't an option. "Mmm, just put yes," I said, which they did, relieved.

We finished the survey, and then we kept talking for a bit.

"Hell," I said, "why don't we go drink a beer?" With this I hoped to project a kind of Steve McQueen swagger, the best of confident American manhood. The Colombian students—Freddie and Cristian—looked almost startled. Really I was desperate for company, and drinking with Colombian students would count as cultural experience, whereas it'd be hard to justify drinking alone in midafternoon.

To them, drinking just then was a curious idea, and they still had to find two more tourists, but could they meet me at seven?

"Sure," I said. "By the way, how did you know I was a foreigner?"

"Height," Cristian, the chubby one, said. "Also you are almost at the door of the hostel."

"Ah," I said. "Well, stick around, and you can probably interview a German woman as tall as me who sooner or later will be getting back from the volcano."

Saturday Night at El Sotareño

Magical realism, that is the name for a movement or idea or style that runs through the literature of Latin America. Stories where people live in cities or villages very much like real cities or villages in Colombia or Mexico, but where a beautiful girl ascends to the sun at four p.m. one afternoon or a Gypsy alchemist dies twice.

The most clichéd observation a visitor to South America can make is that these places do really feel as if they have a magical quality. Baffling sights appear before you, bizarre conversations take form then disappear, you encounter puzzles and moments in your travels that feel somehow enchanted or cursed or called up from some unconscious imagining. You find you soon accept and glide along with events or experiences that defy any logic.

Clichéd. But: It's true, that's how it feels.

For example, El Sotareño, a bar on a street off another street no one can quite give you directions to. Somewhere, that way, you'll find it. Step inside and you are in a small, dark, wood-ceilinged room lit by just a few antique lamps. The walls are covered with posters and photographs and paintings from who knows what decade of players of tango and bolero music. In the corner behind the tiny bar are shelves crammed with a worn library of vinyl records, some of them fifty years old. The bartender/owner, an antique of a man, eyes hidden under the brim of his hat, plays selections of scratched and distant and haunted music. This is a bar worth traveling a thousand miles to get to. Even sitting in it, for hours, drinking and listening, it was hard to accept that a place this fantastic could be real, that it had been sitting on a street somewhere in Popayán my whole lifetime, and long before I was born.

* * *

"Gabriel García Márquez was a dick," said Freddie, the more serial-killery of my Colombian student drinking companions. It was maybe nine or ten at night now, we'd been drinking for three hours, pushing through lulls and awkwardness to get to the realness. If these two were con men or kidnappers, by now I wasn't too worried about it. Freddie joked twice about kidnapping me, which could've been a sign either way, but the truth was he couldn't really pull it off. He had a darkness to him for sure, but it seemed more goth-emo than murderous. He was involved somehow with a dramatic girl then in the hospital for jumping off the Puente Del Humilladero, an old bridge I'd walked under that afternoon.

Cristian, the chubbier friend, was much more gentle, a counselor kind of guy. Accurately named, too, he referenced some kind of Bible study or church group that mattered to him. We had talked for a while about Colombia. For let's say the past twenty years, Colombia's biggest political problem was FARC, a guerrilla army or movement that at times controlled a quarter of the country. Popayán was on the edge of FARC country. At the airport out, I'd seen a military flight of eighty soldiers leaving, tired and relieved after protecting the Easter processions. According to one newspaper, there'd been three bomb threats.

Now we were talking about the just-died king of magical realism, and sometime negotiator or facilitator of negotiations with FARC, "Gabbo."

"Look at Márquez's town, Aracataca. The whole town he got famous from. It's totally poor. Márquez fucked off and went to Mexico City. Once he got famous and rich, he didn't do anything for Aracataca."

I looked to Cristian: "Do you agree with this?" He held up his hands and half shrugged like "I wouldn't put it exactly that way but yeah."

The story goes that Márquez, living with his wife and kids in Mexico City, was driving to Acapulco for a vacation, when suddenly he got the idea for *One Hundred Years of Solitude* in his head. He turned the car around and drove back home and started writing. While, presumably, his wife had an interesting time explaining to the kids why they weren't going to the beach.

One Hundred Years of Solitude is about a village called Macondo and the generations of the Buendía family that lives there. It's incredible. But reading the book by the beach in El Salvador, I can't say I found it totally absorbing. Book lovers and literary types do a disservice to the great masterpieces when they won't admit that some of them are boring. *OHYOS* was, to me, kinda boring. Fully prepared to admit that's my fault. Like I said, I was reading it on the beach. No one would call it a beach read. Márquez was more than Colombia's most famous writer, he was a diplomat, a statesman, a conscience for Colombia. But if these guys wanted to take him down a few pegs, I was happy to let them.

Like a lot of twenty-year-olds, Freddie and Cristian liked to say brash stuff and test outrageous arguments. Fair enough, but then Freddie mentioned, like it was an obvious fact we could all agree on, that Bush and Cheney did 9/11.

"Wait a second," I said, "come on." I looked to Cristian for backup. He put his hands up and half shrugged again and said, "Well . . ."

This got me heated, I admit. Disappointed, too.

The best argument against conspiracy theories, to me, is competence. Pulling off a huge conspiracy would be really hard. Bush and Cheney fucked up everything else—how could they have faked or staged or controlled or whatever 9/11, and gotten away with it? Cheney couldn't even go hunting without shooting his friend in the face. A conspiracy theory is flattering to the conspirators.

For the conspiracy theorist, though, this argument falls apart because he thinks the conspirators did get caught, by him, the theorist. *Claro.*

This happy evening looked about to go afoul. But with a bit of easing on all sides, we agreed to change the topic. Freddie and Cristian asked me if I wanted to go to a party.

Regardless of what they thought of 9/11, the party they described, a birthday cookout, sounded spectacular. With visions of delicious grilled meats and Colombian women dancing in the sweaty night, I said yes and we all got into a cab.

My vision proved very wrong.

Ooooooooo, I realized, when we arrived, *it's so clear now. This party is for losers. Freddie and Cristian are nice guys but they are nerds, and they have taken me to the party of their even nerdier friend.* It was a birthday for an obnoxious dweeb who was watching a soccer game while his mother slaved over a tiny grill, thrilled that her son at least had some friends. That I was there seemed to revive in her some spark of a nearly extinguished dream that maybe her son was a special boy, beloved all over the world.

I did my best to be kind to her in Spanish while also telling her that I did, soon, very soon, unfortunately quite soon, have to get back to town. At midnight was the Easter procession, after all.

Back to town was, what, three miles?

"Hey, Freddie," I said, "I can walk back to town, right?"

"Oh, no," he said. He shook his head. "If you walk back to town, there is a ninety-five percent chance you will get stabbed."

"Stabbed?"

"Yes. I have been stabbed three times. But stay, we are texting a girl, maybe a girl will come."

"Wait, really? Stabbed? I gotta get back to town." We were on a dark neighborhood street somewhere. I had no idea how I'd get a cab here, even how to explain where I was.

"If you walk back to town, someone will come up to you with a knife and make you give them your money, your phone. Even if you do, they will stab you like this."

He pantomimed a light but still forceful stabbing.

I went over to Cristian, who was eating some chips. "Hey, Cristian, Freddie says if I walk back to town, there's a ninety-five percent chance I'll get stabbed. Is that true?"

Cristian held up his hands and half shrugged. Like: "Well, maybe . . . ninety percent."

"Freddie says he's been stabbed three times."

"Yes," said Cristian, "but that's because he always fights or he says something."

Hmm.

With much gratitude and blessings on her son's birthday, I beseeched the wonderful mother to help me sort out how to get a cab. She couldn't really help me. I was stuck eating chips for a while and considering if I'd really, really get stabbed. Surely the stabbers were enjoying the Easter procession, too, no? When a miraculous cab appeared down the street, I chased after it.

That was the last I saw of Freddie or Cristian, but we're Facebook friends.

Easter in Popayán

On the midnight of Easter in the streets of Popayán, they run another procession. But this one is joyous and wild and jubilant. The uniformed men and women from the social clubs or orders charged with carrying the heavy platforms with the statues try to go as fast as they can. Kids are setting off firecrackers and there're meaty and sugary treats. Then at last comes the statue of Jesus, crown on his head, holding demons on chains like captured slaves.

He is RISEN, bitches is the message. A powerful one.

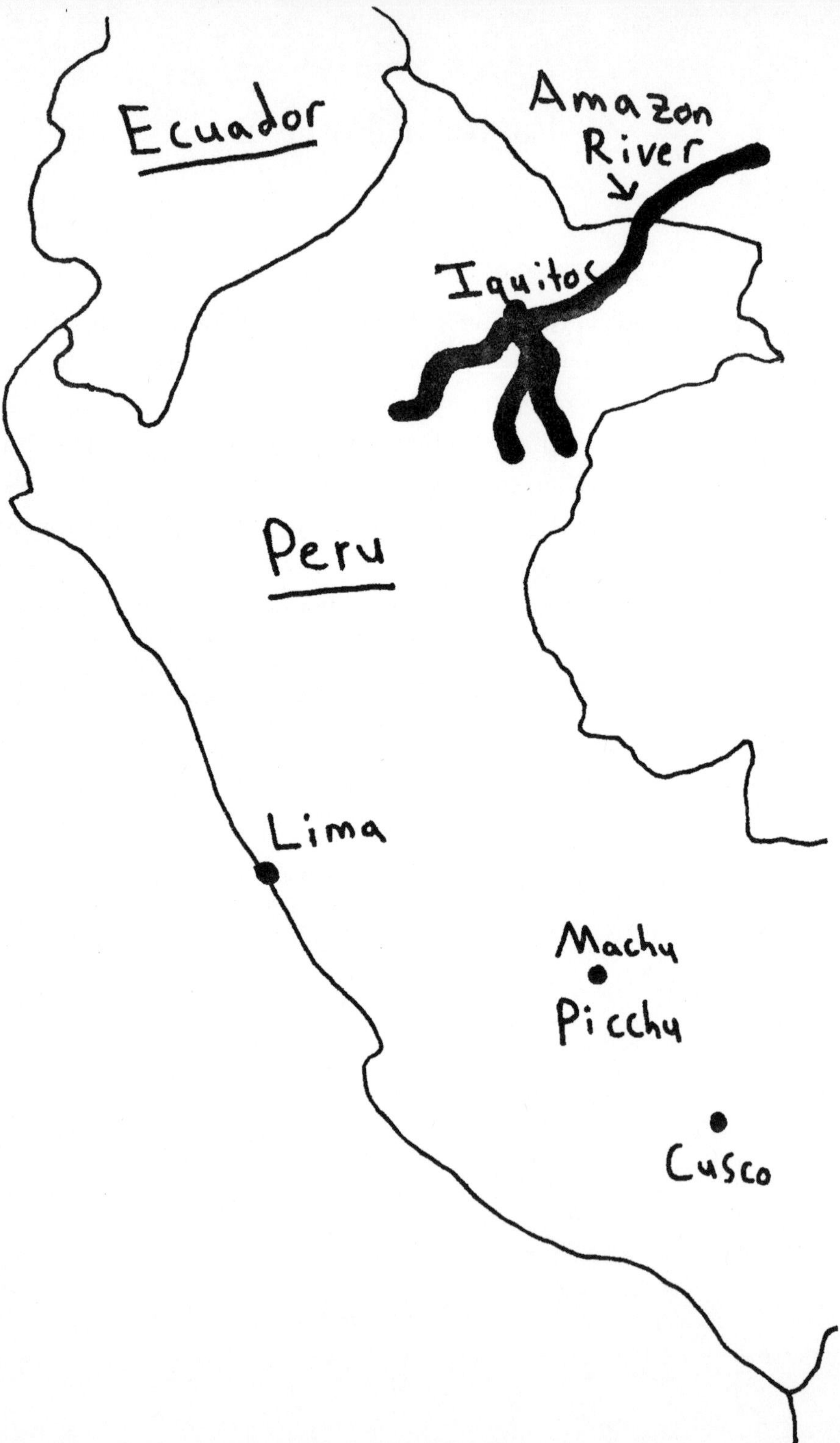
Ecuador
Amazon
River
Iquitos
Peru
Lima
Machu
Picchu
Cusco

The Amazon and Peru

Amazonia

You can read in some places that the Amazon is the widest river in the world, and it is, but what does that mean? The Amazon, like the Nile, floods. When it swells, it can cover with water an area three or four times the dry-season size. Everything within fifty miles of the "banks" of the Amazon, whatever those are, is built to be in a perpetual state of half land, half river. Hills become islands, trails go underwater, whole villages and towns are on stilts where in September there's a ladder and May—when I was there—you step from your canoe into the doorway of your home and hope it doesn't rain much more.

The Amazon disgorges 209,000 cubic meters of water a second. That's something like twelve times what the Mississippi puts out. A journey up the Amazon would be maybe four thousand miles, a thousand miles more than a trip from Los Angeles to Boston, but the Amazon's dozens of tributaries thread out from it like legs from an octopus, so tallying its length is ridiculous anyway.

To call the Amazon a river is too small. The Charles is a river. The Amazon dominates a continent, breathing in and out like an animal of water. A whole half of South America apparently rises and sinks by inches as the Amazon rises and falls. The stretch I would see of it was a hundred kilometers or so, one and a half percent of it. Someday I'd love to go up the whole thing on a boat. But on this trip, I figured, *Hey, it's a river. If I stay in one place, it'll flow past me.*

From the window of the plane coming in to Iquitos was a blanket of trees, dotted in rough proportion by some natural algorithm. Between them was deep thick green. Once in a while, there was some weird aberration like a carved-out airstrip, but you could see pretty far and this was the most biomass I'd ever seen in one look.

"Do you speak English?"

So asked an American woman sitting next to me. From what I'd listened to of her conversation (all of it), she and her husband and another few retired couples from Pennsylvania were flying to Iquitos to start a six-day Amazon River cruise.

"Yes."

"You American? Where are you from?"

"I'm from Boston but I live in California."

"Where are you coming from?"

"Mmm, Lima last," I said. In Lima I'd taken a private tour of the markets led by a Wellesley-educated tour guide I found on the Internet. We mostly discussed optimal practices for getting house cats to drink water while I chewed fistfuls of coca leaves. In Lima, there were department stores where I bought a great shirt and a belt I still wear almost every day. A confused shopboy told me I was too big for the rest of the clothes and asked me where I was from. In Lima you can visit sixteenth-century churches and underground monastery crypts lined with bones and skulls and see the changing of the guard in front of the presidential palace. The food is fantastic, ceviche and flavorful seafood stews. Peruvian Chinese and Japanese food are their own whole cuisines. I'd eaten an enormous fried pork sandwich at the red-and-white-tiled eighty-year-old diner El Chinito (The Chinaman).

Now I was here.

"I've been traveling for a while," I said. "I'm going to the bottom of South America."

" 'Cause me and my husband are sitting here thinkin', *What the hell are we getting ourselves into?*"

I hope somebody picked her up at the airport. Iquitos is a fucking wet crazy jungle mess. What streets there are are packed with motorcycle taxis that either whiz by or sit jammed together in tangled traffic. At the fringes the town is non-streets of wooden docks and alleys and stilt houses and floating markets where you can buy enormous fish that sat out in the humidity all day under attack from flies and chopped-up turtles.

Having to stay somewhere for the night, I picked Casa Fitzcarraldo. *Fitzcarraldo* is a 1982 German movie directed by genius/lunatic Werner Herzog. It tells the story of a manic German, played by Klaus Kinski, determined to drag a riverboat over a jungle mountain dividing the Amazon from a tributary so he can build an opera house in Iquitos. The movie is amazing and crazy but maybe even better is the documentary *Burden of Dreams*, which reveals that the making of the movie was an even crazier project, with natives offering for example to kill Kinski with their blowguns and Herzog rambling on about how "the jungle is an obscenity." Before Kinski, Jason Robards was gonna play the part, but he got dysentery. Mick Jagger was gonna be in it, too, but also gave up. All of them stayed at an old mansion from the days of the rubber boom, bought by one of the movie's executive producers, Walter Saxer, after he couldn't find a reliable hotel. That house is now the Casa Fitzcarraldo, where Mr. Saxer nodded to me from an old wicker chair in the courtyard as I ate river fish stuffed with vegetables and grilled.

The jungle is an obscenity! I agree with you, Werner Herzog. The jungle eats everything. Expose any part of yourself to its air or mud or water and something will bite you, usually an insect. You will not spend five minutes in the Amazon without a bug on yourself. If you don't see the insect on you, then guess where the insects are, because I promise you they are somewhere.

You can prevent this for a few minutes by spraying DEET-based repellent on yourself. DEET is so potent that civilized countries like the United Kingdom and the nations of Europe have limits on how much DEET can be in a repellent. Canada only allows 35 percent. In the USA (fuck, yeah!), where we invented this shit to protect our boys in the Pacific in WW2, you can buy 99.9 percent DEET repellent, but then you have to ask, *Is covering my skin in pesticide better than letting my blood get a little sucked and my flesh a little nibbled on?* It's a balance.

The Amazon is miles of one interconnected, squirming, living biocarpet, with strips hacked or poisoned out here or there, but turn your back for a minute and it will swallow everything into its greenery.

Downriver

T hat is snake." He pointed to a big snake.
Up in the rafters a toucan was hanging around, opening and closing his beak but deciding each time apparently not to say anything. There was a parrot, too.

"Come," my guide said, waving me over to a tree. An anteater walked along one of the branches.

"Sloth," said my guide. Hanging there dimly, soaking wet—it'd just rained—was a sloth. The energized anteater climbed back and forth along the same limb the sloth hung from, as if taunting him. The sloth dropped one clawed arm and let it hang, like he was winding up to smack the anteater one. But he didn't. He blinked his eyes once or twice, which took about a minute. He turned his head and gave up. With sad effort he hugged his three sharp toes back into the branch.

"Do you want to hold the sloth?"

"No, thanks." The sloth seemed like he had enough problems. Nevertheless my guide grabbed him up and held him out to me like a basketball. The sloth looked at me pitifully, his wet fur hung over his white face like a monk's haircut. Then he drooped his head, downtrodden and resigned.

To the truly adventurous the Amazon itself is tame stuff by now. It's been mapped, after all, though geographers and intense kayakers are still exploring where its true source may be, somewhere up in the Andes.

When he left the White House and craved new stimulation, Teddy Roosevelt headed to a mysterious tributary of a tributary to the Amazon, the Rio da Dúvida, a story excellently told by Candice Millard in her book *The River of Doubt*. The British naturalist and travel writer Redmond O'Hanlon worked his way from the Orinoco to the Amazon. By page two of his book *In Trouble Again*, he is describing the toothpick fish that follows the trail of uric acid from unlucky pissers and swims into their urethras. "You must ask a surgeon to cut off your penis," says O'Hanlon.

This tempered my enthusiasm for exploring too deeply into the Amazon.

The brave and insane have rafted and walked and swum all the thousands of miles of this river, thought for years to be unnavigable. An Englishman only a few years older than me named Ed Stafford *walked* the entire thing, which is the craziest way I've ever heard of to see a river. The Canadian botanist and writer and all-around badass Wade Davis hacked his way around the Amazon, sampling and identifying hallucinogenic plants at an age when I was trying to figure out how to get beer.

I say this as almost an apology. Assume this for all parts of the book: I don't claim to be an expert. I'll just tell you what I saw or heard or found out for myself. I'm no explorer, just a curious dope on a wide-eyed stumble.

What I lacked in adventurousness, I also lacked in preparation. "See the Amazon" was a goal, but that's like saying "check out the Internet" or "try sex"—you're not gonna do much more than experience a tiny sample of the vastness that's out there.

My guide, Alberto, had brought me to this place down the river from Iquitos that was a kind of shack/zoo. A tiny monkey ate some fruits and stared at me, then chittered and shinnied up into the rafters.

I'd picked a guide from a company called Maniti Camp Expeditions that had a usable website but still seemed wild enough and with an anything-goes attitude. The Maniti lodge was flooded, it turned out, so my guide took me to a place called Toucan Lodge, which was something like an Ewok village or a cluster of ramshackle tree houses with thatched roofs. Alberto spoke Spanish better than I did, but I don't think by that much. He and the other guide, Pu, spoke to each other in a language that I believe was Yagua. They were the only guys around at Toucan Lodge, although they did not seem to be in charge. In charge, as best I could tell, was an intriguing woman from Spain who wore big black rubber boots like everyone else but also silver sunglasses that looked expensive.

"She got sent out here because the place's accounts are a shambles, apparently, and she told her friend she'd go for six months, straighten it out, but I don't think she knew what she was getting in for."

This told to me by Maddie, an Englishwoman, who seemed to have heard it from a guest before her, passed down like a local jungle legend. Maddie and her Australian fiancé, Mick, whose beard hung down in two tails, were the only other people staying here. They'd been traveling the opposite way from me, south to north up South America, starting with a cruise to Antarctica, on a six-month sojourn that would end for them in Las Vegas, Nevada, where they'd get married. They were about my age and they seemed very happy to have me arrive. Far as I could tell, they loved each other, but they'd spent an awful lot of weeks together in sweaty and exhausting travel, too. They snapped at and teased each other like kid siblings. Maddie, for instance, hinting darkly about Mick's manhood when he failed to catch as many piranha as her, when the guides motored us out to a swampy off-river channel and armed us with wooden sticks and fishing line and hooks and raw chicken. I didn't catch as many piranha as her either and, believe me, she let me know it.

Still. They were fun to be around and go with as our two guides took us on expeditions: to see pink dolphins diving and poking their heads out of the middle of the river, or to climb a rope ladder to a lookout platform high in the trees, where you could see the jungle flooded into a surreal tree-spotted lake as far as the horizon.

One night, eating grilled piranhas and rice, we got to talking about ayahuasca.

Banisteriopsis caapi and
Her Amazing Friends

Ayahuasca is a name for a brewed liquid made from boiling down the *Banisteriopsis caapi* vine with other plants like *Psychotria viridis*. The resulting concoction contains dimethyltryptamine, DMT, a psychedelic compound, and monoamine oxidase inhibitors, which were used in some of the first antidepressants.

You can smoke DMT, and what'll happen is you'll more or less black out and have a rocket-ship ride of fifteen minutes or so of wild visual hallucinations and the feeling of being disassociated from your body, and then it's over. But with ayahuasca, you drink it. The inhibitors allow your bloodstream to take in the DMT, with the result that drinking ayahuasca causes people to hallucinate and also sometimes to vomit all over the place for hours.

About half of this I knew when I got to the Amazon. The other half I'd learn in lots of reading, long after, as I tried to sort out what ayahuasca had done to me.

The Harvard ethnobotanist Richard Evans Schultes studied ayahuasca and its traditional uses as a "plant teacher" among Amazonian peoples, starting in the 1940s. He'd studied hallucinogenic plants from Oklahoma to Mexico before he came to the Amazon. On his trail came pilgrims and seekers and lost souls and the curious and writers and people seeking relief from opiate addiction or psychological trauma or spiritual boredom or confusion. In a famous tale, William S. Burroughs once rambled on about his wild visions while on ayahuasca, to which Schultes replied, "That's funny, Bill, all I saw was colors."

There are ayahuasca retreats in Ecuador and Peru and Brazil, some of them unsurprisingly sketchy. I'd heard of people importing Peruvian aya-

201

huasca shamans for healing ceremonies and New Age retreats up in Malibu, not twenty miles from my house, but those never seemed like people I wanted to take hallucinogens with. Ayahuasca in Malibu felt off. Here in the Amazon, at least it seemed organic.

"When I drink ayahuasca, I am like I am drunk." Alberto laughed when we asked him about it. "Many visions." Pu smiled grimly. The Spanish woman teased us with a feline voice: "Will you try this?"

Well, hell, why not? Here was a trip for sure. I'd tried a few different brain-chemistry-affecting substances in the past and always had a pretty fun time. Surely this Amazonian plant couldn't do me much harm. And besides, I couldn't let the Spanish woman get away with teasing me.

Alberto and Pu told us if we wanted to try it, they'd take us to the shaman's house. Down the river, and then a long walk. A two-hour trip.

Maddie wasn't game. Mick was, but he judged that maybe his future wife wouldn't appreciate his leaving her alone at a rickety lodge while he went off into the jungle to do home-brewed hallucinogens that can last ten hours. He wondered if the shaman could be convinced to come to us.

Alberto and Pu looked at each other. "Is better to go to his house."

"Well, that's not gonna happen," said Mick.

Pu shrugged and suggested this problem could be solved for fifty dollars.

The shaman came to us.

Late after dinner, Pu and Alberto and Mick and I sat in the dark by the hammocks in the netted-in dining area of the lodge. Pu and Alberto were going to drink, too.

The shaman, a raisin of an old man, sat in front of a single candle. The black brew he'd brought burbled inside a glass Coke bottle.

In preparation for the drinking, the shaman began a chant. A low singing whisper. There were snatches of phrases from the Catholic Mass in Spanish and words from some language unknown to me, and he blew sometimes on a little whistle or paused to smoke in a ceremonial style from a fat loose cigarette of leafy tobacco he'd rolled himself. He fingered along on something like rosary beads.

We sat in the dark, ignoring mosquitoes and other unseen biting insects, for twenty minutes, half an hour.

When the shaman was ready, he poured for each of us a serving of his brew into a wooden ladle. The taste was foul, like liquid dirt. My stomach contorted, just enough to send a message like *Hey, this drink is terrible, buddy.* A bucket for vomiting sat in the middle of our circle, but I rode out the wave. We all lay back in the darkness.

Time passed. Mick vomited a bit. Pu went halfway between vomiting and just a good, thorough spit.

The shaman kept up a low chanting or incantation, very quiet, undisturbing. From peeks around, I could see the guides and Mick sitting or lying, eyes closed. Here and there, Pu and Alberto whispered in Yagua.

Maybe this is a joke for the gringos, I wondered. If so, I saluted its elaborateness and detail. But it didn't feel like a joke.

Ah—and now when I closed my eyes, I could see parades of animated creatures. Their forms kept changing. Now they looked like penguins, now like tiny bears with enormous bright circles for eyes. Keeping my eyes closed was like watching some deranged plotless misedited Pixar movie. But it wasn't unpleasant.

Maybe two hours passed of this. *All right*, I thought in my brain, *what do I do with this?* I knew where I was. It wasn't like I'd zonked out completely. The mosquitoes were still nipping at me, so that was a link to a steady physical reality.

Mick moved to a hammock at some point, and so did I. The bizarro Pixar movie seemed to have ended. The guides were gone, off to their rooms. The shaman still chanted, softly, and then he just stopped and sat. Groggy, sleepy, I went back to my room.

Just about the second I opened the door, my stomach reversed itself and I disgorged, half on the floor and half into the toilet hole, the churned-up remnants of the rice and fruit I'd had for dinner. Purists of ayahuasca insist on a special diet, nothing spicy, maybe no meat. I saw now why.

Interesting plant, I thought, as I flopped myself on the damp mattress.

The Shaman's House

The next morning, Mick and Maddie and I had breakfast. Maddie teased Mick about throwing up, which I guess he'd done in force when he got back to their room.

"Did you see all kinds of jaguars and snakes and faces in plants and so on?" Maddie was smiling. She was a teaser for sure.

"Yeah, it was all right," said Mick. In Australia, this is an appropriate emotional reaction to anything from a rugby match to a wedding to a twenty-year relationship to a funeral.

But when Maddie left, Mick opened up.

"That didn't seem all that powerful to me," he said.

"No, not to me either, really."

"I felt something. It wasn't nothing. But it wasn't . . ."

"No." I didn't mention the Pixar movie.

"Well, not sure what I expected. Glad I tried it, anyway."

Mick and Maddie left that afternoon. I was sorry to see them go, and we made plans to meet up two nights later for beers in Iquitos.

With me alone at the lodge, the guides weren't sure what to do. Alberto suggested perhaps I'd like to see the farm of a guy who, it was communicated, had all kinds of fucked-up fish in ponds.

Yes, I said, I'd like to see that. As a kid, I worked at the New England Aquarium. Aquatic life, fucked-up or otherwise, has always held my interest. But:

"Hey," I asked, "did you guys say it's better to drink ayahuasca at the shaman's house?"

Yes, they both agreed. Much better way.

"Stronger visions," said Alberto.

"Take me there."

To get to the shaman's house, we motored downriver in the boat maybe an hour. We docked and passed through the trees to a village that was more just some concrete shells, some occupied, some not, around a long-unused soccer field.

From there it was another two or three miles up a mud trail. We waded at first through sinks of water up to our waists. But then the trail rose, steadily, uphill, a tough walk in mud that sucked at our black rubber boots. If you stopped for a close look around the trail, you might discover, say, several thousand ants in some relentless campaign of conquest or civic improvement project.

Hot and exhausting, this walk, but it struck me like *Yes, of course, this is how it ought to be. Like a pilgrimage.*

If you are gonna take this drink and its ritual seriously, you couldn't get it delivered. You had to go to the source. You had to go on a journey to some kind of sacred place before you could even begin.

Sure enough, the shaman's house appeared in a clearing, up on stilts, a few chickens running around.

Under the thatched roof in the house, there was one big room for cooking and eating and sitting, and a room behind where the shaman's wife came and went. The shaman was there, and his wife, and there was a girl who was maybe the shaman's daughter or his niece, and there was a toddler who was maybe the shaman's grandchild, who squealed and smiled.

They didn't pay me much mind. They'd set up a mosquito net for me and told me to rest. There was a printed calendar on the wall and a radio and plenty of other things. The house itself, it seemed to me, could've been built in this same place in this same way five hundred years ago.

When the sun went down, the girl disappeared, and the shaman's wife put the toddler to bed, then she went to bed, too.

In the darkness the shaman lit a candle. Alberto and I sat cross-legged. He was gonna drink, too.

"Maybe I have a vision of my mother," he said. *Maybe I would, too*, I thought.

The shaman produced again his Coke bottle, overflowing this time with a tempestuous burbling brew. He began the slow rhythms of his chant.

Whether his incantation was always the same, according to some liturgy, or if it was part the same and part improvised, I couldn't tell you. Maybe he even encoded it with special spells to suit the occasion or his perception of the participants. I had heard Alberto use at one point the Spanish word *brujo*, witch or wizard, which freaked me out a bit. There is said to be malevolent ayahuasca shamans as well as good ones. But this man seemed trustworthy. The casual way he'd played all afternoon with his grandchild was the way, I figured, only a good man would. Maybe under his chant, there was even a sermon of some kind.

After forty minutes, maybe, he poured me out a big spoonful of his brew and I drank it.

At no time in the hours that followed did I not know, like, physically, where I was. Like, on Earth. If you'd asked me, I could've told you: *Lying on the wood floor of the shaman's house. There are mosquitoes everywhere, I can hear the shaman gently slapping at them with a towel. I drank ayahuasca. What're you doing here?* I would've said.

But at the same time, eyes closed, I could perceive myself as a tiny, insignificant molecule connected invisibly to a boundless universe extended to an infinity that rendered any idea of "me" absurd and meaningless. Just a flip of perspective, though—*Whose perspective? What consciousness is even perceiving this?*—and I could see and feel myself as a unity of billions of even tinier molecules in a latticework that shrunk incredibly in size but yet grew equal to the universe in the vastness of its infinity.

Ooooooooo. Kkkkaaaaayyyy, I thought to myself, though my thinking was maybe not exactly in words. Got it. Got it. Got it.

Spectacular visions of vines and life and animals in colors and encirclements like the best illustrations from the finest wonder books for science of the 1950s and '60s appeared, deeper tapestries and shifting faster than I could ever take them in. But that was just a pageant compared to the dawning to me that I was a flick of spirit at most in a cosmos beyond comprehension, but contained within me was the seed of the whole universe and everything in it, too.

Even in that time, I was aware that this is the kind of idea "high" people have all the time. Non-high people, too. This wonder is what the best people on Earth seem to always remind themselves of, touching it and revisiting it through channels of science or religion or art or love or just awe.

Maybe this was just that, in concentrated form. I knew that—still, to feel truly dissolved into it was humbling and scary and wonderful.

What it felt most like, to me, was relief. To be that puny, to be shown or even shouted at by the whole of everything how insignificant an ability one consciousness has to even comprehend. Terrifying and awesome and liberating.

Four hours or so in, I sat up, knowing I would throw up. The shaman nudged over a bucket. Black bilious vomit heaved out of me, like I was shedding my skin from the inside out, as if my body was expelling for me my worst and most devilish contents. One palpable sense I remember is hating the smell of my insect repellent—bad as the mosquitoes were, it seemed awfuller to be covered in poison. The insects that teemed were just the shore of the ocean of boundless life spirit anyway.

When I was done I felt like I'd vomited up every bad thing that'd ever been in me. All that foulness now sloshed around in the bucket.

Also, I had to pee.

As I stepped to the edge of the house, Alberto dreamily said I should put my boots on. *Snakes*, he whispered.

Snakes were not anything I felt like thinking about as I peed. But in that moment, I took it as a test of courage, I guess, or else I was sure that no snake would harm me and I stepped down in just my sandals.

In the clearing, the sky was full of stars like a crude painting of what I'd just seen and perceived myself to travel through. The trees looked like they might bend down and talk to me.

The sun woke me up.

Well, okay, I thought as we walked back down the trail to the village and our boat, *what now?*

It's one thing to see enlightenment for a few hours, and another thing to carry it with you all the next day, and every next day to come.

But happy was what I felt. Relieved.

Whatever it was I'd gone on this trip to look for, I wasn't sure I'd found it. But I was sure I could stop looking so hard. At best, I was a nodule of energy and observation, flickering for a brief time. Go on, good-hearted, wherever we were going, try to perceive and feel and be open. "I," whoever that was, couldn't control or understand even a fraction of everything. Best just to smile and be the finest spot of the infinity I could.

I've read to the end of my understanding about ayahuasca. There's more to read every day. There's evidence that DMT, the psychedelic agent at work, is already in pretty much every living thing, and that the pineal gland of your brain produces it naturally. It's often told that the blend of chemicals from two plants, the DMT from the *Psychotria viridis*, and the monoamine oxidase inhibitors from the *caapi* vine is what produces the hallucinogenic effects. This is suggested as evidence of the holiness or mystery or curious evolution of the brewing of ayahuasca, because how would a shaman know to blend these two plants that don't grow together? It's said sometimes that plants speak to shamans in dreams.

Healers and people invested in ayahuasca as a spiritual idea can be as electrified or as stern about the subject as anybody arguing points of religion. There are also quacks and con artists trading in it. This is a powerful thing.

The great Wade Davis, who anyone who approaches this subject ought to pretty much bow down before, came to the study of ayahuasca as a botanist but stresses in his writings and talks and interviews the ethnographic, too, the anthropology, the sense that setting and cultural understanding and perception can affect your mind as much as the DMT does.

I would never step to Wade Davis, who knew more about the Amazon when I was a fetus than I could ever learn. In a recent interview he has a "back in my day" swagger on the topic of ayahuasca.

"I meet young people who take *ayahuasca* and they speak so positively about the experience," says Davis, "whereas I remember the whole point of *ayahuasca* was facing down the jaguar, being ripped away from the tit of jaguar woman. That was sort of what its point was."*

So says Wade Davis. Before I left the Amazon, I'd meet an American guy who'd taken ayahuasca five times a week for two weeks. "I'd really recommend it," he said, "if you're in any time of transition." He himself had fallen in love with a twenty-two-year-old Portuguese girl he met at the retreat. "She has the power of a much older woman," he said. Regrettably, she was studying to be a shaman and thus had entered a one-year period of sexual abstinence. "It's difficult, to not be able to express yourself in that way, your erotic self," he said. I nodded.

Back on the trail, Alberto didn't stop walking as he turned and asked me, "Did you have visions?"

"Yes."

"Of the jungle?"

"Yeah, the jungle—everything. Did you have visions?"

"Yes," he said. "I had visions of my mother. She is very sick."

"Oh," I said. "I'm sorry to hear that." I was. There didn't seem to be anything else to say about it.

"Yes."

---

*This from an interview with Davis by Paul Luke in *The Province* newspaper of British Columbia, March 14, 2014.

A fluorescent blue butterfly the size of my whole outstretched palm and digits flew along the edge of the trail and alighted on a leaf. It was a bright electric blue, a color I'd never seen a crayon of, not even in a big Crayola 64-pack.

"Look," said Alberto. "This one, it has an eye."

So it did, a spot of gray and white on its wings that looked like a detailed eyeball staring out from the jungle.

Damn, I thought, *what am I drinking hallucinogenic plants for? This whole place is a hallucination.*

Three Commandments of a Brand-New Religion

If I were going to start a religion based on the experience I had on aya-huasca, these would be the laws, as they were revealed to me in my mystic trance.

- *You are not that important.* Don't worry about "yourself." That is a meaningless drop in an infinite bucket, believe me. "You" are a minuscule nothing, and trying to puff yourself up in any way is too pathetic to even be laughable. Imagine a microscopic crumb being like "Er, am I important enough?" Forget about that. Give all that up.

- *You are a part of everything.* You're not nothing, though. What's valuable about you is that you're a tiny spark from the great, infinite energy and spirit of the cosmos. You carry that spark within you.

- *Don't poison yourself.* This one was almost like it was said aloud to me. But: I'm not sure how strict to be on interpretation. What counts as poison? I've ruled out beer and moderate to semistrong doses of quality alcohol. Those are allowed, quite confident in that, I think. After that? I'm not sure. I think you're supposed to eat good nutritious food? I dunno, a lot of religions stronger than mine seem to get lost in the weeds around here.

Those seemed like good rules. But the last thing the world needs is a guy starting a religion based on the revelations he got from drinking aya-huasca twice.

So, on we go.

Best Qualities of
My Good Friend Alan Tang:*

- When you need him, he will appear. Sometimes when you don't need him, too. But: You'll be happy to see him. He will be smiling.
- He is quick. Both his body, which he is constantly jumping up and down like a child (he is thirty-one), and his brain. His brain is going super fast, a million scans a second, and what it is scanning for is comedy opportunities or interesting twists of fact.

That is why I like him, that is why when he was like *I'm coming to South America, where should I meet you, Machu Picchu GALÁPAGOS?!* I was like *Fuck yeah, meet me in Cusco.* Though I played it very cool, ever the brave solo wanderer, to say I was happy to see my old friend would be an insane understatement.

---

*I have used a fake name so the real "Alan Tang" can deny these stories about himself if he so chooses. I don't know why he would, though—if it's not clear, I think he's a tremendous human. His actual name is Alan Yang.

Oh! One More Quality

When he travels, he travels in *style*.

If I let Tang book our hotel in Peru, it would be incredible. Yet *I* would arrive sweaty and worn from my travels, having suffered all kinds of rough nights, and could scoff at his luxury while still enjoying it. A delicious position.

If there'd still been ayahuasca in my system, my body would've ejected this rascally thinking in the form of black vomit, but I guess I was clear.

Sure enough, within minutes of our arrival, we were in his room in the best hotel in Cusco, while a man made us Pisco sours, my clothes in my backpack still jungle moist from the Amazon. Tang was laughing and making me laugh and jumping up and down about the many awesome things we were about to do.

First up: Explore the ancient capital of the Inca Empire.

In the Inca Capital

C usco has 400,000 people, many of them Quechua-speaking people descended from the people who were here long before the Spanish turned up. The Inca laid out the city, diverting rivers to build it. No easy job at an altitude of 11,000 feet, twice as high as Denver. Some people arrive in Cusco and immediately feel sick from the altitude. I kept it together fine, but walking up steep old alleys in a neighborhood like San Blas, I was for sure feelin' it. Diverting a river would've been a big ask, for me personally.

On top of the locals, there is, in Cusco, every kind of hiker and backpacker planning every kind of expedition. It is where you slump exhausted or head out determined for the Inca Trail, or even longer, wilder hikes along the ridges of the Andes on old Inca roads, or down into the roaring rivers at the bottom of the sharp valleys.

Every kind of craft and product and wonderful or mysterious thing from across the Andes and Peru can be found in Cusco. Bear in mind just as an example that in the Andes, they have five thousand types of potatoes alone. You might get sick or exhausted in Cusco, but you will not get bored there. Especially not if you're fascinated by different types of potatoes.

The Rise and Fall of the
Inca in Four Pages

There is so much great writing about the Inca: Kim MacQuarrie's book *The Last Days of the Incas* is fascinating from page one. *Turn Right at Machu Picchu* by Mark Adams is informative *and* funny. The description of the Incas in the great Charles Mann's *1491: New Revelations of the Americas Before Columbus* is so terrific, I had to pull my car over while listening to the audiobook—you couldn't drive and listen to facts that astounding at the same time.

Francisco Pizarro, conqueror of the Incas, was himself illiterate. But among his small company of men, there were a number of literate guys, former clerks and boy secretaries and the sixteenth-century Spanish equivalent of paralegals. This might seem odd, but lots of conquistadors weren't experienced soldiers. They were just ordinary Spaniards who had nothing to lose and figured they'd take a shot at becoming millionaires on some harebrained expedition. Some of these guys wrote accounts, but for my money, none is nearly as good as Bernal Díaz, chronicler of the insane Mexico adventure.

Of Pizarro's four shitty brothers who were with him, all very brave and handsome assholes, only Hernando wrote about it. His account is very flattering to himself and his big brother. So we have that, too.

Felipe Guáman Poma de Ayala, a descendant of Inca nobles who was born perhaps the year the Spanish seized Cusco, wrote a thousand-some-page document. A plea for restoration of the rights of Inca aristocrats, Ayala made his case in part by describing the lives and customs of the Inca. He illustrated his book with 398 drawings. In his old age he sent the only copy to the king of Spain. But it never turned up and was assumed lost. In 1908, at the Royal Library of Denmark in Copenhagen, a German librarian, Richard Pietschmann, found it while poking around in his off-hours from a conference.

So now we have *that*.

The best thing I can do is crib from all these sources and tell you: The Inca were incredible.

When Columbus hit the shore of what's now Haiti, the Inca* Empire was the biggest empire in the world. Ten million people or so lived in it. It stretched 2,500 miles. Down its spine ran one of the sharpest and highest mountain ranges in the world.

To manage it, the Inca built roads that are still there, five hundred years later, up astounding grades and down into rain forest valleys and back up again to altitudes that can knock people out. They did all this without wheels or metal tools.

A system of runners, maybe fueling themselves with coca leaves, took messages and commands and reports, keeping track of numbers and dates and categories with knotted ropes called quipu. Charles Mann compares the quipu system to lines of binary computer code. Everything in the Inca Empire flowed to Cusco. And Cusco was incredibly weird.

In Cusco the main ceremonial square was surrounded by houses of mummies.

Generations of mummies who were treated like they were semi-alive. Female attendants swatted flies away from them and communicated the mummies' wishes. The mummies would even visit each other. What they talked about is anyone's guess.

In Cusco the Temple of the Sun was plated in gold. Loads of silver came in on the backs of llamas. There were llamas everywhere. Also guinea pigs. You would not walk far in Cusco in 1533 without hearing the squeal of a guinea pig.

The emperor wore a cloak made of the hair of vampire bats, and there were alpaca-wool sweaters and hats and rugs. There were great stone aqueducts and canals, and storehouses and castles made of stones that

---

*Charles Mann uses the spelling *Inka*, perhaps in part to jolt the reader to think of this culture in a whole new way.

weighed three hundred tons, twenty feet tall, somehow fitted together so tight you can't stick a pin between them. You could drink *chicha* and eat rich stews and dried fish.

And there were thousands of kinds of potatoes.

In 1533, though, Cusco was on one side of a civil war or a coup.

The Inca Empire was vast, but it wasn't old. By the time Pizarro arrived, it had only been around for ninety years or so. The great founder, not the first Inca ruler but the guy who in two-plus decades of rolling conquest stretched the borders out from the valley of Cusco down into Chile and north into what's now Ecuador, was Pachacuti. When Pachacuti died after ruling for thirty-four years, his son, called Túpac or Thupa, took over. Thupa married his own sister, he conquered along the northern coast, he may have sailed to Easter Island. He died in 1493, the year after Columbus landed. Though no one in Cusco had heard about that yet: It was happening two thousand miles away. Thupa's son Huayna, or Wayna, Qhapaq took over. He ruled for thirty-some years, but then he died of a strange new disease that was sweeping across the Inca realm. This might've been smallpox. His mummified body was paraded into Cusco and added to the powerful collection of mummies already there.

When WQ died, he had perhaps fifty sons. It's unclear what happened, but he either divided his kingdom between two of them or left murky instructions on who was to succeed him, and the empire was split between two half brothers. Huáscar maybe had the nobler mother, and took control in Cusco. Atahualpa, meanwhile, was leading an army up around Ecuador. In the war that followed, Atahualpa barely escaped death at one point, only to turn it around and capture Huáscar and crush his army. Huáscar was made to drink llama piss and then he was led in ropes to Cusco, where all of his wives and children were killed in front of him. Then he was killed.

Around that time, news came that a band of hairy pale monster men had turned up, riding snorting four-legged war animals never seen before.

*   *   *

Francisco Pizarro, the guy who would "conquer" the Inca, had 168 Spaniards with him, some African and Nicaraguan slaves, and 68 horses. They didn't know it, but they'd just landed in an empire three times bigger than Spain.

Pizarro followed the Cortés playbook. He was Cortés's second cousin, in fact, and the older conquistador may have given the kid advice, years ago in Spain. Pizarro lured Atahualpa and his army into the main square of the city of Cajamarca, fired hidden artillery, charged out on horseback, captured the emperor, and killed some two thousand stunned Inca. He kept Atahualpa hostage while the emperor directed his guys to fill a room with gold. The Spanish were so into gold that some Incas thought their horses must eat it. In the end, Pizarro decided to have Atahualpa burned at the stake, for treason or heresy or not telling Pizarro that there was a whole other Inca army out there somewhere. After a priest tried to get the baffled emperor to accept Jesus Christ and the Pope and the Catholic faith, which didn't work, they bailed on the burning idea and strangled him.

To say Pizarro "conquered" the Inca Empire wouldn't be right. At the time of his death, the old Inca world had a guerrilla insurrection going on underneath a Spanish-versus-Spanish civil war. All Pizarro's guys nearly died several times. Plenty of them did die, their heads bashed in or crushed by huge rocks rolled down on them in deadly traps. Pizarro himself was saved from destruction at least once by the timely arrival of reinforcements. The Incas would fight it out for thirty-some years. Pizarro would end up bleeding to death in his own house in Lima, the city he founded, stabbed by conspirators after a dispute with the son of his old business partner. His bones were lost for centuries, though they're now believed to be in a box in Lima's cathedral. In 1572, some Spaniards found the last Inca emperor and his wife hiding in the Amazon. They hauled him back to Cusco and hanged him for religious heresy.

Kind of a bad scene for everybody.

If the Spanish were trying to wipe out any trace of the Inca, they did not succeed. In Cusco you can see the Inca anywhere you go.

Saqsaywaman with
San Pedro and Alan Tang

W HY DOESN'T ANYONE TALK ABOUT *THIS* PLACE?!"
So said Tang, and I agreed. I was also furious to think we might've missed Saqsaywaman.

If you see one thing in Cusco, make it the ruins of the old Inca castle, a fortress on the hill above the city, once so huge it's said it could've held the entire population of the old city, maybe a hundred thousand Incas. Here, there was a ferocious fight between Pizarro's guys and Inca die-hards, the Inca emperor Manco having decided to fight to the death against the Spanish after his two immediate predecessors had been burned at the stake and strangled right before being burned at the stake, respectively. From the towers of Saqsaywaman, Incas had jumped to their deaths, landing on piles of bodies of their comrades.

We were extra stimulated perhaps because we had taken some San Pedro.

Wade Davis, in his pamphlet *Sacred Plants of the San Pedro Cult* (Botanical Museum Leaflets, Harvard University, Vol. 29, No. 4, Fall 1983), writes that "the high northern Andean valley of Huancabamba, Peru, is the centre of an extraordinary moon-oriented magico-religious healing cult, a fundamental feature of which is the nocturnal ingestion by patients and curandero of the mescaline-rich San Pedro cactus (*Trichocereus pachanoi* Britton et Rose)." In a more casual interview, Davis recounts how he took "heroic amounts" of San Pedro and had to be stopped from telegramming his professor, "EUREKA! we're all just ambulatory plants!" ("That wouldn't have gone over so well," says Davis.)

Sure, I wanted to try that. I'd been telling Tang about my experiments so far with South American hallucinogenic plants. He was very game. To my surprise, the first guy I asked at the first weird little occult shop I found in Cusco said he had some, and sold me a baggy of greenish-blue powder he took from a drawer in his desk. Whether this was really ground-up powder extracted from the native Andean *Trichocereus pachanoi* I couldn't say for sure, but it definitely made me feel weird.

"That giant green mound over there is pulsating and then disappearing," said Tang, staring into the distance. "That's good, right?"

I had to agree the ground seemed a little more wobbly than usual, but it seemed fine. Nearby, a kid played with her baby sister while a llama worked its gums and looked on. There were a few stray llamas, and a few stray German tourists, both odd creatures but friendly and harmless. An hour before sundown, and we were climbing around on the gigantic rocks and immense walls of Saqsaywaman—it is pronounced more or less like "sexy woman," there's no need for a false maturity. Below was the whole long valley, the city of Cusco from the ancient plaza and the cathedral, stretching out and growing up the sides of the slopes beyond.

Astounding place, the ruined castle of a fantastical kingdom. Peering into the valley, I couldn't help but be astounded by the Incas and by everything that had grown up since, everything you could see on this April Tuesday in Peru.

"DAMN!" said Tang, who says stuff enthusiastically. "AND WE HAVEN'T EVEN SEEN MACHU PICCHU YET!"

How to Get to Machu Picchu

If you're hard-core, you can walk. The trip can be as long as you want. There are something like 25,000 miles of remnant Inca roads and trails. You can hike for forever in Peru.

If you take the "classic Inca Trail," you'll walk for four or five days. You'll start at a high altitude where air is thin and go up another four or five thousand feet, through cloud forest, past old Inca temples and way houses. You'll have to go with a guide company, because the government only gives out a limited number of permits. Porters will carry most of the stuff for you. Hikers are always sheepish about this, trying to be tough, but the guide companies will smile at you and pat you on the head and most likely you'll end up agreeing you'd never make it. If you're truly hard-core, you can find your own guide and insist on carrying your own stuff, but it isn't easy. It's prohibited to go up there without a guide, which is maybe as it should be. Foreigners hauling off all the best stuff from Peru has been a problem for half a millennium now. Can't blame them for wanting to supervise their own trail.

What counts as a real adventure is an electric subject travelers of all stripes can get anxious or hot about. Maybe that's how it should be, too. The human urge and desire to seek adventure is noble, as a species one of our best qualities. We like it in ourselves and others, and we should admire great examples of it and be inspired to push ourselves. We're all on our own level, though. For some its brave to haul yourself to the store, while for others the Inca Trail is a bit of a joke, easy stuff for vacation warriors.

To treat Machu Picchu like the epic goal of a quest, like a place of pilgrimage, is a good instinct. I'm down with the folks who seek out a bit of challenge, who believe you appreciate stuff when you earn it. This is a very New England way of thinking, I get it.

But: Knowing what I've told you about Alan Tang, do you think we slogged on humid trails for four days and arrived sweaty and exhausted and unshowered for dawnrise over the Gate of the Sun? No. This dude was on vacation and he had come to do it right. He had booked us on a comfortable train where they serve you a magnificent lunch with all the Pisco sours you can drink while a band plays Peruvian music and you glide along with the Sacred Valley out your window until you are delivered to a train station, where you are transferred to an air-conditioned bus and brought up right to the edge of the cliff, where you can suddenly gaze down on the boggling ruins on the narrow green plain high on the shoulder of the mountains.

What *Is* Machu Picchu?

I f there were no ruins in Machu Picchu, it would still be a spectacular spot worth a long trip to see. You go up a zigzag road on the side of a mountain, then you're looking across a ridge, very narrow, two hundred meters, two football fields or so from dropping cliff edge to cliff edge. On the far side, the ridge narrows and narrows and drops out of sight and then rises up again to form the sharp peak of a mountain, Huayna Picchu.

Oh, but there *are* ruins. Terraces, the remnants of drains and fountains, more than a hundred and fifty buildings, towers, baths, storehouses, temples. . . . Actually: Who knows what they all are?

Yale assistant professor Hiram Bingham discovered these ruins in 1911. By "discovered" I mean he heard about it and had a map with MACHU PICCHU marked on it and he paid a local guy at the bottom of the mountain to take him up there. But, fair enough, he was the first guy to photograph it, and write about it in *National Geographic*. The ruins as he saw them were overgrown and wild, but still stunning.

Bingham was sure what he'd found: the lost city of the Incas. Historians knew there was one. After Pizarro, the Incas had hidden out somewhere for nearly forty years. Somewhere, there was known to be a mysterious city. Any Spaniard who got close was killed. A captured friar was taken there, but then pretty fast he was tortured and killed. This lost city was called Vilcabamba. It was known to be big, with large temples. But in the end it was burned, and the location forgotten. If any Quechua farmers passed down the knowledge of it, they didn't tell the explorers who came looking. In time, historians read of the lost city in old documents, became obsessed with it. There were a few scant clues. But no one could find it.

Bingham declared that he had. He'd found the lost city. Vilcabamba was Machu Picchu. He became internationally famous. He was elected governor of Connecticut, and then to the US Senate, and then reelected. While in the Senate, he got in trouble for letting a lobbyist act as his representative at a committee meetings on tariffs, which was a little blatant, even for the semicorrupt Congress of the time. Then he got beat by a Democrat.

Here's the thing: Hiram Bingham was not totally honest. He must've known that he hadn't really found Vilcabamba. The descriptions of it weren't really like Machu Picchu. The lost city was still out there. He was fudging. Typical Yale behavior. Since Bingham, a variety of eccentrics and explorers have, it seems, found the real Vilcabamba. It's overrun by jungle. Thrilling to archaeologists, but not nearly as picturesque for tourists.

The irony is Bingham had found something maybe more amazing. Machu Picchu wasn't the rumored lost city. So what the hell was it?

Well, maybe it was a remote shrine-city populated by sacred female virgins. That was another idea Bingham had. A very sexy one. You can't accuse him of not having cool ideas.

A kind of royal resort, says Kim MacQuarrie. A hilltop estate for the court of Pachacuti, the greatest Inca emperor of all. Like Camp David, sort of.

Maybe it was a monastery, a religious center. An Incan university, a place to study astronomy and engineering. A sort of health spa, perhaps. A sprawling vacation compound for the tens of illegitimate royal children and their families.

My favorite idea, the one Tang and I looked for evidence of as we climbed around, a beautiful morning for a mountaintop ruin, is that Machu Picchu was a prison. Like an Incan Alcatraz, for high-born prisoners or political or religious dissidents or something. You look at it that way, and for all its majesty, it can start to seem depressing. There's no way you'd escape from there, not unless you were ready to jump a thousand feet off a steep cliff into an unseen ravine and hope you hit something squishy.

What to Do at Machu Picchu

☐ **Take pictures.** This is the number one most popular activity there by a mile. No wonder, it's dramatic background. At this point we probably have enough pictures of Machu Picchu. But people like to have their own, and it gives you an activity.

☐ **Take stuff in and out of your backpack**. Saw a lot of people doing this one. I did it plenty myself.

☐ **Explore.** This one I recommend. If you get away from the main ruins, there're all kinds of crazy sites to discover. There's a sheer cliff wall where once was slung a rope bridge. I'm glad it's not there anymore, or I would've had to walk across it, which would've been terrifying.

☐ **Feed an apple to a llama.** There are llamas grazing around on Machu Picchu, as there should be, as there have long been, perhaps. My Amazon friends Mick and Maddie had come from this way. They'd given me the good tip to bring an apple, which apparently llamas enjoy. So they did. You should see them chomp and tooth-mush and gum away at the apples. Tang would agree that was the highlight of the trip. Girls gathered around with joy to watch our apple-happy llama.

☐ **Ponder?** Muse aloud or imagine in silence the wondrous lives that once were lived here?

Kind of a weird question, maybe, what to do at a place like Machu Picchu, but I kept running into it. The main thing about Machu Picchu is to see it, take it all in, gaze upon it, gape your jaw in wonder. Gape you will, it is a wonder for sure. That gape is worth the whole trip, I agree. But gazing upon something . . . that takes, what, twenty minutes? Then what do you do?

I'm not sure I know. Nor did anyone else. They were led around by guides, took pictures, took stuff in and out of their backpacks, looked around at the place, and looked around at each other.

Tang and I went off and climbed around, tried to see the inside of everything we could, studied the stones, and searched for clues that maybe, just maybe, this was once the most inescapable prison in the world.

Now it was the end of April. A month or so before I had to be back in Los Angeles to start a new TV writing job. Not a ton of time to see 2,966 miles, but I work fast.

First, though: Tang and I took a detour to meet our friend Amy Smozols and see one of the most special places on Earth.

A place in fact that's as close as possible to feeling like you're not on this planet at all.

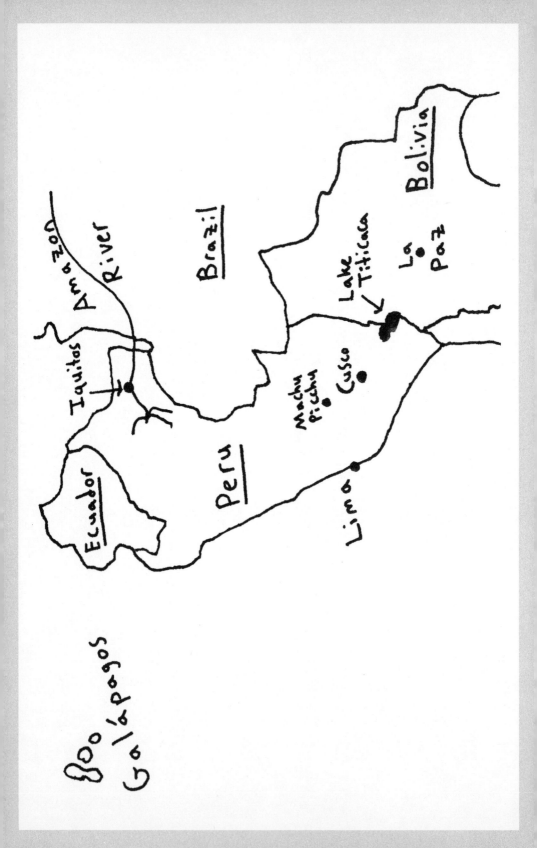

The Galápagos and Bolivia

Away Team Mission to the Galápagos

Technically, I guess the Galápagos are outside the range of the book. Though they're part of Ecuador, and thus "in" South America, they're almost six hundred miles out in the ocean. That's far enough to be its own world.

The Galápagos are a bunch of volcanic islands, divided by the Equator. There are eighteen serious islands, the biggest sixty-two miles across, and four "minor" ones, one of which is called Nameless Island, which is a funny paradox.

The reason why the Galápagos are so special is that they are full of animals. Wild, wonderful, weird animals.

Because they are isolated on faraway islands, these animals could evolve in bizarre and specialized or just surprising ways. So there are crabs that look like they're painted blue and red, and birds with enormous fire-truck red air sacs under their beaks that they can inflate and deflate, and blue birds with huge ridiculous feet, and tortoises that can live to be 170.

On most of the islands, there are no people, there are only animals. The animals have never been bothered much by people. For generation after generation the animals could get weirder and weirder without anyone bothering them or hunting them.

When these animals see people now, they react the same way they did when Charles Darwin saw them in 1835. They act like you're nothing. They walk right up to you and then past you, ignoring you completely. You can walk right up to them, stare them in the eye. If they stare back at all, it's to say, "What? Who gives a shit? Are you gonna fuck me or fight me? No? Okay, well, you're none of my business and not my problem then," and they get back to sitting on their nests or rolling in the sand.

We saw: SO many sea lions and Nazca boobies and red-footed boobies, and frigate birds with flush red sacs under their beaks, both Great and Magnificent. We saw swallow-tailed gulls and flightless cormorants, terns and egrets and herons and pink flamingos picking tiny shrimp out of the mud. Oystercatchers and plovers and all kinds of finches. Plus at least three types of iguana and a giant tortoise.

It's so strange and wonderful. You step onto some island forged into topographic curiosity by geology and weather over millions of years, and walk past whole harems of female sea lions, the alpha male eying his rivals, the pups flopping around and flipping sand on themselves, and past nests of blue-footed boobies and scattering crowds of Sally Lightfoot crabs, and whatever other far extreme of the branching tree of life is passing by.

Darwin was sailing around with the British navy as, like, a guest naturalist when he saw the Galápagos. On these islands, he said, "We seem to be brought somewhat near to that great fact—that mystery of mysteries—the first appearance of new beings on this earth."

YAAAS kween! That is how I want my scientists to talk and think and write! I love when scientists invite me to join them on their humble journey near to the great mystery of mysteries!

Darwin, you deserve it all, dude.

Memory of a Nerdy Childhood

As a teen boy I used to read *The New York Times Book Review* every Sunday. Listen, I'm not saying I was a cool teen. But reading that thing every week allows you to gloss through summaries of all the best new books out there. Before long your talents at intellectual bluffery will be through the roof and you can fake your way through college and on into highbrow cocktail parties with ease.

When I was fourteen a book came out called *The Beak of the Finch*. The writer was Jonathan Weiner, and the story he told was about two scientists, Peter and Rosemary Grant, who'd been studying the varieties of species of a kind of small bird called Darwin's finches. For twenty years they'd camped out on an extinct volcano in the Galápagos, examining and measuring these birds. They took drops of blood from every finch on their island, measured their legs, and photographed their beaks. Their study took in more than 20,000 birds. What they found was that evolution was even more dramatic and fast than Darwin realized.

Life is tough for these birds. There are droughts and dry years. What the Grants discovered was that their finches would adapt quickly. A new generation would have bigger beaks, for cracking open the hardest seeds. If it flooded, the next generation would have smaller beaks, to collect lots of tiny seeds. Out in the wild, they'd found and shown evolution at work.

At the time Weiner wrote this book, almost half of Americans didn't believe in evolution. He carefully and patiently described it happening and showed how it worked. It's a great book. Weiner won a Pulitzer Prize for it.

When I heard about this book, I didn't care about finches. I still don't, really. To me, finches are in the bottom half of Galápagos animals in

234 The Wonder Trail

terms of overall coolness and interest. But ever since I read about it, I wanted to go to the Galápagos.

Half the people on the boat to the Galápagos had a story like that. They'd seen a documentary when they were kids, they studied wildlife photography, they'd dreamed about the Galápagos for years.

Now we were here.

Good Company

Strange and wonderful creatures are what you go to the Galápagos to see. Just in case, I'd brought two with me. My favorite thing about sailing around the Galápagos was hanging out with my friends Alan Tang and Amy Smozols.

Amy Smozols* is small in size, has a deep voice, seems to subsist entirely on alcohol and cigarettes, yet she is never tired nor does she ever speak in anything less than perfect, articulate sentences that are almost always insightful and funny. Weak men and women are afraid of her, and strong men and women are attracted to her. If you are someone truly badass, like a billionaire biotechnical entrepreneur who rock climbs or like a brilliant surgeon who is also charming, Atul Gawande or something, get in touch with me and perhaps she will judge you worthy of her. She started out as a high-powered New York lawyer but hated lawyering and became a comedy writer and producer. She helped to launch Jimmy Fallon's *Tonight Show*. Despite intense drive and a cool steeliness, she is one of the most sentimental people I've ever met. She loves Christmas and friendship and presents and animals and families and children.

One night on the boat, she ran out of cigarettes. She went into the office of the ship's bursar, a serious Ecuadorian.

"Someone on this boat has cigarettes. I need to buy them."

The bursar of a ship is a powerful guy. He's in charge of the money and supplies. He doesn't take orders from just anybody. Usually just the captain. But the voice of Amy Smozols is a voice of command.

The bursar looked her in the eye, picked up the phone, and issued some terse commands in Spanish. Within sixty seconds, some poor sailor from the bunks below scurried into the bursar's office with a pack of cigarettes.

---

*I've changed her name in case she'd prefer to stay anonymous, but I don't know why she'd want to; if it's not clear, I'm in awe of her. Her real name is Amy Ozols.

The bursar told him to give Amy his cigarettes, for which she gave the sailor forty dollars.

Amy Smozols and Alan Tang are two of the greatest conversationalists I know. They will both stay up as long as people are drinking and laughing and being funny. If they're around, that will be like three a.m., minimum. A word that no comedy writer will ever use without some irony, but which is sadly useful, is *riffing*—picking up and playing with an idea or a joke and seeing how far it can take you down exploratory roads of comedy. A fancy-pants way of saying "joking around."

That was the best thing we did in the Galápagos—riffed and joked around.

There are all kinds of boats that'll take you to the island. We were traveling in style for five days at sea. At the stern of the boat was a bar, and in the evenings, there would be a red-jacketed barman who spoke no English and was one of the coolest men I've ever seen. Every night after the day's activities, we drank and talked and laughed and looked out over the water. One night at two or so in the morning, an officer of the ship invited us to the bridge. He showed us everything, and then he took us out on the deck and pointed out the constellations of the equatorial sky. We stayed awake to watch the sun come up. An incredible marriage or some magnificent kids or some epic love affair will have to come along before the memory of that night gets knocked too far out of the top slots in my Best Times Ever file.

For all that drinking, I promised I wouldn't miss a single activity on the boat. Every day, there were little expeditions. We'd climb into a motorized panga and head out on an away team mission to the day's crazy island.

Hungover, it could be tough, but when I stared at a baby sea lion rolling itself around happily on the wet sand, my body seemed to agree this was terrific and pull itself together.

Second-Best Thing: Snorkeling

As wonderful as the land life on the Galápagos is, more stunning still is to jump in the water with a mask on your face and look down. In one single look one morning, my eyeballs could see five sea turtles at once. There were hammerhead sharks and octopi and fish by the thousands, Galápagos penguins darting through the water, and shelves and walls of coral for a hundred feet down. Thousands of pounds of biomass acting out their lives in a single glance right in front of you. And there diving for his supper, shooting through the water like a conscious torpedo, a Galápagos penguin.

Dropping dynamite or cyanide on coral reefs as a way to go fishing isn't unheard of in the world. That's a pretty blunt example of the freakish power humans have acquired for ourselves over the Earth. A coral reef in the Galápagos could take a hundred years to develop, supporting thousands of creatures in webs of intertwined dependence and development. A bad oil spill or some dumped chemicals could kill it all in a few hours.

Luckily, that doesn't seem too likely. The Galápagos is a protected national park. Our power as a species is exponentially out of whack with all the other species. We're a freakish development. Unless we're freakishly good at understanding that, at controlling ourselves, we'll wipe the whole world out and ourselves with it.

Everybody knows that, of course, any kid could tell you that we have to take care of the Earth and all that. But we have to remind ourselves about it, over and over again. Seeing the complex miracles of life on Earth that are all over the Galápagos, you're like "Riiiiiiiiiiiiight, insane harmonious, blossoming tapestry of nature, wondrous but fragile, got it, got it. Remind me again later, but I see it now. We *can't* screw this up."

Witness to a Heroic Deed

O n this boat were many retired people, from England and the United States. Our best friend was a former photographer for the US Postal Service. I hadn't known that the US Postal Service had photographers, but this man explained that over a long and happy career he'd photographed post offices, and postal workers on their rounds, and postal excellence, generally. He was charming and ebullient and had great stories, and a loving partner, who'd knitted him thin gloves to protect his hands from the sun when he was out photographing.

There were only two young kids. They were with their parents, a handsome English executive and his Czech-born wife, a veterinarian. They were like a family from some fantasy about families, the kids curious and thoughtful, the parents attractive and healthful.

One day we were out in the panga motoring through a mangrove forest, when the wife tipped her head back and lost her sunglasses.

Our guide, a terrific Galápagos-born naturalist, tried to fish them out with a long pole. He could spot them but not quite grab them.

"Too bad," said the wife, accepting the loss gracefully. "Those were my favorite."

Without a moment's hesitation, the English father took off his shirt, looked to the guide, who shrugged a permission, and dove headfirst into water full of rays and fish and all kinds of unknown creatures. He disappeared, and then he popped back up thirty seconds later with his wife's sunglasses.

It was such a manly act, so decisive and brave and competent, that the whole boat applauded him. He was assured, coyly, by his wife of a reward to come in private. His sons looked at him, burning into their brains a memory of their father demonstrating exactly manhood at its most valiant. While by no means unique to England, deeds like that are what made Britain great, I thought. And for all the neat and freakish features of the animals of the Galápagos, there's not one that would do *that.*

I doubt I'll ever see that guy again, nor do I know his name, but I think about him every so often, as he gave me an example of how to be.

"Going to Town"

There are some people in the Galápagos. Galápagonians is not what they're called, I don't know why. Some European settlers in the 1920s and '30s tried to make it, canning turtle meat or in various eccentric lifestyles, but it's not an easy place to live. Poor farmers and fishermen from mainland Ecuador moved there, looking for a better life. Some of them found it. Our main guide grew up in a big family of kids of the Galápagos. When he was a boy, he had to hide on the boat over because his mother didn't have the money for tickets for all of her children. Now he tried to train other young people to be naturalists and guides and make a life sharing and protecting the wildlife of the islands. A lot of the crew of our boat were native Galápagonians.

One night, late at night, Alan, Amy, and I were up drinking, as usual the last passengers awake by far, when we saw some of the crew get into a panga boat. They were going to a little town on the island of San Cristóbal.

In a frenzy I hollered over the side and waved and asked if I could come with them.

There was a reason for my passion: I've always been fond of the phrase "going to town" to mean really going nuts. Like "Last Saturday night a bunch of folks came over to my house and we got out the whiskey and just went to town."

These guys were *literally* going to town. What kind of next-level island debauchery were they going to get up to in their one night off?!

Of course, the last thing they probably wanted was to chaperone some gawky tourist on their one-night shore leave. So they acted like they didn't understand and smiled and waved and launched the boat as fast as they could.

Fair enough. Still. When I remember the Galápagos, I'm haunted a little by my failure to truly go to town. Animals are great and all, but what humans get up to—that's what's really great to be a part of.

A few days later we were back in Ecuador. My friends went back to their regular lives, and I went on to finish my trip down South America.

I didn't have much time. In two weeks I had an appointment in Santiago, Chile.

But first: Bolivia.

Oompa-Loompa Hunting

World travelers, people who have an addiction to the rush of going places, find each other. They find me, at least. I meet them everywhere I go, even at home.

When two of these people cross paths, what can happen next is a game of "where's the weirdest place you've been" poker. A one-upping of trips or adventure. You must play with caution in these contests. Plenty of people have mic-drop trump cards. "I took the Norwegian mail boat in winter." "I spent six months cooking at a research station in Antarctica." If you inflate your tale even a tiny bit, you risk getting trumped by your competitor: "Oh, you took the Trans-Siberian Railway? Were you in second class? Everything interesting happens in the second-class cars," etc.

A particular form this can take is seeking out the most exotic, remote, and strangest people. Curious people are interested in curious places, that's a terrific thing about humans. But this search can enter odd territory. It can become Oompa-Loompa hunting.

Oompa-Loompas, you'll recall perhaps, are the green-haired, orange-faced small people or creatures who work at Willy Wonka's factory in *Willy Wonka & the Chocolate Factory*. I'm talking about the 1971 movie here—there are Oompa-Loompas in the book, too, but seeing them on screen is what made so traumatizing an impression on so many children of my generation and beyond.

Wonka tells us the Oompa-Loompas come from Loompaland, which is nothing but "desolate wastes and fierce beasts." "A Wangdoodle would eat ten of them for breakfast and think nothing of it," says Wonka. The orange-faced little people appear relieved to be locked in a factory making candy instead.

"Oompa-Loompa hunting" is a phrase coined by my friend Professor

James McHugh. I wouldn't mess with him when it comes to exotic adventure. Professor McHugh teaches Sanskrit at the University of Southern California. When he's in Los Angeles he's always being invited as the faculty guest by blond girls to sorority dinners. When the school year's over, he's dodging snakes in the basements of ancient Indian temples while he looks for forgotten manuscripts. Hard to say which setting is more full of pitfalls and hazards.

One night we were eating at a Thai restaurant in LA, and we were talking, as one does, about Laos. I asked Professor McHugh if he'd ever been to Laos. Seemed like a reasonable thing to ask: On top of Sanskrit, Hindi, Bengali, Thai, Spanish, and French, it wouldn't be that odd if James had picked up Lao.

He hadn't, but he was interested, like I was. Landlocked Laos was strange enough before it was colonized by the French. The blended culture preserved there sounds like it must be worth a trip. In Vientiane, Laos, you can find exquisite shops making French pastries in the middle of the steaming jungle. You can visit the Plain of Jars, where there are thousands of mysterious basins carved from huge stones. The best guess of archaeologists is this was once some prehistoric graveyard that sprawled for miles.

"Man, I'd like to go to Laos," I said.

"FORGET Laos, dude," said a stranger to my left. Professor McHugh and I turned abruptly. "Sorry to interrupt. But Laos is *over.*"

"Excuse me?"

"It's done. I thought it'd be cool, too. It's not. They put a friggin' highway through the whole place, man. Now it's just like any other place."

I doubted that very highly, but we thanked the guy for the tip and saving us a trip to Laos. He went off into the night.

"See, that drives me BATTY!" said Professor McHugh. He's allowed to say that, he's English. "That's Oompa-Loompa hunting."

Professor McHugh pointed out that Western adventurer cool guys and girls can be so insistent on finding the weirdest, oddest, most backward people.

"But everywhere is interesting!" said Professor McHugh. I couldn't agree more. "People say they hate Bangkok because it looks like LA. 'Get out of Bangkok,' they tell each other. Well, sure, on the surface, Bangkok looks like LA. But then in some strip mall you can find a temple where people worship the embalmed corpse of a middle-aged woman who died in, like, 1998. Why do you have to go out to the jungle looking for people in funny costumes?"

Professor McHugh makes a great point.

On the other hand: It's tempting. Who isn't interested in what happens to people who are isolated, remote, left in their own deep valleys and rugged countries, only glanced at, at most, by the rest of the world? Who doesn't want to see the last holdouts against a global monoculture? When we hear of some pocket of people preserving their culture, how can you not root for them, a little?

Not if they're, like, ISIS, I guess, lighting people on fire and so on.

Maybe worshipping the vulnerable cultures of the world might be a luxury and fetish of people who are safely part of the dominant forces and culture that are making traditional cultures so vulnerable.

Who knows? I'll tell you this much: If you're looking for strange pockets of preserved culture, you will find them in landlocked countries.

Mongolia, Bhutan, Tibet, Afghanistan, Ethiopia: Landlocked countries are *fucked*. They don't have any ports! Ninety percent of everything traded goes by ship sooner or later. For these countries, all those things are at least a full, possibly unfriendly country away. They can't get stuff in and they can't get stuff out.

Circumstances can get crazy in a landlocked country, *fast*. Nobody in the outside world might hear about or process the situation until it's off-the-charts nuts. Switzerland and Austria seem okay now, but nobody can tell me they're not pretty weird there. Liechtenstein and Uzbekistan are *double* landlocked. If you can tell me *anything* about what's going on in either of those countries, I'll be impressed.

Landlocked countries, especially the rugged, mountainous ones, can preserve cultures like time capsules.

Bolivia is landlocked. Whole swaths of the country are a swamp, and whole swaths are salt pans and desert. The part that's all mountainous is, like, the best part. That's where they put their semi-capital, La Paz. Their real capital is in Sucre, closer to the silver mountain of Potosí, but after they'd stripped that out, the government took off, I'm told.

In Bolivia, the women in the market straight-up do not want you to take their picture. This is a shame, because they are wearing tiny bowler hats such as were fashionable for men in Britain in the 1890s, and flowing homemade dresses. Whether they don't want you to take their picture because of concern for their souls, or they just don't want to be props for your Instagram, I'm not sure. Ask them and they will refuse. In La Paz, Bolivia, you can buy a dried llama fetus with which to bless a new house.

How to Survive Prison in or Become President of Bolivia

La Paz is at an elevation of almost 12,000 feet, which is ridiculous. Just to cap the whole thing off, I stayed at the tallest hotel I could find. Out the window, I could look down at the US Embassy, a building not warmly thought of by many Bolivians after several decades of clumsy and sometimes murderous Yankee muddling in local affairs.

In the middle of La Paz, on perhaps the most beautiful square in the city, there is a prison, called San Pedro. There's a hole in the roof of the prison, and out of this hole to waiting messengers in the park are thrown packages of refined cocaine.

The officials of this prison do one thing: Keep prisoners inside. Even that they don't do very well. But once you're inside San Pedro, you're on your own. The first thing you do is rent yourself a cell. If you have money, you can rent quite a nice one. You can eat at restaurants within the prison. If you don't have any money, you might sleep under the stairs. The prisoners have elections and run their own society.

At one time, the residents of this prison made extra money by giving tours. An Australian named Rusty Young heard about this, went up to have a look, and got a tour from Thomas McFadden, a black Englishman who'd been caught at the La Paz airport smuggling cocaine. He'd ended up in San Pedro, where he eventually figured out the system and organized a half-decent life for himself. He had, for instance, a girlfriend, an Israeli backpacker who'd come and stay with him for weeks at a time.

Rusty Young and McFadden collaborated on a book called *Marching Powder*, which is incredibly interesting, I recommend it. It's good to read just as like a manual for how to get along in life. McFadden is a gifted charmer and survivor. He was tossed into prison half-starved, friendless, alone, sticking out, and not speaking Spanish. Everyone wanted to kill him because they assumed he was American. But he made his way, became a prison tour guide, and from what I hear, he is now back in England someplace with an astounding story to tell.

I was taken to see San Pedro—the outside—by a terrific tour guide from Red Cap Walking Tours. (If you find yourself in La Paz, get with these guys.) The guide suggested that while you could maybe still find a way into San Pedro, he did not recommend it due to incidents of rape and stabbing. I decided then and there I had nothing to add to McFadden and to not spend time and energy bribing my way *into* a scary prison.

The guide walked us, winded, on to the Presidential Palace, and called our attention to the third-story balcony.

"In Bolivia, the traditional way to become the president is to throw the previous president off the balcony," our guide explained, before pointing out lampposts from which unlucky political figures have ended up getting hanged.

Balcony throwing is no longer the preferred method. The current president of Bolivia, Evo Morales, was elected in 2009. He's from the Movement for Socialism party, the son of subsistence farmers of the Aymara indigenous people. Of the seven children in his family, only three survived to adulthood. When he was a kid, 25,000 miners in his hometown got put out of work. His family moved to the Andes and became coca farmers. This was in the 1980s, when the United States was providing helicopters to send UMOPAR (it stands for, in Spanish, Mobile Police Unit for Rural Areas) up into the mountains to burn coca farms. These guys were not super cool. Morales says he was present when UMOPAR, with DEA help, massacred twelve villagers at the town of Villa Tunari.

Morales eventually became the leader of a coca growers' union. He nearly won election in 2002 but got edged out by Gonzalo Sánchez de Lozada, who had hired James Carville and a bunch of other ex-Clinton campaign guys as consultants. The next year, after an economic crisis and protests Morales helped to organize, Sánchez de Lozada had to resign. He lives in the United States now and gives speeches at business schools.

Bolivia is trying to extradite him to charge him for deaths during the protests.

As far as I can tell, Morales is fairly popular, though known to be very strange, maybe even a bit mystic. He's said to rely on omens from his dreams. He plays for a soccer team called Sport Boys. He suggested that Barack Obama's speeches at the United Nations have been "a discourse of war, of arrogance, and of threats to the peoples of the world. That also is a discourse of extremist fanaticism." He's on track to be the longest-serving president of Bolivia since the 1830s.

Everywhere you go in Mexico and Central and South America, you'll find Catholic images blended with native traditions. The images of the Virgin Mary, say, might look suspiciously like the mountain deities worshipped by local people long before missionaries ever arrived. Halfhearted compromises no doubt settled on at last by exhausted proselytizers who just needed to move souls past the heaven goal line. In Bolivia, they didn't get very far at all. There's an eighteenth-century church in La Paz, sure, but carved right onto the outside wall you can see Pachamama, the Andean Earth mother goddess, tits out, giving birth to the world.

Lake Titicaca

What kid doesn't want to visit Lake Titicaca? If my childhood was any indicator, Lake Titicaca gets mentioned in every geography book for kids, no doubt because they know kids will enjoy the name, perhaps saying the name aloud or luring adults into saying it. I dunno, maybe kids today are more jaded now, what with YouTube and whatnot, but I bet they still like it.

As any kid who dreams of impressing Alex Trebek at the National Geographic Bee knows, Lake Titicaca is the largest lake in South America. It's the fifteenth-largest lake in the world by volume, although that includes what I consider to be a bullshit lake in Antarctica, so let's say fourteenth. The lake is almost as big as Puerto Rico. It is also, notably, one of the "highest" lakes in the world in altitude, at 3,812 meters, or two and a third miles, above sea level.

Once you've traveled in South America a bit, Denver's brag about being "the mile-high city" starts to seem pretty lame. Try a *two*-mile-high city, like La Paz, that is itself encircled by mountains that are taller still! You might as well be in space.

Well, okay, maybe that's too much, but it does feel like another world, if not another planet. The air is thinner, the colors are crisper, the sun is more intense. It's a tough place, the people are tough, but it does seem half-magical. Just ask a llama with her half-shut eyes and what looks like a smile on a face that's either dopey or blissed out.

Bolivia is huge: almost twice as big as Texas. What I saw was a tiny sliver from La Paz to the shore of Lake Titicaca, out a bus window. That alone was plenty to take in.

Bolivia is undeveloped: Twice as big as Texas it may be, but it has less than half the people. I don't know if you've seen Texas, but it ain't exactly crowded. So imagine Bolivia. True, much of that territory is white salt flats that stretch for miles, or high desert plateaus covered in fine sand, or 20,000-foot mountains. But even up here, in the north, not far at all from the de facto capital, the grass rolls on undisturbed. A tiny farmhouse here and there, many of them that look like they were built by their current inhabitants. Old women in their traditional clothes sit by the side of the road, waiting for a bus or a person or maybe they're just sitting. And: llamas.

Amerians are always comparing things in size to Texas, while of the windswept portions of the world, they always say, "It looks like Montana."

Well, the land above Lake Titicaca does look like Montana. I've seen Montana. Sweeping plains, barren, that roll out to snow-covered mountains of impossible size.

Except here: llamas.

On the Bolivian shores of Lake Titicaca, there are a few towns. Most tourists who come to the lake come through the Peru side, where you can take a train. There you can visit a floating market of reed boats, even sleep out on a reed island. That's across the lake, though.

Where I went was Isla del Sol, a short boat ride across the waters of the lake.

A Hippie Theory

A little more than a year after I got back from Lake Titicaca—just yesterday, in fact—it was the Fourth of July. Late at night at a party, I got to talking to a girl who I can fairly describe as pretty hippie'd out. Blond and cute, she had spent some months in India as an actress playing the wrong girl for the hero in Bollywood movies.

"Where's next?"

"I want to go to Lake Titicaca."

"Oh, actually, I was just—"

"It's a magical place," she said. "There are stone ruins there, and no one knows how they built them. The stones are . . . some really big size. And the further back you go, the more ancient the culture, the bigger the stones were."

This *might* be true, I don't know for sure. I don't *think* it's true. Definitely not worth interrupting somebody at a party over.

"No one has any idea how they built them."

This is also, I guess, true. *I* don't know, though I've looked into it a little. The most likely theories seem to be the most boring, like: lots of work and rolled logs. Impressive organization must've been involved.

"They didn't use the wheel. But they had wheels, in children's toys."

This: I'm not sure about. The people of North and South America, before Columbus, did not use wheels and axles like they invented in the ancient Middle East. They had round things: calendar stones, millwheels. As for the toys, about this there is some controversy. The best example are some objects that might've been children's toys, or else some kind of funeral offering, found at the Olmec site of Tres Zapotes, now in the Museo de Antropología de Xalapa, Veracruz, Mexico. They are animals with a hollow tube that might've allowed an axle with wheels to be fit through, to make them roll. The debate about wheeled toys in pre-

Columbian America is a hot one. Among the strongest researchers are Mormons, seeking to explain passages in the Book of Mormon, which describes chariots in ancient America.

The last thing I wanted to do at a fun Fourth of July party, though, was discuss the scholarly dispute over the pre-Columbian wheel.

"They had very strong fibers and ropes and wonderful materials," she said. This is totally true. The Inca and the Maya made rope bridges of impressive strength from the fibers of their indigenous plants.

At this point a guy who was maybe her boyfriend joined the conversation. "Yeah, and hemp. Washington, Jefferson, all those guys were growing hemp. For ropes, but you know they were smoking it. Probably in a blend. The tobacco plant is a cousin to the marijuana plant."

This I didn't know but I think it is true. Anyway, we got on that topic for a while.

If she was wrong about the details, she was right that Lake Titicaca is magical. Some hippie-type travelers from around the world have discovered this, but it's not nearly the thriving bazaar of yoga and meditation retreats that is Lake Atitlán. On the Bolivian side, the feeling of Lake Titicaca is wide emptiness, with water so blue it's like a color from a wild kids' cartoon.

On the Isla del Sol, in the middle of Lake Titicaca, not sure what else to do, I walked up and across the island as far as I could, up steep steps from the shore that're said to date back to the Incas, or even before. I walked past an old church that didn't look much used lately, and a few farms. On the trail, there were donkeys passing along without too much supervision, knowing and accepting, it seemed, what they were here to do and what paths to follow. Only a few llamas in the walled fields, woolly, kept around for show maybe, or out of deep llama-fondness.

I sat, looked back across the lake. As otherworldly a place as I'd ever seen, but the beauty of it was a touch harsh, the landscape on the far mountains semi-bare, the few boats on the lake almost disappearing on the vastness of the surface.

Welp, I guess that's Lake Titicaca, I thought.

On the boat back, I sat on the roof with a half-Indian Englishman and his girlfriend who'd biked down here from Colombia.

"How was that?" I asked.

"Quite nice, actually," said the girlfriend. "A bit exhausting at times as well."

She stared off, across the lake, and off to the snow-covered mountains of impossible size.

What a very English way to summarize a trip of several thousand miles.

Simón Bolívar

Bolivia is named for Simón Bolívar, the Liberator, a Venezuelan Creole aristocrat who dreamed of a united South America free from Spanish rule. The revolutions he led are turning points in the histories of what are now Venezuela, Colombia, and Ecuador, too.

The career of Bolívar is complicated. In the wild swings of his career he became president of Venezuela twice, first president of "Gran Colombia," first president of Bolivia, and president of Peru. I can't say I'm an expert on the man: I have not, for example, read all thirty-two volumes of the memoirs of Daniel Florencio O'Leary, the Irish-born son of a butter salesman who became Bolívar's close aide. But it seems like you'd be cheated in a book about the southern half of the Western Hemisphere if I didn't try to round up the facts on the guy who has the most per capita statues of anyone in South America. There's even a statue of him in New York's Central Park.

As a boy, Simón Bolívar was raised, mostly, by his family's slave, Hipólita. The Bolívars had owned copper mines in Venezuela since the earliest days of the country. When he was a teenager, like a lot of South American aristocrats, Simón was sent to Europe for a bit of finishing. It's claimed in some biographies that he watched the coronation of Napoleon at Notre Dame Cathedral in Paris and was inspired to achieve a similar greatness. Like Napoleon, Simón was not a big guy: five foot four, maybe. Other chroniclers say that Simón skipped the coronation because he was disappointed in Napoleon for abandoning the true cause of freedom. Either way, he'd seen an example of a diminutive near-nobody who rose to head an empire.

French military officer Henri La Fayette Villaume Ducoudray Holstein, who served with Bolívar, thought all this time in Paris hadn't done the guy much good: "He remained a number of years, enjoying at an early period, all the pleasures of life which a rich young man, with bad examples constantly before him, can there easily find." With disapproval, Ducoudray Holstein says that Bolívar loved to talk about Paris: "His physiognomy became animated, and he spoke and gesticulated with such ardour as showed how fond he was of that enchanting abode, so dangerous to youth. His residence in Paris, and especially at the Palais Royal, has done him great injury. He is pale, and of a yellowish colour, meagre, weak and enervated."

Ducoudray Holstein didn't think much of Bolívar in the end. He found him full of "monstrous faults," like epic womanizing, laziness, and yelling at everybody all the time and making sarcastic remarks about them when they were gone. In his *Memoirs of Simón Bolívar*, Ducoudray Holstein scoffs at the great-man theory. Instead, in a fantastic phrase, he says that Bolívar was "the sport of circumstances."

Back in Venezuela, young Simón joined a revolutionary army, and through skill and betraying some of his fellow officers he rose to the top of it. In 1813, he issued the Decreto de Guerra a Muerte, the Decree of War to the Death, in which he announced that any Spaniards who didn't actively support independence for Venezuela and Colombia could expect to be killed. It's a pretty dramatic read: *May the monsters that infest Colombian soil, and have covered it with blood disappear for good; may their punishment be equal to the magnitude of their treason, so that the stain of our ignominy is washed off, and to show the nations of the universe that the sons of America cannot be offended without punishment.*

By this time the Spanish Empire was in crumbles. Napoleon was destroying Spain. You can't help but feel bad for the poor Spanish soldiers who died fighting Bolívar's armies at the battles of Boyacá and Carabobo, and the Spanish officers he executed. At Carabobo, Bolívar's loyal dog Nevado got killed, too.

Bolívar himself owned slaves, but after the black president of Haiti, Alexandre Pétion, became an ally, he abolished slavery. "It is impossible to say with any certainty to which human race we belong" was Bolívar's attitude. He himself was pretty mixed up, racially.

But Bolívar was a big believer in "president for life" type arrangements, and lifetime senates and noble titles. In the nations of South America, he believed, leaders would require an "infinitely firm hand." He'd hoped to unite all of what he'd liberated into one big nation, but it wasn't to be. Betrayals and conspiracies undid him. With local rebellions springing up, he divided his dreamed-for republic into present-day Venezuela, Colombia, and Ecuador.

Dodging assassination only with the help of his mistress toward the end of his life, Bolívar decided it was time to go into exile in Europe. He died before he made it.

While he was president of Venezuela in the 2000s, Hugo Chávez got into the idea that Bolívar must've been poisoned. His body was exhumed to check it out, but there wasn't much evidence.

In the last line of his *Memoirs of Simón Bolívar,* Ducoudray Holstein has this to say: "The worst of Bolívar's acts is the last, where he has impudently thrown off his flimsy mask, and declared that 'bayonets are the best, the only rules of nations.' This pernicious example, it is to be feared, will be followed by other chieftains, in the new Spanish Republics."

The more you read about the founders of other nations, the more you realize why early Americans revered George Washington so much.

Chile and Patagonia

Chile: The Longest, Skinniest Country

I f you spend a lot of your spare time looking at maps (and who doesn't?), then you've gotta be fascinated by Chile. Look at it down there, the slender country. The only country with the body shape of a runway model. A slice, a sliver of Earth hugged for 2,600 miles of coastline by the Pacific.

What's down there?

Let me give you one answer: lots and lots of true nothing.

My travels in Chile began in Iquique, since that was the northernmost place I could fly to from La Paz. It was a shame to skip the salt flats of southern Bolivia, but salty wasteland takes a while to cross, and I had an appointment in Santiago in a few days.

Iquique is a charmless and tsunami-prone former nitrate port. About a month before I turned up, Iquique had been hit by an 8.2-magnitude earthquake, which might be part of why the streets had a desolated feel. During the earthquake, almost three hundred women escaped from a local prison. Some of them were still on the loose, though quite a few had eventually turned themselves in. My taxi driver did not have what I'd call a can-do attitude, but his job wasn't easy on the dark streets, lights out everywhere. Only with many mutterings that mounted in volume did he finally find his way to the address I had for a youth hostel, said by my Lonely Planet guide to be Iquique's "place to be."

If it ever was, it was no more. Deposited on the dark doorstep, I rang the bell for, oh, probably forty minutes or so until a sleepy woman in a bathrobe at last arrived. She showed me to what appeared to be maybe her son's bedroom, and disappeared. I was the only guest in this hostel, if it really was the hostel. Maybe I'd gotten the address wrong somehow and become the uninvited guest of a luckless Chilean woman. She wasn't thrilled about the situation, that was clear enough. She did have me sign my name in a little book, though. That felt at least kind of official.

In the Atacama Desert of northern Chile, there were once hundreds of refineries for the extraction and processing of potassium nitrate, saltpeter, a valuable fertilizer and firework ingredient. The synthesizing of ammonia, the Great Depression, economic shifts, chemical advances, all this in time destroyed the saltpeter business. The refineries of the Atacama became ghostly industrial wrecks. Ghost towns, or ghost mines.

The abandoned works at Humberstone and Santa Laura are just forty-eight kilometers from Iquique, and are the most spectacularly abandoned of all. Now UNESCO World Heritage Sites, they're not much visited, most people being not all that interested in decaying industrial complexes in harsh and remote desert. It's said the iron of the buildings and the old gates creak and moan in eerie symphony with the sun and wind. In photos, Humberstone looks like the loneliest place in the world, stripped of everything, the conveyor belts crumbling, pathetic graffiti on the walls of the old hospital sunlit through holes worn into the concrete. Just enough to remind you that people were once here, but everything warm or human hauled off or eaten away by the dust.

Man, I would've liked to see Humberstone. As I lay in my child's bed in Iquique, I couldn't sleep from wondering if I should wake up at four in the morning, which would maybe give me time to get a car and make my way out there. (On Humberstone-related sites, you are highly advised against hitchhiking—it's not dangerous, you just might be stuck there for days.)

But you can't see everything in this world. If I have to skip something, I guess I'll pick a rusting, decrepit nitrate works in a bleak desert that, also I should note, is said to be spotted with a few land mines from the days when the abandoned mines were used as concentration camps for political prisoners.

Instead, I took a bus to San Pedro de Atacama, legendary hippie oasis of the Atacama Desert.

Austenland (2013, PG-13)

The scenery wasn't bad. Ten or even twenty minutes of it: That could've been amazing.

The bus ran first south, Highway 1 running in Chile just as it does in California, pressed up to the coast, dropping off into thin beaches and then the Pacific. Hardly any waves here, not enough for surfers to make anything of it. Just the softest lap of water, or dramatic breaks against scattered and jagged rock.

On the other side of the highway, sharp and immediate, a steady ridge of mountains. Enough mountains that no one lived here, seaside. We passed through one grim port town, and a few clusters of what must've been seasonal houses or fishing camps, constructed in a flimsy way, maybe so if you lost yours in a tsunami, you could shrug it off.

Then: We turned inland and crossed through the mountains. Now: the desert. The Atacama, one of the harshest, hottest, and driest places on Earth. There are stretches of the Atacama where it's gone twenty years or more without raining. Punishing country where there are long stretches of nothing, nothing to either side of the highway, nothing for miles.

When I say nothing, I don't mean a little something, a cactus or a sagebrush or a few rocks here or there, like in Texas or Arizona or California's Mojave. I mean nothing, nothing but red-brown sand all the way to the unbroken blue sky. No clouds out here—clouds are moisture. In the Atacama, there is no moisture. There is nothing.

In the Atacama, the air is so clear that where the red earth meets the blue sky on the horizon, the colors stay so vivid it's as if they were right up next to your eyeballs.

Very cool, absolutely. Worth seeing. Very cool thing to see.

But, I mean: The bus ride was seven hours.

To break the monotony of the trip, an indifferent female attendant who was above average in size walked to the front of the bus and put on a movie.

Now: Let us say you are transporting a busload of almost entirely Chilean men, most of them on a long journey to or from work in the mines.

What movie would you choose to play for these men?

The movie the attendant put on was called *Austenland*. It came out in 2013, and it stars Keri Russell and Jennifer Coolidge. It tells the story of Jane (that's Keri Russell), a young American woman who loves Jane Austen so much that she spends all her money to go to, like, an adult camp or theme park or resort in England where you pretend to be Jane Austen characters and gigolos in period garb pretend to seduce you. Only, Jane doesn't know they're only pretending, so she gets her heart broken. But then a decent Jane Austen actor guy (Bret McKenzie from Flight of the Conchords), who is playing a stableboy in the fake Jane Austen land, actually does love our Jane or comes to love her.

Jennifer Coolidge plays Jane's friend.

I could understand the plot of the movie, because I am fluent in English. I could listen to the English under the dubbed Spanish.

For the other men on the bus, I'm not sure it was so clear. Another problem is that many of the jokes play on how snooty English people pretending to be nineteenth-century landed gentry talk, versus how modern American women talk, and also regular English people, and then the Americans do silly versions of the English snooty way, and so on. *How were these jokes re-created in Spanish?* I wondered. Listening hard I tried to divine it but could not hear the way. Chilean Spanish is already itself famously crazy and hard to understand, even by other Latin American Spanish speakers. So that's another wrinkle.

The guys on the bus were not laughing at the movie. I will say they were mostly all watching.

How had this movie been chosen? Surely the bus could play whatever movie it wanted. I doubted the Chilean desert bus company had a deal with Sony Classic Pictures Entertainment that mandated they show *Austenland*. Someone must've chosen it. Why? How?

My best guess was that the indifferent attendant wanted to see it. I looked to her, at the back, to see if she was enjoying it. No: She was watching, but her posture and face were still very indifferent. Her arms were crossed in stern nonenjoyment.

The best solution I could think of was that she had come to despise the men on the bus. Truly hate them. Why? I can't say. They seemed inoffensive to me. Maybe it was the way they smelled.

She devised a twisted penalty for whatever crime she had found them guilty of. Whenever she bought the DVDs, she tried to select at the market the movie these men would least enjoy. The movie the furthest from their tastes. Her sole, meager, perverted pleasure as she rode the bus was watching them sit, imprisoned, as their wills gave out and they sank in their seats and watched.

Hey, I'll tell you this, people have done stranger things in the Atacama Desert.

ATVs, Hot Dogs, and
Relationships in the Atacama

"Why did you do that, Steve?"

Not angry, not accusing. Just asking. Why had I done that? Gotten the wheel of the ATV stuck, wedged quite tight actually, in a concrete drainage channel.

Oh, lotsa reasons. The exact cause was I guess I assumed the ATV could bounce or jump over such obstacles, like G.I. Joe's and Cobra's do in cartoons. Even over ditches slightly wider than their tires. Also because the ATV had sorta seemed to want to go that way, and I wasn't assertive enough to tell it not to. Biggest core reason is that I wasn't giving full attention to what I should've been: steering this monstrous machine.

A truck came along. We flagged it down. The guy helped pull us out, with a noble minimum of side-eye and smirk at the gringo idiot, and went on his way.

Juan was my guide. He was taking me out to see some good and roadless parts of the desert.

In San Pedro de Atacama, there is a main street of red packed dirt, and along it are rows of low buildings made of red clay and caliche. Skinny but friendly street dogs follow you around—the oldest joke in San Pedro is to call it San Perro, Saint Dog.

Some of the buildings along the main street have clay and woodstoves inside and make great food, and some have little offices that book tours out to sites in the surrounding area: the Valley of the Moon, or high shallow lakes where flamingos pick their way along, or even overnight expeditions to the Bolivian salt flats. And, of course, a volcano.

I'd already been, at four in the morning, out to El Tatio, where you can watch as the rising sun warms underground water and sends fumes of hot steam up through vents in the rock. You can bathe in a hot spring, if you want, or an indigenous Atacameño will sell you skewers of grilled guanaco for breakfast. The bus was full of Brazilians, and the tour guide enlisted them to vote loudly as she moved her hair around in different possible styles, from *ridiculo* to *muy atractivo*. We stopped at the sixteenth-century church at Machuca, bright white with bright blue doors, standing alone on the red hillside, an almost comical display of missionary optimism.

Today, though, felt like it needed something more adventurous. So I found Juan. He lived outside of town in a house with a dog and some trucks and his drum kit and a girlfriend I never saw. I knew we would get along because his rooms were a mess but the walls were covered with maps. Places he'd been and places he wanted to go, all over South and Central America and the world.

"You have to dominate the beast," he said, as I mounted again my now unstuck ATV.

"Got it," I said. To my surprise, I did. I made it clear to the ATV I was in charge now. I dominated the beast, and there were no more problems. We tore off again.

Farther on down the trail, Juan flagged me over and we stopped under a tree.

"This is a special tree," Juan said. So it was, I could see that. It was the only tree around for what had to be miles. Looking at a photo of it now, I believe it was a Chilean mesquite tree, but before Juan could tell me about it, he got distracted by a text.

If you can get texts out here, I thought, *then game over. The unknown realms of the world are gone. The whole planet's connected and the mysterious places are gone.*

"I'm sorry," he said. "I'm having a problem with my girlfriend." We were speaking in English, which Juan spoke very well, mainly, he said, because of watching movies.

"Oh," I said. "I'm sorry to hear that."

"Yes." Juan was almost exactly my age, also never been married. He stared off.

"What kinda problem?"

For the next twenty minutes, under the shade of the mesquite tree, he told me. We discussed and considered aspects of his problem with this woman. Sometimes I offered similar cases for comparison, in case they might be helpful. He considered them, and nodded. He added more to the story, and a description of this woman's character, both her exciting qualities and her troublesome ones. He told of warning signs, past disputes, upsetting revelations. He told of his own life, of his sisters, and his family, and we discussed how the patterns and ideas of our youth can express themselves again later, in ways we may not even realize. How we form our notions of what can be accepted, and what cannot be tolerated. Juan made an accounting of his own behavior and possible misjudgments. The mysterious and sometimes contradictory and baffling nature of women's minds and wills and emotions were considered as well. We ate some almonds from a bag and drank some water as we spoke.

In time the conversation came to an end, as all such conversations must, in a melancholy but not unhappy agreement between us that some difficulties won't ever offer even the small relief of being wholly comprehensible, and must be simply accepted. You must accept, choose, and try to move on.

"What can you do?" he said after a long while.

"What can you do?" I agreed. We got back on our ATVs and kept going.

After some rough country, we rode up and stopped at a salt deposit, a jagged wall of exposed crystals, drooping and dripping like stalactites. Juan said that you can hear a kind of creaking music the salt makes as it expands and contracts in the heat of the sun.

"So now we will be quiet for a few minutes."

We were. The salt tower tinkled and hummed like a trippy tune played by some faraway or celestial instrument.

We rode on and came to the rusting shell of an abandoned bus. Truly in the middle of nowhere. How did it get there? We dismounted and discussed it for a while, the conversation turning to the abandoned bus in Alaska and the adventurer, told about in the book and movie *Into the Wild*. Then we talked about Eddie Vedder's album written for that movie. Juan was a musician, and into music. He'd wanted to go to school in California to learn to be a music producer, but in the end his father told him they couldn't afford it. So he went into tourism. His big gigs were leading packs of rich middle-aged Brazilian men on motorcycle trips into Bolivia.

We talked about girls more, too. The town of San Pedro has a semi-mystical, hippie reputation. The light, the air, the colors, the dreamy formations in the desert, the laid-back vibe, the dirt roads: Strange people wash up there, and many backpackers, but it's a small town. If he broke up with his girlfriend, Juan figured, it might be a long time until he found another. He was a good-looking dude, both rugged and intelligent. Surely hippie backpacker chicks must pass his way?

"You can hook up with the tourists," he said, "but that is a lot of work for little pay."

We thought about that for a while.

Then it was lunchtime.

On the edge of town, there was a true hole-in-the-wall, more a shed than a restaurant, that Juan recommended to me. He'd told me to get whatever the day's special was. That day it was two hot dogs and some kind of refreshing floral lemonade for 3,000 pesos, less than five dollars. Chileans are serious about their hot dogs. They don't just boil up some garbage, they grill their hot dogs properly. At this place they lined the bun with guacamole and a tomato salsa—a Chilean specialty known as the *completo*.

I know what you're thinking: guacamole and salsa on hot dogs? Do we need to bomb and invade Chile and teach them Correct Ways? But I tell you, it was delicious. My beard was salty and I was dusty and thirsty and this lunch was so satisfying I ate it and then ordered it again and ate it a second time.

I'd hired Juan only for the morning. What had I been planning to do with my afternoon? Visit the museum or some bullshit? No. Of course not. Obviously, I should control the monster and blast around the desert some more. I texted Juan.

"Well," he said when we met again. "That's it. We talked, and she is moving out."

"Whoa. Fast."

"When I make a decision, I make it. There is no point in going back and forth."

"When's she moving out?"

"Right now. She is there now."

"Damn."

"Yes." We stood there a while. "She used a word to me that I cannot allow to be used to me. After that, it was it."

"Man."

"C'mon. Best thing to do is take a ride."

So we went, in the late afternoon, out into the desert again. The other direction this time. We rode out to a deep round sinkhole of water. Along the dry reeds at the lip, some boys were daring each other to jump in. We watched the first one go. By his reaction the water must've been friggin' freezing. We rode on across lands owned by the indigenous people. We stopped so Juan could talk to a friend of his, and show me a kind of solar-heated toilet they'd installed just off the road. He was impressed with it and showed me its innards, though between my memory and a jumbled schematic I drew in my notes, I admit that I can't quite explain its workings. The sun somehow heated human waste to create energy, I think? That maybe powered a compactor of some kind, too. Very little water was involved. This toilet was provided for those who came to visit a wide but very shallow turquoise lake, studded with spikes of white crystallized salt. Shoes off, we walked out into the water.

In the mountains beyond, we could see the home of ALMA, the Atacama Large Millimeter Array, where sixty-six radio telescopes beam out through the clear moistureless air of the desert and study merging galaxies forty million light-years away. With our feet on the crunching salt and our legs cooling in the water, we talked more about music and women.

Juan had worked in the Amazon for six months, hunting turtle-egg poachers.

He had come to San Pedro a bit of a hippie, he said. "Then I started my business. Once I had a business, *immediately* I stopped being a hippie."

I asked him if he'd ever been to Paraguay. My time here in South America was running out, and one country I could now see I wouldn't have time to visit was Paraguay. In Paraguay, in the eighteenth century, Jesuits tried to create a utopian society that lived by the principles of their order, out in the jungle. They did not succeed, but the ruins of their old missions are still there, overgrown. Landlocked Paraguay has had a sad history. During the pointless and catastrophic War of the Triple Alliance in the 1860s, ten-year-old boys were sent to battle with farm tools. It is said in some books that half the population of Paraguay died in this war, and almost seven out of every ten men. This seems inconceivable. I've tried to research it, but there just aren't great records on the historical population of Paraguay. Who can say? All I can say is it sounds like a sad place.

"Yes, I've been there," said Juan. "Go to Paraguay if you want to see animals." On the savannas and dry forests of the Chaco of Paraguay, there are all kinds of jaguars and tapirs and deer and anteaters and giant otters.

"What about people?"

Juan shook his head. "Paraguay for animals."

The sun was starting to set. So we mounted up and rode back to town in the low orange light. There was a girl at my hotel who I thought could perhaps be Juan's next girlfriend. She was cute and small and smart. She told me she'd studied for a semester at Ole Miss.

"Wow, what was that like?"

She smiled and rolled her eyes and said, "Long story."

Juan came inside to see if she was there, but she must've been off that night. He shrugged, we shook hands, and he left.

I hope they've met by now. If I'm being *really* optimistic, I hope they invite me to their wedding.

Aliens of the Atacama

There are some strange and enormous artworks in the Atacama Desert. One, the Mano de Desierto, is a thirty-six-foot hand emerging from the sand off the highway, south of Antofagasta. It was built in 1992 by Chilean sculptor Mario Irarrázabal.

Another is the Atacama Giant, a geoglyph about 400 feet long, carved into a sloping hillside. It shows a square-bodied, spike-headed creature like a bad guy from a 1980s video game, and was believed to have been carved sometime after AD 1000. It's suggested that watching how the moon aligns with his head could tell farmers when to plant their crops. This seems crazy to me. There're easier ways to figure out what time of year it is than carving a 400-foot giant into the rock and sand.

No, I think the message of both these works could be a much simpler one: a natural human desire to try to express the feeling you get in the Atacama. Namely: *It's fucking weird out here.*

In reading up on the Atacama on the ol' Internet, I came across stories and photos of the "Atacama Humanoid." This is a skeleton, six inches long, allegedly found in a bag in a ghost town somewhere in the Atacama. With an elongated, ovalish head and oval eye sockets, it looks, frankly, like an alien. Like the versions of aliens I used to see re-created on *Unsolved Mysteries* and TV conspiracy documentaries when I was a kid.

(I was very into TV conspiracy documentaries when I was a kid. If Fox 25 advertised an alien autopsy, you can be damn sure I was setting the VCR.)

Professor Garry Nolan, who studies immunology and microbiology at Stanford's Baxter Laboratory (and also has a great photogenic look for a scientist), inspected this skeleton and determined, to his satisfaction, that it was human. A child, probably an indigenous Atacameño child, born with all kinds of birth defects. How his or her skeleton ended up in a bag in a ghost town, and now in a private collection somewhere, is a story perhaps less startling than an alien appearance, but no less poignant and strange.

You can still find online many alien conspiracy buffs clinging to the Atacama Humanoid. They scoff at how the so-called scientific community always tries to shut down dissent and keep the truth hidden from us. The conspiracy buff's attitude is appealing to me. In a way, it's optimistic. An insistence that the world can't possibly be as familiar and clumsy as it appears to be, that someone out there is keeping from us powerful secrets that could change everything.

With its moistureless air and almost no artificial light, the Atacama Desert is one of the greatest places in the world to see stars. The nights I was there fell around the full moon, the worst time of all for stargazing. Still, from the dirt roads out of town, I could look up and see the sky thick with scoopfuls of distant stars, thousands at a glance.

There are places in the world—Iceland, Death Valley, the Atacama—that feel like another planet. They make you feel like you're stranded on some mysterious planet somewhere in the vast enormity of space.

Or, rather: They *remind* you that you're stranded on some mysterious planet somewhere in the vast enormity of space.

Because, of course, you are.

At least all of us are stranded here together.

Che Guevara

In 1951, Ernesto Guevara was a twenty-three-year-old medical student in Buenos Aires, Argentina. His buddy, Alberto Granado, had a motorcycle they called La Poderosa. The two of them were drinking yerba maté tea and talking.

"Along the roads of our daydream we reached remote countries, navigated tropical seas and traveled all through Asia," says Guevara in his memoir *The Motorcycle Diaries.* "And suddenly, slipping in as if part of our fantasy, the question arose:

" 'Why don't we go to North America?'

" 'North America? But how?'

" 'On La Poderosa, man.'

"The trip was decided just like that, and it never erred from the basic principle laid down in that moment: improvisation."

I hear that. The two of them set off on a nine-month motorcycle journey, across the pampas of Argentina, over the Chilean border, to Valparaiso, Santiago, up north through the Atacama and the Andes, to Iquique, to Bolivia and Lake Titicaca, over into Peru, to Cusco and to Macchu Pichu, and on to Colombia. Almost a reverse of the trip I'd taken.

In my own fantasies for a while I'd thought about going Guevara style, riding a motorcycle across Latin America. So I learned how to ride a motorcycle. Quickly, I decided it wasn't my nature to ride motorcycles, and what's more, it seemed like there could be nothing more douchey and poseur-y than trying to redo what Che did.

It would feel wrong, though, to put down a book about the southern half of the Western Hemisphere without saying something about Che Guevara, whose image and ideas are everywhere.

The nickname Che came from the way Argentines talked: a bit like if

Argentines started calling an American guy *bro*. If you've heard of Che Guevara the revolutionary, you might be surprised like I was when you read *The Motorcycle Diaries*. It's not mostly a radical political document. It's a travel book. Che spends much more time talking about schemes he and his buddy pulled to steal wine, or get free meals, than he does about overthrowing governments. For a while their goal is to get to Easter Island, which intrigues them, but they don't quite make it. Che talks about the diarrhea he had, and the problems of taking along a little dog on their motorcycle. A constant obsession is how they're going to get more yerba maté. Che's father was a yerba maté farmer for a while. The stuff's highly caffeinated, and Che appears totally addicted to it.

In the legend of Che, the sight of workers struggling in the American-owned copper mine at Chuquicamata, the struggles of poor Communists in the Chilean desert, the hard lives of the indigenous people of Peru and Bolivia, and the sufferings of the sick they helped while volunteering for a week at a leper colony in the Amazon inspired him to take up a life of revolution. "What needs to be done," he says, "is to get rid of the uncomfortable 'Yankee-friend.'"

He went back to Argentina, finished his medical degree, but then he was off again. He was in Guatemala when the American-backed coup toppled the socialist Jacobo Arbenz. He wrote his relatives and told them he'd become a Communist. In Mexico City, Che befriended the Castro brothers. He was with them when they sailed to Cuba on the *Granma*, a small yacht crammed with eighty-two revolutionaries.

Only maybe twenty of them survived the next year. The *Granma* is now encased in a glass box in Havana, a monument to the revolution. When Fidel Castro took over Cuba, three years after they landed, he made Che minister of industry and president of the National Bank. This last job, Che used to say, he got when he misunderstood Castro asking for an *economista* as asking for a *comunista*.

Smarter people than me have spent years of their lives trying to figure out Che Guevara. Oliver Stone and Steven Soderbergh and Walter Salles all tried to make movies about him, with different amounts of success.

Mandy Patinkin plays him, a dreamlike version of him, in the musical *Evita*.

Che did, absolutely, send people to be executed by firing squad. Jon Lee Anderson, who has more knowledge about Latin America in one cell in his brain than I ever will, and who wrote a 672-page biography of him, says that Che's executions were never once of "an innocent." Che also encouraged relations between Cuba and the Soviet Union, and he helped bring to Cuba the Soviet missiles that sparked the Cuban missile crisis.

Che visited the United States in 1964. At the UN, he gave a fiery speech calling out the United States for its racism. He appeared on *Face the Nation*, too. You can see a clip of it on YouTube. Che smokes a big cigar, he takes his time, and he has crazy swagger. You can see that the besuited journalists have no idea what to do with this guy.

What happened between Castro and Che in Cuba might never be sorted out. But Che left. Che went on to try to start a revolution in the Congo. Then it was on to Bolivia.

On October 13, 1967, Special Assistant for National Security Affairs Walt Rostow sent President Lyndon Johnson a very brief memo with an attached file, still classified. "This removes any doubt that 'Che' Guevara is dead," it reads. He'd been captured and killed by Bolivian troops, with help from the CIA. Supposedly his last words were "Shoot me, you coward! You are only going to kill a man!"

After the motorcycle trip, Alberto Granado went back to Argentina and finished his studies. When the Cuban Revolution prevailed, he accepted an invitation from his old friend and helped train doctors there. He continued his research in genetics, and he died in Havana in 2011. "He was not compromising," Granado told the BBC about his old friend in 2005. "It wasn't easy unless you shared his vision and believed in it."

Now he's on a million T-shirts. You won't go far in Latin America without seeing Che's face. I've read as much as I could about Che, but I can't say I've come close to figuring him out. On his main point, that the United States was extracting all kinds of wealth from Central and South America without much of it trickling down to the people there, he was absolutely right. He also believed in violent revolution, which I myself, as a Yankee-friend, am not too psyched about.

But I will say this: He was a very good, and sometimes very funny, travel writer.

If I were as full of life and energy as Che, I would've taken a motorcycle from the Atacama to Santiago. But I had an appointment to meet my friend Fabrizio in Santiago, and I couldn't be late. So instead, I slept on a short flight.

The Museum of Memory

When the jets from your own air force are bombing your own pres-idential palace, your country is having a bad day. On September 11, 1973, that happened in Santiago, Chile. By the end of the day, Chile's president, Salvador Allende, went on the radio.

Allende had become the president after a messy election in 1970 in which he won the most votes but not a majority. He was "left leaning," which is to say he pushed for things like more spending on housing, free milk for kids, improved relations with the USSR and Castro's Cuba, and nationalizing copper mines. His style of economics and foreign policy was not exactly in line with what US president Nixon and National Secu-rity Advisor Henry Kissinger wanted, and so they conspired to destabi-lize his power. You can hear them talking about it on White House recordings. Strikes and political disputes turned into a national crisis. Now, General Augusto Pinochet of the Chilean army was commanding tanks and troops in the capital.

On the radio, Allende said, "At least my memory will be that of a man of dignity who was loyal to his country." Then he either shot himself or was shot.

Immediately after the coup, thousands of Chileans were rounded up in the national stadium. In the years that followed, Chileans who pro-tested the dictatorship of Pinochet were electrocuted or shot or thrown out of helicopters or taken to secret concentration camps in abandoned nitrate mines. Some of Pinochet's guys were blown up or assassinated by opposition groups.

There were all kinds of opposition to Pinochet: unions and journalists and indigenous people and miners and intellectuals. They fought with each other plenty. But in 1988, they managed to unite themselves enough to rally a majority of the country to vote no in a referendum on the military dictatorship. Pinochet stuck around as a senator for life, making the case until his death that hey, maybe I was tough but you guys needed me. When he died at ninety-one, he was wrapped up in all kinds of legal cases involving torture, kidnapping, murder, and possibly having his army build a lab to make "black cocaine," a mixture of cocaine and various chemicals.

This isn't ancient history. Almost all of this happened in my lifetime. There are coworkers and friends, maybe even married couples in Chile, who voted on opposite sides of the No referendum. There are families that were destroyed and neighbors who betrayed each other during the military junta who are still neighbors today.

The story of all this is told at the Museum of Memory and Human Rights in Santiago. It's an incredibly cool building, designed by a Brazilian architectural team. The afternoon I was there, a bunch of seventh graders were on a tour. To me they seemed to be spending most of their time bouncing toward and away from each other in patterns that no doubt told stories of growing crushes and explosive friendships and awkward affections. But some of them watched the videos.

In the videos, you could hear people tell about being kidnapped and sexually assaulted and tortured, of losing sons and sisters and parents. You could learn about the so-called Operation Television Withdrawal, where the exhumed bodies of executed dissidents were thrown from airplanes into the ocean. You could hear about La Cueca Solo, where one person alone would do a traditional Chilean dance as a kind of protest over the fate of her partner, who'd been disappeared. You could watch news footage of the huge celebrations in the streets after the No vote.

Much of what happened in this time is murky or rumored or lost in secret or destroyed documents. The Museum of Memory felt extra powerful to me because it seemed to make no judgments. Mostly, it just showed things—an electrified bed, an underground newspaper, a poster—and played images of people saying, *This is what I saw. This happened to me.*

Quite a place. My friend Fabrizio had told me this was the one thing I had to see in Santiago. Now I'd done it and I was relieved I was free to party and joke around with a strong candidate and my personal choice for Funniest Guy in Chile.

The Funniest Guy in Chile

When Fabrizio Copano was a boy living in Los Angeles—Los Angeles, Chile—he heard about an American TV show called *Seinfeld*. To watch the show, he had to download it over a modem. An episode took two days to download. Imagine the crushing frustrations this boy experienced when the Internet went down or his mom knocked out the modem plug with her vacuum at, like, hour thirty-one.

On *Seinfeld*, Fabrizio saw a man standing with a microphone telling jokes. This didn't really exist in Chile. He decided he wanted to try it. So he went to tango clubs and asked them if he could stand up with a microphone for a few minutes and tell jokes.

To the owners of the tango clubs, this seemed ridiculous, but he was a cute fourteen-year-old kid, they said okay, so he started doing it. The tango club patrons were amused by this. More and more came.

"They liked that it was a New York thing. It sounded sophisticated. Soon magazines were writing about it and saying this is something they do in New York," Fabrizio said. That's how he brought stand-up comedy to Chile.

Now Fabrizio is twenty-seven and he has a popular late-night talk show on Chilean TV.

"It's hard because I run out of celebrities. There are only like eleven celebrities in Chile. I just interview them over and over again."

I met Fabrizio when he was in Los Angeles, California, seeking help for a movie idea where he would play a boy seismologist who discovers a conspiracy by the rich people in Chile to cause earthquakes so that Chile can separate from South America and go to Europe. This movie got made and came out and was an enormous hit and now Fabrizio is even more famous.

In Chile, anyway. In the US, nobody knew who he was. I took him to

Universal Studios, because he wanted to see the Simpsons ride, which is indeed great. I really liked him and thought he was funny.

"Hey, Fabrizio, what do your parents do?" I asked him on the Universal Studios escalator.

"They are architects."

"What kind of architects?"

"Bad ones."

When he left, I told him I'd visit him in Santiago someday. You know Americans, we are always promising to visit Santiago. But I went and did it.

"Was I supposed to bring you weed? An American stand-up told me it is always polite to bring comedy people weed when they visit."

That was said by Paloma Sales, a friend of Fabrizio's and another Chilean comedian, who met us out for dinner. Very gracious and nice, a lovely person, Paloma. Her stand-up is incredibly filthy.

Paloma could speak English easily. She had gone to the American School of Santiago.

"All these schools. American School, French School. My school was just school. It wasn't even Chilean School. It was school!" said Fabrizio.

"Duh," said Paloma, "that's because you were poor."

That night, Fabrizio took me to his stand-up show. Chilean Spanish is a mixed-up rapid-fire of contractions and slang, and I couldn't understand most of the words. The comedians, though, were very expressive, so a lot of the comedy got through. One guy had a bit, for example, which unless I'm really mistaken was about the technical challenges and possible mishaps of giving oral sex to a woman. The crowd could relate. Another guy was dressed kind of like a Chilean Marilyn Manson. From the slow release of laughs mixed with groans and oooooooooohs, I could tell he was trying to find the most offensive things he could think of, lead the audience right to the very edge, pull back, and then when they got relaxed again, he'd shove them over.

"Hey, Fabrizio, I have to ask you something." This was the Sunday after. We were driving with Fabrizio's girlfriend to the beautiful (and UNESCO-listed) seaside city of Valparaiso, an hour down the coast. "Yesterday, I went to the Pablo Neruda house, La Chascona."

"Oh, yes. This is one of the most famous things to see in Santiago."

"Okay, is it possible . . . I don't know a ton about Pablo Neruda, but . . . did you think . . . was he maybe . . ."

"Oh, yes, he was totally an asshole. Yes. My friends and I have discussed this."

This was a huge relief. The Nobel Prize–winning Chilean poet Pablo Neruda has, like, a halo of sainthood around him in Chile. He was an advisor to Allende, he'd served as Allende's ambassador to France for a while. He died just two weeks after the coup, and his funeral procession became a kind of protest march. Some say Pinochet had Neruda poisoned.

Neruda had three houses that are now national monuments. Each is a kind of masterpiece of 1970s collector kitsch and swinger style. The one I'd visited was named for Neruda's longtime mistress. "The crazy-haired lady" is a cloddish translation.

"She was always attractive despite the many responsibilities she took on," said my audio guide to the house, in a luxurious accent.

"Neruda delighted in surprising his guest by emerging from secret passageways of the house." The audio guide went on at some length about how constantly delightful Neruda was, how he saw his house as a ship and himself as a captain, how guests stayed all night captivated by him.

Quickly, I became convinced that actually going to one of Neruda's dinner parties must've been an insufferable nightmare.

Fabrizio was with me. While still driving, he managed to do a vivid impression of Neruda popping out all over the place. "It's me! Neruda! Aren't you delighted?" and his guests forcing themselves to act amused.

Look, Neruda is a great poet, he was a glorious artist full of vitality and the joy of life, his brief poems on love are heartbreaking, blahblahblah. I'm just saying I prefer comedians.

*   *   *

Before hitting Valparaiso, we strolled by the Pacific in Viña del Mar, Chile's halfhearted version of Monaco or Atlantic City, with beachfront casinos. On the boardwalk, vendors were selling squirt guns for kids, glow sticks and beach towels, portraits of Michael Jackson, and odd pieces of folk art. A guy was offering to write your name on a grain of rice.

"The writing your name on a grain of rice—that is not so impressive anymore," said Fabrizio as we passed by. "I mean, 'Cool, it's my name and it's very small.' I have a phone in my pocket that can play movies."

Nearby, a guy was playing moaning versions of classical tunes on a four-foot saw. At his feet were a pile of CDs for sale. Fabrizio, his girlfriend, and I considered his art for an appropriate amount of time, say thirty seconds.

"Playing the saw—okay, yes, that is good. But: He has *albums*?"

Fabrizio suggested I Google image search the mayor of Viña, a woman named Virginia Reginato Bozzo, so I did.

"Yikes." She was quite something.

"Yes," he said, laughing. "It's okay to make fun of her because she's right-wing and terrible."

We went on to the squares and old shipping buildings by the water in Valparaiso, where Fabrizio spotted a statue that delighted him. It was of Arturo Prat, a Chilean naval hero of the 1879–1883 War of the Pacific.

"This guy! We love this guy in Chile, he's everywhere." It's true, you can't go far in Chile without crossing an Avenida Arturo Prat. He looked distinguished in the statue, with a sword and flag, towering above some sailors below him. But Arturo Prat brought out a boyish giggly delight in Fabrizio.

"The thing is, he was a loser! His ship, it was getting destroyed by the Peruvians, so he jumped onto their ship, and the Peruvian sailor, he grabbed a . . ."

As he searched for the word, he mimed a pan.

"A pan?"

"Yes! Yes! They hit him on the head with a frying pan."

"Really?"

"Yes! They killed him with a pan! Now he has a statue." He shrugged and smiled. "That is Chile."

"They should put the pan on the statue," I suggested.

"Yes! Yes, it should show the moment of him getting hit with the pan! That would make a good statue."

Chile did win the War of the Pacific, and the results resonate down to today. The war cost Bolivia its seacoast, which they're still aggrieved about. In the years after the war, Chile had a monopoly on the nitrate trade, which allowed the country to get a lot richer a lot faster than its neighbors. In 2007, Chile gave back to Peru some books their soldiers had stolen during the war 120 years before.

As for Prat being killed by a frying pan, I suppose I could research that. But if it isn't true, I'll be too disappointed, so why bother?

On the streets of Valparaiso, children saw Fabrizio and squealed and pointed him out to their siblings. He played it cool, but of course he enjoyed it. His girlfriend kept him humble. Valparaiso is like a twisted puzzle version of San Francisco. A seaport bustles under steep hills packed with dense mazes of streets that you can climb and descend on rickety elevators and funiculars that creak like wooden roller coasters. We took a boat tour of the harbor, where Fabrizio and his girlfriend laughed the whole time as the tour guide, a gruff ex-dockworker, spent most of his time with the microphone talking shit about the incompetent harbor master. Back ashore, we ate huge bowls of seafood stew and drank Austral beer at an upstairs restaurant with photographs of Marilyn Monroe on the pink painted walls. Fabrizio's girlfriend couldn't really speak English, just Spanish and Portuguese, but she communicated very well through funny videos she showed me on her phone. She took us to a spot she knew, a former jail turned into a kind of arts collective where young people were lying out on the grass, and Fabrizio and I listed episodes of *The Simpsons*.

Between the wild colors on the painted houses of Valpo, the container ships moving their colored LEGOs in the harbor, and the crooked angles and the stairs and streets of the city, we took good Instagrams. It was late

May, but here in the Southern Hemisphere, that was autumn. Joking around with friends, stopping for beers and meat pies and pastries, exploring an old harbor city, watching the sun go down over the water from high up—it was a great Sunday. In the darkness, before heading back to Santiago, we drove up one of Valparaiso's steepest, most treacherous streets, built like the world's insanest skateboard run, to La Sebastiana, Neruda's vacation house. But it was already closed.

"Man, this guy can't stop fucking us!" I said.

He did his best possible impression of Seinfeld cursing the name of his horrible neighbor Newman.

"NERUDA!"

Sandwiches of Chile

There is an area in which Chile is unsurpassed by any nation in the world and that is sandwiches.

Perhaps not in "variety of sandwiches," but in "particular excellence of their top sandwich," Chile can hold its head proud.

I speak of the *lomito*, or the *chacarero*, a sandwich served on a round bun that is soft but with some tenacity. Inside is thinly sliced, seasoned, grilled steak, with fresh slices of tomatoes, green beans still with a snap to them, and chili peppers, perhaps sautéed. To substitute thinly sliced pork is acceptable as well.

A variation is the *Italiano*, so called because the mashed avocado, tomato, and white cheese creates a beautiful color combination that resembles the Italian flag.

Across Santiago and across Chile there are *fuentes de soda*, soda fountain restaurants where the unfriendly women wear blue-and-white uniforms, the decor is from some antipodal version of the 1950s, there are paper napkins tessellated into spiraling towers, cold beer is on tap, and you eat at the counter as fast as you can and are then encouraged to immediately leave.

The greatest of these is the Fuente Alemana. I went to the one on Avenida Libertador Bernardo O'Higgins 58 once for lunch and then the next day, right when it opened, for breakfast. If you are truly serious about sandwiches, sooner or later you want to get there, too.

In Patagonia

In Patagonia, near the bottom of the world, the wind swirls in such hard and twisted patterns that the wizened trees have no idea how to grow. Their branches contort out in confused, desperate jigjags like a many-armed, hyperactive dancer frozen in wood. They look like trees from a nightmare. Some of them are bent at the trunk and lie, alive but forever knocked over. From the bus, most of what I saw were worn-out old *estancias*, sheep and cattle ranches. When we got to Puerto Natales in the afternoon, it was starting to snow.

In Patagonia in 1895, a German explorer named Hermann Eberhard found, in a cave, a collection of bones of humans and prehistoric animals. He found, too, a reddish pelt. This was hung on a tree, discussed, and shown to visitors. A few European scientists heard about it and came to Patagonia and started poking around its caves. They found even more fur and skin, and they determined it had come from a mylodon, a giant sloth long thought to be extinct. Perhaps living mylodons still roamed unknown Patagonia. The English reporter H. H. Prichard of the *Daily Express* was sent to hunt them. He didn't find any. Nor did I, though it wouldn't shock me too much if I heard of one in Patagonia. The mountains don't look conquered at all. They have a vast and looming spookiness like they could hide any number of surviving Pleistocene Megatheria. With a few Chilean women, I took a van ride to visit Eberhard's cave. They have a good statue of the giant sloth, standing on his hind haunches, half smiling, like he's mid–dance move.

"Patagonia" doesn't have an exact border. It's a term for the huge stretch of sparse grassland that makes up the southern half of Argentina and Chile. Maybe a million square kilometers with, on average, two people per kilometer. The name was given by Magellan, who got it, it seems, from a giant monster in a Spanish chivalry novel he was reading. The explorers and conquistadors, the ones who could read, were always read-ing fantastical novels of knights and adventures.

In Patagonia are great glaciers of ice as big as small mountains. You can climb with ladders and ice axes or be deposited on them by helicop-ter. And there are spires and walls of rock, like Fitz Roy, which rises up like a gigantic middle finger to rock climbers, taunting them and chal-lenging them. The American climber Chad Kellogg climbed it in Febru-ary 2014 but was killed in a rockfall on the way down.

In the Southern Hemisphere summer—December, January, February—swarms of backpackers trek in Patagonia. They hike routes like "the W," staying at wooden *refugios* along the way. Lately, Patagonia's become es-pecially popular with Israelis, traveling for a while after finishing their military service. In 2012, a fire allegedly started by an Israeli backpacker and whipped by the Patagonian wind burned sixty miles of forest in Tor-res del Paine National Park.

By the time I got to Puerto Natales, though, most of the backpacker shops were closed up, and the town was very quiet. The next morning, I rode into the park with a vanload of Chilean tourists, mostly retirees. By the side of the road, there were patches of ice and snow. Herds of free-ranging guanacos, lean and spry, tugged up mouthfuls of grass. The van driver took us to a waterfall, and to perfect cold lakes dotted with a few pink flamingos. It was glorious but it got me pretty sleepy. Somewhere between stops, I fell asleep with my face against the window.

A bump to the head woke me up as the van wildly fishtailed. We'd slid, out of control, on a patch of black ice in the road. Now we wobbled help-less toward the rocky drop-off at the edge. One of the Chilean women let out a horrible, agonized scream. A true death scream, a scream like you may as well abandon all dignity or pretense to courage and wail like a baby because before you're finished, you and everyone with you will die.

Only: We didn't die. The bus driver calmly rode out the skid, when he could get some traction he braked, and then, danger passed, he hit the gas and drove on.

It was awkward after that. It was awkward in the van, since we'd all seen and heard this woman shriek like a dying coward at what turned out to be nothing. It was awkward at the gift shop, and it was awkward all the way home.

Where the Andes drop off into the ocean in western Patagonia, there are deep fjords where chunks of ice crack off from sloping glaciers into the black water. With what was, I think, a company retreat of drunken Chileans, I sailed out on a tour boat to Parque Nacional Bernardo O'Higgins, named for the Irish Chilean hero of the Chilean War of Independence, whose father had trekked back and forth across the Andes building shelters and creating the Chilean postal service. Bernardo became supreme director of Chile, but a coup led by his former friend deposed him and he sailed away from Valparaiso, never to see his native country again. Our boat docked at an old *estancia* on a remote island, where we had a barbecue and I ate with a Chilean mother and her two sons. They were both fans of Fabrizio Copano's comedy.

The place where I stayed in Puerto Natales, Kau Lodge, claims to have developed the idea of "contemplation activity." Wonderful term, I'm into it. One of my contemplation activities was sitting alone in the lobby, drinking good coffee, petting the lodge dog, and reading an issue of *Rock and Ice* magazine that profiled Edurne Pasaban, a female Basque mountaineer who decided to climb all fourteen of the 8,000-plus-meter mountains on Earth. In a bout of depression mid-quest, she tried to kill herself and was confined to a mental hospital, but after she got out, she finished. She also carried on an affair with the married Italian climber Silvio Mondinelli. (This was a good article, and can be found in issue number 204, written by David Roberts, may he prosper.)

Sometimes I walked outside, along the wrecked tracks of a railway that had once served an immense meat-rendering plant, and looked out onto the waters of Seno Última Esperanza, Last Hope Sound.

Truth is, writing about my own minuscule explorations in Patagonia seems silly when the place is already the subject of one of the best travel books of all time.

Bruce Chatwin

In his grandmother's cabinet when Bruce Chatwin was a boy, there was a piece of leathery skin. His mother told him it was the skin of a brontosaurus. His grandmother's cousin, Charley Milward, had sent it as a wedding present. Charley Milward was a sailor who'd been shipwrecked off Punta Arenas in Patagonia, and began life again there.

In the best version of the story, the "brontosaurus skin"—it was probably a bit of giant sloth—always fascinated Bruce Chatwin, until one day, when he was thirty-four and working as a journalist for London's *Sunday Times Magazine*, he went to interview the Irish furniture designer Eileen Gray at her apartment in Paris. She was ninety-three years old. On her wall was a map of Patagonia.

"I've always wanted to go there," said Chatwin. Eileen Gray told him to go there for her. So Bruce Chatwin sent his boss a telegram that read GONE TO PATAGONIA FOR FOUR MONTHS and took off.

In the book Bruce Chatwin wrote, *In Patagonia*, he tells of eating toffees with the Scottish owner of the Estancia Lochinver, and he has an audience with His Royal Prince Philippe of Araucania and Patagonia, an eccentric Frenchman said to have bought the title from the descendants of another eccentric Frenchman who first claimed it for himself. He walks into the remote Chubut Valley, where the descendants of settlers still spoke Welsh, and he follows the trail of two mysterious American cowboys called Evans and Wilson, aliases perhaps of Butch Cassidy and the Sundance Kid, who hadn't died in Bolivia after all. He speaks to an old priest and doctor of theology, anthropological theory, and archaeology, who tells him that in the sixth millennium BC, the men of Patagonia hunted the native unicorn to extinction. Chatwin spins yarns about the Brujería sect from the island of Chiloé, who could change into animals, reverse the course of rivers, and see the secrets of anyone's life in a crystal stone called the Challanco. He tells about Alexander MacLennan, the Red Pig, who hunted the native Ona people of Tierra del Fuego with his rifle, and about Jem Button, a native boy hauled away to England, where he met King William IV and then returned to Patagonia on the *Beagle*, traveling with Darwin. When he arrived back home, Jem Button reverted to his Fuegian name, Orundellico, and may or may not have killed some English missionaries.

Chatwin retells some of the exploits of Charley Milward, his grandmother's cousin, and finds his old house in Punta Arenas. Then at last he visits the Cave of the Giant Sloth. Digging around, he claims he found himself another piece of sloth skin.

When *In Patagonia* was published in 1978, it became a bestseller. Backpackers with dog-eared copies started turning up in the Chubut Valley, to the startlement and sometimes anger of the Welsh sheep farmers. To a certain kind of literary-minded traveler, Chatwin became an icon. He was an electric presence, and photogenic: The author photo of him with his boots slung over his shoulders is exactly the look a lot of travelers aspire to. The Moleskine notebook takes its name and design from a specialized notebook he describes that he ordered from a Parisian stationer. He was onto something. When Chatwin had come, Patagonia was still rancher country. Now it is, among other things, the name of a company with $600 million in annual revenue. From their company website: *Patagonia brings to mind, as we once wrote in a catalog introduction, "romantic visions of glaciers tumbling into fjords, jagged windswept peaks, gauchos and condors." It's been a good name for us, and it can be pronounced in every language.*

Almost as interesting as Bruce Chatwin's book is his life story, told in a 1999 biography by Nicholas Shakespeare. Chatwin had a "gift for instant intimacy," Shakespeare says. People were always inviting him to stay at their summer house and introducing him to their most interesting friends. Chatwin was an art dealer for a while, studied archaeology for a time, and spent three years trying to write a book that would prove that humans by nature were nomads. When "warped in conditions of settlement," we go crazy with "violence, greed, status-seeking or a mania for the new." We'd walked out of Africa and we never should've stopped walking was Chatwin's idea.

He lived up to it. He was apt to head to Niger and Cameroon for three months, or a few weeks in the Sudan anytime he felt restless. He'd send his wife letters suggesting "we meet somewhere in Western rather than Central Asia on or around Aug 25."

Elizabeth Chatwin met Bruce when they both worked at Sotheby's auction house. On one of their first meetings, Elizabeth remembered Bruce eating a tin of caviar without offering her any, and then asking her to buy him an Hermès diary, then inviting her to a dinner, an invitation he canceled at the last minute because there were already too many women coming. Bruce sometimes told people they'd met on an archaeological dig in Persia. A few years later they were married, even though Elizabeth knew Bruce was bisexual.

Chatwin made a lot of things up, and he hid a lot of things, too. He was a "polymorphous pervert," said one (female) lover. He had strings of male lovers, too. He left his sexual adventurers out of *In Patagonia*, though he apparently slept with at least one of the boys he describes. Invention, the blending of fact and fiction, didn't seem to be a big deal for him, it was part of the art. He shrugged off accusations from critics.

When his health started to give out, around age forty, he told friends he'd gotten a rare Chinese fungal infection, perhaps "from eating a slice of raw Cantonese whale." He told someone else he'd caught a disease from bat feces. But he knew he had HIV. At age forty-eight, he died in the South of France, and his ashes were scattered near the ancient town of Kardamyli in Greece.

The Australian poet Les Murray, who knew him, said of Chatwin, "He was lonely, and he wanted to be."

Maybe that's what it takes to write a true masterpiece of a travel book. Myself, by the time I got to Patagonia, I was lonely and I didn't want to be.

The Bottom

The first guesthouse I'd tried in Punta Arenas, capital of Magallanes and Antártica Chilena, was already closed for the winter. But the owners, a young couple, made me a cup of tea anyway. They told me not to miss the cemetery in Punta Arenas.

"It's the most beautiful cemetery in the world."

It might just be. The next morning before the sun came up, I walked out to the cemetery gates. Inside were white marble tombs, mausoleums for landowner families that got rich in the sheep boom of the 1890s. The cemetery gate was paid for by Sara Braun, a daughter of Baltic German Jewish immigrants who inherited from her husband and then ran herself an empire based on sheep raising and seal hunting.

I climbed up the hill overlooking the town, and could see across the water to Tierra del Fuego.

Welp, I thought, *that's it. That's pretty much the bottom.*

There was still Puerto Williams to visit. That'd been my original destination all along, the southernmost city in the world. I could hop a plane and check it off.

Meh, I thought. *What's over there, buncha sheep and oil wells? I'll catch it next time.*

I mean, I could keep going to Antarctica, but really, what would the point of that be? Time to go home.

Don't get me wrong, there was plenty I was still curious about. The tepui plateaus of Venezuela, say. Pain in the ass to get there, but it looks worth seeing. And hadn't I skipped entirely the Llanos Orientales of Colombia, where gauchos have the roughest rodeos in the world? Could be an interesting time. Quito, I really should've seen. And it was a shame, really, that I'd skipped Belize entirely.

Maybe I could keep at it. Just: Never stop. Keep wandering until I'd exhausted the world. How about Bhutan? Grassy Lesotho, and the cows of Swaziland? Ireland and Italy: There're two whole worlds right there. Those I'd been to, and I still wanted to go back.

But when I scrolled back through my memory of all the wonders I'd experienced, what mattered more than anything was people. Even strangers had become, in a few hours, more important to me than any wonder I saw, any mountain or ruin. And those were strangers. What about the people I loved? The people I loved the most were all back in the United States. They were hanging out in Los Angeles, drinking in New York, going to bed in Needham, Massachusetts.

People are what's best in the world, I say. Or maybe "people are *who's* best in the world." Quote me both ways. People are what's most interesting, too. People are who's most interesting.

For one last Chilean sandwich, I stopped at Lomit's. *SANDWICHES PARA SERVIRSE Y LLEVAR. LOMITOS—SCHOPS—TORTAS—HELADOS—BEBIDAS.* I ordered a *lomito Italiano*.

"*Perdon, amigo. De donde eras?*" A kindly looking older guy sitting next to me at the bar had taken a break from talking to his friends and turned to me. I told him I was American.

"Your Spanish is very good," he said to me, in Spanish. This wasn't true, but I was proud of it anyway. "Are you spending long in Patagonia?"

No, I told him, I was, in fact, leaving that afternoon.

"Well," he said, "if you come back, give me a call. I give tours of this area. Out to see the penguins, to Tierra del Fuego."

"Do you ever go to Puerto Williams?"

"Yes, sometimes. There's not much there."

"I'll come back sometime and go there," I told him, and he gave me his business card. A German name. He said his ancestors had immigrated here in the 1880s.

That afternoon I flew back, by way of Santiago and Panama, took a taxi back to my house, plopped my bag down on my floor, and let my cat consider my return. The next day, I went back to doing my stuff, and tried to spend as much time as possible with the people I loved.

At night I wrote this book. Through which I hope you went on a kind of a trip, too.

Now that it's done, I'm thinkin' about going to Honolulu. The Hawaiian Islands are super interesting. Forget that they were once called the Sandwich Islands, after John Montagu, 4th Earl of Sandwich, who had an affair with the opera singer Martha Ray while his wife was going insane, and who probably invented the sandwich so he could eat roast beef without looking away from his gambling. How about when the last queen of Hawaii, Liliuokalani, who married a Boston ship captain, spent five years imprisoned in the 'Iolani Palace writing songs? Did you know that twenty-three sets of brothers died when the USS *Arizona* was sunk at Pearl Harbor? How terrible is that? Hawaii sounds like a paradise, but it seems to shimmer just out of the grasp of so many of the people who have passed through there . . .

Could I do the Kalalau Trail barefoot? I wonder . . .

(*Free Offer for a Bonus E-Book*)

Back before I wrote this book, I had an idea to write a book called A Trip to Canada. *I spent three weeks in British Columbia, the Yukon, and the Northwest Territories before it truly dawned on me that* A Trip to Canada *is literally the most boring title ever for a book.*

Anyway, I assembled the wreckage and if you'd like to read it, e-mail me—helphely@gmail.com—and I'll send you the PDF for free.

The one rule is you have to have bought The Wonder Trail.

(If you got this book from the library, but you still want a copy of A Trip to Canada, *well, write me. I'll probably send it to you anyway.)*

(If you stole this book, then fuuuuuck you, dude.)

Appendix

Female Travel Writers

Writing this book and looking at my bookshelf, it occurred to me, I have a strong bias toward travel books written by guys. That might be because men are more likely to brag or write books or publish books, or they've historically had all the time and money and reason to travel, and most of my books are old.

But whatever, it's like 95 percent to 5 percent. I'm sure I have all kinds of biases, but this one I noticed, and when you notice a bias, you should try to correct it, right? So I did. I tried to read books by female travel writers.

Here are, for my money, some of the best ones:

Freya Stark, *The Valleys of the Assassins and Other Persian Travels.* Now, that is just a baller title, by an obvious baller of a woman. Freya Stark got half her hair ripped out in a factory machine when she was a teenager. In World War I, she was a nurse. In World War II, she wrote propaganda in Arabic. In between, she wrote some twenty books about one incredible adventure after another.

Eleanor Clark, *The Oysters of Locmariaquer.* This isn't really a book about a trip, but it is about a place she was visiting, on the coast of Brittany, where the men harvest oysters and the women have all kinds of drama happening. Sometimes she goes a little nuts with it, just sometimes, just my opinion, like it can't possibly be as heartbreaking as she describes it. But maybe I'm just getting cynical in my old age. I hope not! Anyway, great book.

Elizabeth Gilbert, *Eat, Pray, Love.* Okay, the first time I tried to read this, when it was already superfamous, I was like *What the fuck?* I mean, in the first few pages, this bitch is in *Connecticut* and she has her fucking *dream* job traveling the world for fancy magazines, a fucking dream husband who was *also* rich, a dream life with an apartment in New York City *and* a house in the country, who had everything she admits she ever wanted, and then is like "I was crying on the floor because there had to be *more for me!*"

But: I kept reading. Now I think it's like a spiritual masterpiece.

Elizabeth Gilbert is hypnotizing, and I understand why thousands of people pay to hear her talk on Oprah's The Life You Want Tour. She's obviously got something figured out.

Cheryl Strayed, *Wild.* To many women I know, Cheryl Strayed is like something better and stronger and more heroic and valuable than a saint. I'm definitely not gonna mess with her or them: all respect to this book. One thing about this book is that it was a good, like, I guess reminder to me that when women walk around in strange places, they are constantly being stared at and preyed on by men. Whereas I could stroll the streets and nobody was gonna think about me much at all. That's an advantage, I'd say.

Dervla Murphy, *Full Tilt: Ireland to India with a Bicycle.* Here's the first sentence of this book: "On my tenth birthday a bicycle and an atlas coincided as presents and a few days later I decided to cycle to India." Then she did. Dervla is an Irishwoman, and she is tough and no-nonsense and sharp. I can't help but think she'd find a lot wrong with the way I traveled, but hey: I'm not as clearheaded as she is, I'm doing the best I can.

This book is great.

Early on in it, Dervla Murphy says, "The temptation to make myself sound more learned than I am, by gleaning facts and figures from an encyclopedia and inserting them in appropriate places, has been resisted."

Well, obviously, in my book the temptation hasn't been resisted. I hope I'm not being dishonest. The truth is, I think part of my *job* here is to glean facts and figures, from encyclopedias and whatever else I can find, and insert them in appropriate places, so you can have them, Reader. It's part of my service as writer.

I promise you I'm not just trying to make myself sound more learned. I make no claims at learneditude.

Anyway: I love you, Dervla!

(I can picture her curtly dismissing my cheap American affection.)

When he was twenty-seven, in 1953, **James Morris**, a newspaper reporter, was at the base camp of the British Mount Everest Expedition when Edmund Hillary and Tenzing Norgay reached the summit for the first time. He wired the news, in code, to London and broke the story. His book about this, *Coronation Everest*, is pretty fun. A few years later, in 1964, James started transitioning to Jan Morris. Jan has written a bunch of great travel books: To pick one more or less at random, how about *The Great Port: A Passage Through New York*. Or *Journeys*. Bow down to Jan.

Guides (Human)

If you're a gawky idiot who bumbles through eleven countries, the number of people from whom you must seek help is obscene. If you're any kind of person, you should try to thank all of them in person, and I tried to, but here are some people I thought I should double-thank.

Marco of Croozy Scooters. I endorse this man and his business. His patience and generosity to a traveler was one of the finer displays of coolness and good character I can remember. If in San Cristóbal, why not check out Croozy Scooters?

The people of *Mayabell*, in Palenque. These people were unusually good to me in many ways and I loved being in this place.

The journalist and the graphic designer who were very patient with me in answering many questions about Mexico. Thank you.

Guatemala Pam, I tried to change enough of your story that it will never unravel, yet keep enough of it so I could share some of your human amazingness.

Miah and *dude* at La Tortuga Verde, thanks for talking to me about surfing.

Owner of La Tortuga Verde, I was mad that you called TV writing pablum for the masses. But I loved being at your place, it was very special.

Thanks to *Brent Forrester*, who gave me a lot of experience and ideas and enthusiasm about these countries.

Captain Rich of Panama Canal Fishing. Awesome man.

The *captain* of the *Jaqueline*. Two captains in a row who seemed really competent and admirable.

The A-Team. I mean, goddamn guys, just keep it up. Special thanks to Veronica for the kidnapping story and answering many tedious questions.

Lena of Tilberg, what a good person you are.

Popayán guys, thank you for the good times. Please review the evidence on 9/11.

Pat Hobby and his *wife*.

Mick and *Maddie.*

Walter Saxer of Casa Fitzcarraldo in Iquitos, who told me many good stories I can't put in this book.

Amy Smozols and *Alan Tang.* Times.

Juan of San Pedro. Not his real name.

Fabrizio Copano and *Isadora*, what a great day, I'll have that forever. Thank you.

The *Chilean dudes* in Puerto Natales, you were very welcoming when I was probably at the end of my tether.

The *man at the bar* at Lomit's in Punta Arenas.

Guides (Books)

Books are made out of other books. I don't think I would've done any of this if I hadn't read *1491: New Revelations of the Americas Before Columbus*, by Charles C. Mann (2005). I can't say enough about this book. Every page is so interesting. Charles C. Mann is so good at learning everything and then sharing it with you in the best way. This book is what got Tenochtitlán, the Maya, the Inca, the Amazon, and the whole world of Central and South America so deep into my head that finally I was like, *I better go have a look at this.*

To sort out how to get where I wanted to go, and also where I wanted to go, the number one helpful source was anonymous people in the Lonely Planet Thorn Tree forums and on Wikitravel. So, thanks everybody.

The other incredibly important start was **all the Lonely Planet books I used**. Everyone who travels knows these books; they are amazing! You probably know the founders' story, too, how Maureen and Tony Wheeler drove across Asia in a van and then published a pamphlet called *Across Asia on the Cheap: A Complete Guide to Making the Overland Trip.* (Now, there's an example for us all!)

Now the company is owned by an American billionaire, which can't be good. Anyway, these guides are indispensable, these are the ones I used and who wrote them: *Mexico* (John Noble, Kate Armstrong, Ray Bartlett, Greg Benchwick, Tim Bewer, Beth Kohn, Tom Masters, Kevin Raub, Michael Read, Josephine Quintero, Daniel C. Schechter, Adam Skolnick, César G. Soriano, Ellee Thalheimer); *Guatemala* (Lucas Vidgen, Daniel C. Schechter); *Nicaragua* (Alex Egerton, Greg Benchwick); *Costa Rica* (Nate Cavalieri, Adam Skolnick); *Panama* (Carolyn Mc-Carthy); *Colombia* (Kevin Raub, Alex Egerton, Mike Power); *Peru* (Carolyn Mc-Carthy, Carolina A. Miranda, Kevin Raub, Brendan Sainsbury, Luke Waterson); *South America on a Shoestring* (Regis St. Louis, Sandra Bao, Greg Benchwick, Celeste Brash, Gregor Clark, Alex Egerton, Bridget Gleeson, Beth Kohn, Carolyn McCarthy, Kevin Raub, Paul Smith, Lucas Vidgen); *Chile & Easter Island* (Carolyn McCarthy, Jean-Bernard Carillet, Bridget Gleeson, Anja Mutić, Kevin Raub). I mean, Celeste Brash? These people have the coolest names.

The third-most important book I read has to be *Breaking the Maya Code* by

Michael D. Coe. Just a terrific fun read packed with information that fired up my whole brain.

Oh, but maybe that book is tied with *The Conquest of New Spain* by Bernal Díaz. One of the most incredible books I've ever read, no joke. I read the translation by John M. Cohen, who must be great at his job.

Here Are More Books That Were Important to Me:

True Histories by Lucian, translated by Keith Sidwell. It's pretty clear that Lucian was hilarious, but how do you translate that from the ancient Greek? Admirable job by Sidwell.

The Travels of Ibn Battuta edited by Tim Mackintosh-Smith. What a boss.

2666, *The Savage Detectives*, and *By Night in Chile* by Roberto Bolaño. All fiction, but hugely enriched my understanding and helped me build a picture of the Mexican border, Mexico City, and recent history in Chile.

Letters of Cortés, translated by Francis Augustus MacNutt. This guy. I will say, I believe Cortés was genuinely obsessed with spreading Catholicism and wiping out the pagan religions he found. Whether that makes him better or worse I don't know.

The Conquistadors: A Very Short Introduction by Matthew Restall and Felipe Fernández-Armesto. Great book, really helps you understand these guys and where they were coming from.

Seven Myths of the Spanish Conquest by Matthew Restall. Superinteresting work that shows how complex what happened was, how it can't be chalked up to simple causes and easy stories.

History of the Conquest of Mexico and *History of the Conquest of Peru* by William H. Prescott. Prescott, so far as I know, never went to Mexico or Peru. He wrote these books in Boston. Also he was blind in one eye from getting in a food fight when he was at Harvard. Yet when the books came out in the 1840s, they were considered towering achievements of history. At the time of the war with Mexico, a copy of Prescott's book was on every US Navy ship, and many army officers were said to have taken it along for inspiration during their march to Mexico City.

The Broken Spears: The Aztec Account of the Conquest of Mexico by Miguel León-Portilla. Translations of Nahuatl versions of the baffling events that had just befallen them.

The Aztecs: A Very Short Introduction by David Carrasco. Coulda been shorter.

The Interior Circuit: A Mexico City Chronicle by Francisco Goldman. A good but sad essay by a writer living and exploring and grieving in Mexico City.

Ambivalent Conquests: Maya and Spaniard in Yucatan, 1517–1570 by Inga Clendinnen. A dense, complex picture is revealed but in a way that's graspable and clear.

Yucatan Before and After the Conquest by Friar Diego de Landa, edited and translated by William Gates. Hey, man, de Landa's got a lot to answer for, since he burned so many Mayan books, but this book is fascinating.

Incidents of Travel in Central America, Chiapas, and Yucatan and *Incidents of Travel in Yucatan* by John L. Stephens, engravings by Frederick Catherwood. If these guys were still alive I would want them to be my friends.

The Spectacle of the Late Maya Court: Reflections on the Murals of Bonampak (The William and Bettye Nowlin Series in Art, History, and Culture of the Western Hemisphere) by Mary Miller and Claudia Brittenham. The leading scholar on Bonampak, a tremendous achievement, the passion is contagious, but it does seem like they kinda focus more on rapturous odes to the beauty and not the torturing.

Popul Vuh by unknown sixteenth-century Mayan writer(s). I read the version translated by Dennis Tedlock. Just a Mayan romp through the underworld with talking gourds and so on.

The Aztec Treasure House: New and Selected Essays by Evan S. Connell. Fantastic book by a great American writer, who muses and considers the lost worlds of Mesoamerica.

Demanding Democracy: Reform and Reaction in Costa Rica and Guatemala, 1870s–1950s by Deborah J. Yashar. And thanks to Marika for recommending it.

Mandate for Change 1953–1956: The White House Years by Dwight D. Eisenhower. Dug up this book to find what Ike thought about the Guatemala coup. Man, read those pages, and you see it: how the foreign policy establishment in the White House bossed around and toyed with Central America like a crummy branch office.

Salvador by Joan Didion. Damn, this lady can write about a body dump without once breaking her cool.

The Columbus Conspiracy: An Investigation Into the Secret History of Christopher Columbus by Michael Bradley. My man Miah recommended this on the beach in El Salvador. Conspiracy that has it all: the Cathars, the Holy Grail, mysterious African sailors, treasure pits, FDR and the New Deal, the Masons—it's great.

Columbus and the Quest for Jerusalem: How Religion Drove the Voyages That Led to America by Carol Delaney. Not beach reading, exactly, but paints a really fascinating picture of Columbus as a true religious fanatic driven more by bizarre visions of reaching Jerusalem than by money or gold or exploring or whatever.

The Business of Empire: United Fruit, Race, and U.S. Expansion into Central America by Jason M. Colby. I mean, he walks you through the whole story, but it's pretty much what you'd expect.

Mosquito Empires: Ecology and War in the Greater Caribbean, 1620–1914 by J. R. McNeill. Okay, you don't have to read this whole book, but do yourself a favor and read the first paragraph of the preface where J. R. McNeil talks about being poor and lonely and sad as a young researcher in Seville, thankful that at least he didn't have to get eaten up by mosquitoes.

Sweetness and Power: The Place of Sugar in Modern History by Sidney W. Mintz. I'm told by my friend Professor James McHugh this is a classic in the field.

Inevitable Revolutions: The United States in Central America by Walter LaFeber. Good book on all the messes we made and how we either didn't clean them up or in cleaning them up made worse messes.

The War in Nicaragua by William Walker. I gotta say, I liked the guy more after I read his book than I did before. You get why Walker got acquitted at his trial after his first effort to invade Mexico: He makes a powerful case for himself.

Walker: The True Story of the First American Invasion of Nicaragua by Rudy Wurlitzer. Deeply weird compilation of materials apparently released in connection with the movie.

Tycoon's War: How Cornelius Vanderbilt Invaded a Country to Overthrow America's Most Famous Military Adventurer by Stephen Dando-Collins. The one flaw here, I think, is that Dando-Collins is sometimes so excited about his story, which is admittedly amazing, that he moves faster than we can keep up with.

The Path Between the Seas: The Creation of the Panama Canal 1870–1914 by David McCullough. This man is a complete boss and this book is astoundingly great. Something amazing on every page. I stole facts from it up to the exact level where it'd be criminal.

Crossing the Darien Gap by Andrew Niall Egan. This guy is a great writer and a brave and calm explorer. Not just saying that 'cause he wrote a five-star Amazon review of my last book.

Under the Black Flag: The Romance and the Reality of Life Among the Pirates by David Cordingly. Not that relevant to my book but a great read.

Empire of Blue Water: Captain Morgan's Great Pirate Army, the Epic Battle for the Americas, and the Catastrophe That Ended the Outlaws' Bloody Reign by Stephan Talty. Most readable book about Morgan I know of.

Blood and Silver: A History of Piracy in the Caribbean and Central America by Kris E. Lane. Kinda stiff for a book about pirates, but maybe that's the point.

Sodomy and the Pirate Tradition: English Sea Rovers in the Seventeenth-Century Caribbean by B. R. Burg. I can't tell if this guy is joking or not.

Violent Delights, Violent Ends: Sex, Race, and Honor in Colonial Cartagena de Indias by Nicole von Germeten. Okay, this book didn't inform my book too much, but whatever, it's full of amazing and sexy stories.

Killing Pablo: The Hunt for the World's Greatest Outlaw by Mark Bowden. A specific story about a specific moment and maybe a pulpy way in, but the fact is this book really helped me start to sort out Colombian history.

One River: Explorations and Discoveries in the Amazon Rain Forest by Wade Davis. Crazily compelling story by the world's most badass ethnobotanist/journalist.

DMT: The Spirit Molecule: A Doctor's Revolutionary Research into the Biology of Near-Death and Mystical Experiences by Rick Strassman. Sometimes bogged down by Strassman's lengthy explanations of the regulatory difficulties he faced when he tried to do research on DMT.

The Last Days of the Incas by Kim MacQuarrie. Terrific, readable, exciting historical storytelling.

The First New Chronicle and Good Government by Felipe Guaman Poma de Ayala. For me, the illustrations were better than the text. You can see those online at the website of the Royal Library of Denmark. I had the paper edition translated and abridged by David Frye, too.

Narrative of the Incas by Juan de Betanzos, translated by Roland Hamilton and Dana Buchanan. Kinda meh.

History of the Incas by Pedro Sarmiento de Gamboa. Gamboa's assignment was to make the Incas look bad. Somehow, it's still one of the best sources we have.

Wildlife of the Galápagos by Julian Fitter, Daniel Fitter, and David Hosking. How you gonna tell your boobies apart without this book?

The Voyage of the Beagle by Charles Darwin. Just a guy on a ship falling in love with crazy animals and science.

The Beak of the Finch: A Story of Evolution in Our Time by Jonathan Weiner. A must-read for anyone curious about what it's like to live with your wife on a remote island for twenty years measuring finch beaks.

Marching Powder: A True Story of Friendship, Cocaine, and South America's Strangest Jail by Rusty Young and Thomas McFadden. Amazing, entertaining, recommended.

Memoirs of Simon Bolivar and of His Principal Generals by Henri Louis Ducoudray Holstein. This guy wasn't shy about sharing his opinion, but I don't know enough to tell you how much he's lying or not.

Simón Bolívar: Essays on the Life and Legacy of the Liberator, edited by David Bushnell and Lester D. Langley. Not for the casual reader, but these guys are serious about their stuff.

The Motorcycle Diaries: Notes on a Latin American Journey by Ernesto Che Guevara. It's interesting how honest Che is about his diarrhea. I used the 2003 translation published by Ocean Press and the Che Guevara Studies Center.

Che Guevara: A Revolutionary Life by Jon Lee Anderson. What a huge accomplishment to write this book, on top of being one of the most badass reporters ever. Jon Lee Anderson knew more about Central and South America before I was born than I ever will.

The Bolivian Diary of Ernesto Che Guevara by Ernesto Che Guevara, edited by Mary-Alice Waters. In my opinion, by this point Guevara had fallen in love not with lifting people out of poverty but with violent revolution itself. The means he used became so destructive that he set back the goals he fought for. Che's crime, if he has one, was that for decades young men and women who wanted change followed his example and picked as their tool guerrilla warfare.

In Patagonia by Bruce Chatwin. Way better writer than me, went farther out, wrote a better book. But: I didn't make anything up.

Bruce Chatwin by Nicholas Shakespeare. The man's true story is almost better than his writing.

I also read a lot of articles and websites and newspapers and pamphlets. I really tried not to get anything wrong, but if I did please let me know at helphely@gmail.com.

By the way, I should note here that I made up that Ponce de León quote at the beginning of this book. I'm not even sure if Ponce de León was literate. Just seemed like a good quote the world could use.